MANAGING THE UNDESIRABLES

MANAGING THE UNDESIRABLES

REFUGEE CAMPS AND HUMANITARIAN GOVERNMENT

MICHEL AGIER

Translated by David Fernbach

polity

First published in French as *Gérer les indésirables* © Flammarion SA, 2008

This English edition © Polity Press, 2011

Polity Press
65 Bridge Street
Cambridge CB2 1UR, UK

Polity Press
350 Main Street
Malden, MA 02148, USA

ISBN-13: 978-0-7456-4901-6
ISBN-13: 978-0-7456-4902-3(pb)

A catalogue record for this book is available from the British Library.

Typeset in 10.5 on 12 pt Sabon
by Toppan Best-set Premedia Limited
Printed and bound in Great Britain by the MPG Books Group

The publisher has used its best endeavours to ensure that the URLs for external websites referred to in this book are correct and active at the time of going to press. However, the publisher has no responsibility for the websites and can make no guarantee that a site will remain live or that the content is or will remain appropriate.

Every effort has been made to trace all copyright holders, but if any have been inadvertently overlooked the publisher will be pleased to include any necessary credits in any subsequent reprint or edition.

For further information on Polity, visit our website: www.politybooks.com

CONTENTS

v

CONTENTS

Part Three After the Camps . . .

ACKNOWLEDGEMENTS

The present work is based on field studies undertaken between 2000 and 2007 in the refugee gathering spaces in Kenya, Zambia, Liberia, Sierra Leone and Guinea, and also to some extent on the West Bank. These studies were spread over a number of journeys, each lasting anything between two weeks and over three months, in collaboration with the local teams of Médecins Sans Frontières (MSF). I have to thank first of all these various MSF teams (French, Belgian and Swiss sections) for their always warm and helpful welcome. Discussion with officials from this organization and with staff at the MSF foundation's research centre[1] made it possible for me both to prepare my investigations and to present their results on my return. Löick Barriquand, Jean-Hervé Bradol, Ron Brauman, Emmanuel Drouihin, Marie-Christine Férir, Coralie Lechelle, Denis Lemasson, Marc Le Pape and Françoise Saulnier-Boucher all helped me with their knowledge of the humanitarian world and particular sites, as well as with valuable operational advice, questions, suggestions and encouragement. Fabrice Weissman, Xavier Crombé and Sophie Baylac were kind enough to read and comment on certain parts of the present book. I hope that they will see it as an attempt to repay the support and interest that they lent to my project.

My research was conducted in the framework of the ASILES research programme.[2] The discussions that I had with the thirty or so research staff and doctoral students involved in this programme provided valuable support for my investigation. I have to thank them all. More widely, the activities of the scientific network TERRA (Travaux, Études et Recherches sur les Réfugiés et l'Asile, www.terra. org) provided a stimulating context for me as well as for everyone else who has contributed to its existence in the last five years or more.

ACKNOWLEDGEMENTS

As is necessarily the case with work over several years that combines field study with the public presentation of research findings, several oral and written interventions preceded and prepared for this book between 2002 and 2008. Everyone who invited me to share these reflections, discussing and commenting on them, will hopefully find in the present book an echo and extension of our exchanges, as well as a token of my gratitude.

I must thank Sylvie Fenczak for her belief in this publishing project and the proof of her benevolent patience. And finally, thanks to Mariana and Antonin once again for their coaching and patience.

LIST OF ACRONYMS USED

ACF	Action Contre la Faim (Action Against Hunger)
ACT	Action by Churches Together
AI	Amnesty International
AMERA	Africa and Middle East Refugee Assistance
ANAFÉ	Association Nationale d'Assistance aux Frontières pour les Étrangers
ARACEM	Association des Refoulés d'Afrique Centrale au Mali
BCR	Bureau de Coordination des Réfugiés
CARE	Cooperative for Assistance and Relief Everywhere
CFDA	Coordination Française pour le Droit d'Asile
CRA	Centre de Rétention Administrative
CRASH	Centre de Réflexion sur l'Action et les Savoirs Humanitaires
CRR	Commission des Recours des Réfugiés
CVT	Center for Victims of Torture
DRC	Democratic Republic of Congo
ECHO	European Commission Humanitarian Aid
EEC	European Economic Community
ERM	Enfants Réfugiés du Monde
FRONTEX	European Agency for the Management of Operational Cooperation at the External Borders of the Member States of the European Union
GISTI	Groupe d'Information et de Soutien des Immigrés
GTZ	Deutsche Gesellschaft für Technische Zusammarbeit
HCR/UNHCR	UN High Commission(er) for Refugees
ICRC	International Committee of the Red Cross

IDPs	Internally Displaced Persons
INGO	International non-governmental organization
IPD	Internal Patients Department
IRC	International Rescue Committee
IRD	Institut de Recherche pour le Développement
IRIN	Integrated Regional Information Networks (the OCHA information service)
JRS	Jesuit Refugee Service
LURD	Liberians United for Reconciliation and Democracy
LWF	Lutheran World Federation
MDM	Médecins du Monde
MPLA	Movimento Popular de Libertação de Angola
MSF	Médecins Sans Frontières
NGO	non-governmental organization
NIMBY	'Not in my back yard'
NPFL	National Patriotic Front of Liberia
OCHA	Office for the Coordination of Humanitarian Affairs (a UN agency)
OFPRA	Office Français de Protection des Réfugiés et Apatrides
OIM/IOM	International Organization for Migration
OXFAM	Oxford Committee for Famine Relief
PWJ	Peace Winds Japan
RENAMO	Resistencia Nacional Mocambicana
RUF	Revolutionary United Front (Sierra Leone)
SADR	Sahrawi Arab Democratic Republic
SBRs	Soomaali Bantu Refugees
STC	Save the Children
ULIMO	United Liberation Movement of Liberia for Democracy
UN/UNO	United Nations Organization
UNAMSIL	United Nations Mission in Sierra Leone
UNDP	United Nations Development Programme
UNICEF	United Nations Children's Fund
UNITA	União Nacional para a Independência Total de Angola
UNRWA	United Nations Relief and Works Agency for Palestinian Refugees
VOA	Voice of America
WFP	World Food Programme
ZAPI	Zone d'Attente pour Personnes en Instance

Introduction: From Vulnerable to Undesirable

Imagine . . .

Imagine a single world without conflict, made up of little secure worlds whose mutual connections, whether by road, underground or computer network, are themselves protected by gateways and identification systems hypersensitive to the sound of a person's voice, iris and skin texture. Imagine peace, cleanliness and the absence of disease, an eternally temperate climate, children who are to a marvellous degree wanted, planned and happy. Imagine a daily life without mishap or disturbance, in communities of identical interest (over-sixties, golfers, families with dogs, Krishna worshippers). This part of the planet, diverse and consensual, is called the 'World'.

This world seems to include all available space, the whole breadth of the terrestrial globe, as it were. But this totality is no more than a mirage, delicately maintained by flat screens and mirrors that are scattered throughout all public and private spaces, in which each person can imagine and view themselves, maintain their mind and their body, and deliciously cultivate a sincere self-concern. The other reality remains invisible, even though its existence is not totally unknown: large parts of the planet are separated off, behind high walls and barriers or across long stretches of sand or water, at the heart of deserts and forests. Other human beings live there. The world's 'Remnants' – that is what they're called – populating countless camps, kilometres of transit corridors, islands and marine platforms, and enclosures in the middle of deserts. Of variable size (from a few square metres to the area of several towns and villages combined), each camp is encircled by walls, barbed wire and electric fences, or imprisoned simply by the dissuasive presence of the emptiness surrounding it.

From time to time, some of the Remnants enter our world for brief visits. Their entries and exits are made through narrow corridors, under the filter of cameras, fingerprint readers, detectors for weapons, viruses and bacteria, captors of thoughts and memories. The queues at the checkpoints are long, and the people in them are not always certain of reaching the other side. Those who manage to do so work on the construction, upkeep and cleaning of the world's cities, weeding and harvesting plantations and gardens, before returning to sleep and await the next day in their enclosures, devoid of dreams.

The world's statisticians regularly count the Remnant population. VLCOs (Very Large Charitable Organizations) are charged with keeping these inhabitants alive. Meetings are regularly held in the world's parliament, however, to decide whether, and until when, we should still remain responsible for the Remnants. Groups of scholars reflect on the best way of eliminating them – one solution being to leave them to die in the desert. Several indices show that a certain part of the Remnants are in the process of self-destruction. It is reported, for example, that some people hurl themselves against the barbed wire or injure themselves with fire, while others attack their loved ones and even kill them. The results of this 'violence against themselves' require emergency treatment, say the representatives of the medical VLCOs: this is a new form of distress that justifies a new deployment of volunteers. More lives to save! But long discussions start up again on the usefulness of such actions in relation to their costs: 'Who will pay for the survival kits?' asks one elected representative. The charitable organizations decry such cynicism and launch great campaigns for funds to save those relegated from the human condition from dying out. A coordination of VLCOs is established with the name of 'Endless Emergency'.

Endless emergency: walls, camps, deserts

We need not continue with this fiction, which hardly counts as imaginary. Just bringing all the facts together is enough to create a fictional effect, even one of science fiction. And yet almost all the facts just mentioned are already reality – the hundreds of African camps revealed by each new conflict, each new massive displacement of population due to war, famine, violence, as if Africa had no other option of survival except that of becoming the twenty-first century's continent of camps; or the Palestinian territories of the West Bank, with the long wall separating them from Israel, under construction since June 2002 – 408 kilometres already built by May 2007 (56.5 per cent of the projected total), and sealed by a combination of ditches, trenches, barbed wire, electric fences, electronic barriers and concrete walls 3 metres high.[1]

The reality of the world today, and not the fiction of novels set in the future, is also that of the Afghan asylum seekers in Australia who were held until 2003 in military-humanitarian camps at Woomera, where some of them killed themselves by hurling themselves against the barbed-wire fences; or in the same part of the world, on Nauru and Christmas Island, where the Australian government has built large detention camps for asylum seekers prevented from entering its territorial waters. It is the reality of dozens of Sudanese exiles (27 according to the police, but over 150 according to human rights organizations) killed by the Egyptian police in the centre of Cairo on 30 December 2005, after having been deprived of their rights by the UN High Commission for Refugees, whose representative himself requested the Egyptian government to expel the Sudanese. It is that of the European frontiers made tighter by the hardening of security policy after 2002–5:[2] borders of many kinds, dotted with sophisticated control systems, high barriers (Ceuta, Melilla), waiting zones for travellers without a visa (there are 100 of these at French sea ports and airports), or again administrative detention centres for foreigners and asylum seekers (30 or so in France in 2007). It is also, more widely and in the same period, the reality of the detention camps for immigrants systematically established on the other side of the Mediterranean, in Algeria or Libya, where some African 'illegals' are sent back and abandoned in the desert with no means of survival, eventually to die.

This then is not a science-fiction tale, but an actual development in the world with prospects that are likely to be highly pessimistic. If all this continues, in fact, camps will no longer be used just to keep vulnerable refugees alive, but rather to park and guard all kinds of undesirable populations. This movement is already under way: for several years now people have been speaking of a 'return of the camps' to the borders of Europe, and the growing interest of historians over the last few years in the camps established in France from the beginning of the twentieth century seems indeed to express questions born of this actuality.[3] If the twentieth century in Europe was the 'century of camps',[4] what is happening on the world scale today

3

is the extension and greater sophistication of various forms of camps that make up a mechanism for keeping away undesirables and foreigners of all kinds – refugees, displaced, 'rejected'. In a world context dominated by the national and inter-governmental obsession with controlling mobility and frontiers, it is possible to draw up an inventory of these camps.[5] What purpose do they serve today, from the Sangatte 'hangar'[6] to the Palestinian camps in Nablus, via the network of camps for displaced persons and refugees along the Mano River (Liberia, Sierra Leone and Guinea)? The diversification in the forms of camp, the widening of frontier zones, the increased control of wandering populations – all this today adds up to consolidating a partition between two great world categories that are increasingly reified: on the one hand, a clean, healthy and visible world; on the other, the world's residual 'remnants', dark, diseased and invisible.

Managing the undesirables: the disturbing ambiguity of humanitarianism

The 'very large charitable organizations' of our little fiction are not in a different world. If the history of the camps displays on a world scale a control of movements and a distancing of certain populations treated differently, most often foreigners – if it thus displays a *police* mentality of confinement and separation – today's humanitarian organizations have made a speciality for themselves of 'managing' these spaces and populations apart. Humanitarian intervention borders on policing. There is no care without control. Today, NGOs and all those working for humanitarian intervention find themselves caught in a process that is seemingly pragmatic, but far too powerful for humanist goodwill. The development of the refugee camps from the 1960s and 1970s in the Middle East and Asia, then from the late 1980s on a massive scale in Africa and to a lesser degree in Central America and Eastern Europe, were only the anticipation and preparation – 'morally correct' as vulnerable lives really were saved at this time – of a political strategy and control technique that closes the gates of the 'World' to all these undesirable 'Remnants'. This takes place behind the wonderful screen of the interventions of rescue, protection, reconstruction and 'peace building' conducted by humanitarian organizations and UN agencies. It is this development, already visible today, that has steadily led me to investigate the formation of a global mechanism that I will refer to here as humanitarian government. My argument aims to put in relief the control that this mechanism ensures over extra-territorial spaces ('out-places' as I call them) and a section of the world population – outcasts and pariahs of all origins – who are both undesirable and vulnerable.

I shall mention in this book the effects of a functional solidarity, 'organic' in the Durkheimian sense, between the humanitarian world (the hand that cares) and the police and military ordering (the hand that strikes) on the part of the world as a whole. I do not see this connection as an institutional one, and certainly not a manipulating intentionality that need only be denounced for the critique of humanitarianism to be complete. The work of the anthropologist is not to denounce scandals, nor to 'reveal' hidden intentions that would serve to fuel the moral or ideological condemnation of humanitarian action that regularly appears in humanitarian, political and media milieus. Rather than any idea of denunciation, I prefer to say – and demonstrate – that the connection is contextual and functional, that individual intention acts only within this 'place' of humanitarianism in the world's social, moral and political order, and to understand on this basis how humanitarian action today is always deeply ambiguous. It has a power of life and death in the space assigned to it, but also and above all a major role in the transformation of individual lives, of social and cultural models, in the places where it operates. My position seems to be both more radical in relation to the forms of domination specific to the humanitarian mechanism, and more respectful of the individuals acting in its framework – of their intentions if not always their ideas.

The anthropologist, less polemical and more critical, is able to think in a manner less tied to immediate events; criticism here is based on the available data – even those that do not seem useful in operational analysis – and on a fundamental freedom of action and expression. This does not mean fatalism or defeatism – quite the contrary. Rather than a 'system' proceeding unconsciously by itself, humanitarianism is an unstable arrangement made up of networks, leaderships and values. Each person involved can, if they want, constantly criticize their own action in relation to its contexts and its effects in the world as it is. The case of the refugee camps, which the present book will study in depth, is an example of this, and certainly the most complete today as regards the disconcerting ambiguity of humanitarianism. But this goes beyond just the space of the camps; all spaces created today by intervention under the humanitarian banner echo this ambiguity on all sides. It is in this direction that I have been forced to expand my research, and to situate refugees among all those others today who likewise find themselves devoid of state protection or recognition and constitute a whole world of undesirables, to situate the refugee camps among the many present forms of *encampment*, and finally to situate the forms of power that are locally observable in the globalized perspective of humanitarian government.

Observation, participation, commitment

What I offer here is the result of a lengthy investigation and in-depth reflection, based on a series of fieldwork studies conducted over seven years (2000–7) in the refugee camps. More precisely, these were the three camps at Dadaab in Kenya (in 2000); the Maheba camp in Zambia (2002); and, in the Forest Region of Guinea (2003), the two camps of Boreah and Kountaya (Kissidougou region), the Kuankan camp (Macenta) and the three camps around Nzérékoré, as well as the transit centres on the Liberian frontier; also included were the camps of the Bô-Kenema region and the transit centre of Kailahun in Sierra Leone (2003); the displaced persons' camps of the Bong region and the surroundings of Monrovia in Liberia (2004 and 2007); and finally the camps of Balata and Askar at Nablus in the occupied West Bank (2005). Towns and villages situated close to these camps – or at certain stops on the routes taken by refugees, 'internally displaced persons' and 'returnees' – have also been the object of specific studies, as at Kailahun (the Sierra Leone – Guinea – Liberia border region in 2003) and the Foya region (Lofa county, Liberia, in 2007).

In this book I shall describe and analyse in detail several of these refugee camps. They provide information on the distinct treatment of the individuals and groups that form part of the world's 50 million 'victims of forced displacement'.[7] But I shall not try to argue for the institutional existence of a 'population' of which all definitions and measurements are the object of controversy as regards the categories of identification used to construct them (you are only a 'refugee' because an institution decides to classify you as such, after having previously considered you as 'illegal', 'asylum applicant', 'tolerated', etc.). Nor shall I try to validate the figures – so often approximate and contradictory, and sometimes quite imaginary – that are produced in order to quantify these categories, and whose fluctuations essentially derive from changes in identification that depend on the institutions that count and recount categories of individuals at the same time as they name and rename them.[8]

The position that I take in defining the object of research (and the place of the researcher) is a different one: it makes institutional strategies an object of study and analysis; it is detached without being too distant; it includes the whole network of humanitarian arrangements while requiring the researcher's personal presence within this in order to be attentive to its details. It is from this attention to detail, to the grains of dust that jam the machinery, the recalcitrant words of individuals about the roles assigned them, that the ethnologist can learn and transmit most.[9] This procedure will make it possible to describe (as ethnographer) and understand (as anthropologist) a modality of social organization that is deployed on a world scale and treats a section of the planet's population according to a special regime, that of humanitarian government – an organization and a regime that are always observable at the local level.

My involvement in the voluntary organizations of the humanitarian movement, however, has been another important source of knowledge and reflection. Indeed, my work with Médecins Sans Frontières, initially necessary to gain access to the camps with full independence,[10] was transformed into a stronger commitment following my election to the executive council of MSF-France in 2004, and again in 2007. Without losing anything at all in the way of freedom of speech, I find that a critical posture towards the humanitarian 'apparatus' and the political contexts of its interventions – a posture that is something of a 'hallmark' of MSF, even if the reality is more contradictory[11] – goes well together with my own commitment to the humanitarian movement: critical and reflective, as well as being attentive to crises and their human consequences.

This book, therefore, contains not only the results of my ethnographic observations in the refugee camps,[12] but also an echo of the debates raised by those who travel the world with the object of assisting populations in distress. Is a critical commitment to humanitarian action possible? What is it that transforms the terrains of humanitarian action into places of anthropological experiment in the broad sense of the term, i.e. where the contemporary experience of alterity is put to the test? Is all humanism 'trapped' in the way that humanitarian action is today? What can be done?

Finally, if the reader of these pages is willing to accompany me in this investigation between terrain and theory, we shall reach a radical critique of the foundations, contexts, and political effects of present-day humanitarian action. Everything then has to be reconceived and recommenced. What future are 'emergency' interventions and the spaces they create moving towards? Can other utopias be opposed to that which, paradoxically, is in the process of stifling international solidarity after having wanted to reinvent it? Beyond the end of the camps, will we be able to create the conditions for a reinvention of asylum and refuge, a reinvention of the city and of solidarity?

Part One

A World of Undesirables, a Network of Camps

— 1 —

Refugees, Displaced, Rejected:
The Itinerary of the Stateless

Recognizing, identifying and describing those people who are said to be entitled to humanitarian intervention could lead to fieldwork on identities and recognition – two concepts that have 'worried' the social sciences for several decades. Such a study, however, is immediately vitiated by the presence on the ground of a different kind of investigation: one aiming to define in law and in practice (sometimes violently) categories of identity to be used to classify and sort individuals as refugees, displaced, disaster victims, tolerated, detained, rejected, in order to integrate them, expel them or keep them waiting.

Following the establishment of the United Nations High Commission for Refugees in 1951, one might have expected this body to create the conditions for a space of recognition and speech, by guaranteeing (physical and legal) protection and respect for the human rights of those individuals who had lost these in their state of origin and had not yet recovered them either in the state receiving them or another. The creation of this institution, and the universalist message it was intended to bear, had a connection with the Cold War: the Western world wanted to be the land of asylum for the 'good' victims of communism.[1] The status of refugee was defined by the UN's Geneva Convention of 1951, precisely when the UNHCR was founded. The definition of 'refugee' in this Convention reflected the universalistic aim of 'protecting' the stateless, being broader than the status of 'political refugee' that had previously been in use, and that international institutions refer to as 'conventional'.[2] Gradually, however, a function of control (whether in the application of asylum policies or in the management of camps) came to accompany that of protection, and very often to dominate it.[3]

11

This development confirms what we have known ever since the measures for reception of foreigners adopted in France in the nineteenth century: every policy of assistance is simultaneously an instrument of control over its beneficiaries.⁴ Even earlier in history, the first charitable activities, according to Jean-Christophe Rufin, former president of Action Contre la Faim (ACF) and now French ambassador to Senegal and Gambia, were 'means of political and social control'.⁵ Thus, in the seventeenth century, the almoner Vincent de Paul, who founded a number of orders giving aid to the poor, abandoned children and vagabonds exposed to disease, already embodied a certain 'prehistory of humanitarianism'. What an unexpected success his enterprise had! Very rapidly, the state and its police decreed the internment of those very populations as a condition of official responsibility for them: 'The monarchy took over the work of Saint Vincent de Paul for its own purpose. It saw this as the opportunity to complete its control over society, including its margins, the poor and the sick, and all those on whom poverty had conferred a paradoxical and dangerous freedom.'⁶

The proximity between the functions of investigation, control and care, between acts of assistance and police actions, is accompanied today, in the first decade of the twenty-first century, by ever more frequent and commonplace 'slippages' in the exercise of power over the lives of immigrants and refugees – either recognized and documented, tolerated or declared 'illegal'. As we shall see right away, these slippages relegate the stateless to the very limits of life – limits from which they initially believed they had freed themselves. But, given the dead who pile up at the borders or against the fences of government or international authorities, it is important to seek the meaning of such events by widening the focus. What is sketched out in the pages that follow is an overall understanding of the development of the question of 'displaced populations', of exile, the stateless and the right of asylum, in the twentieth and twenty-first centuries. If it is a matter of course for institutional categories to be arbitrary, changes have gradually been made in the identities assigned to displaced persons, and in their political, police and humanitarian treatment.

The researcher scarcely has any option but one of deconstruction, to take up this term of Derrida's that denotes both an epistemological stance and a manner of seeing and experiencing the present world. My study thus questions any pretence to a 'sociological realism' that consists in taking constructed categories as realities in themselves.

Commentaries on a massacre

In Cairo, on 30 December 2005, a horrific massacre took place, in which the Egyptian police killed dozens of Sudanese (27, including 7 children, according to official figures; over 150 according to certain lawyers and voluntary organizations). Somewhat over 1,000 people had gathered to demand 'resettlement' (re-establishment in a third country), having occupied for the last three months a park located close to the compound of the UNHCR, which refused to satisfy their demand. They declared that they were the target of anti-Black racism by the Arab Egyptian population, and that it was impossible for them to return to their country which was still partially at war – the two justifications required for any demand for transfer to a third country to be acceptable.[7] At the same time, however, the UNHCR announced the objective of repatriating 60,000 Sudanese in the first half of 2006 from neighbouring countries, including Egypt. The demonstrators, two-thirds of whom were at this point the recognized responsibility of the UNHCR – they held either 'yellow cards' (temporary asylum) or 'blue cards' (refugees) – were led by a group that called itself 'The Voice of the Refugees' and was quite familiar with their rights. Barbara Harrell-Bond,[8] who was in Cairo at this time and in contact with some of the demonstrators, explains that they

> wanted to present a united front of their demands, and insisted that they came from all parts of the Sudan, that they were not just southern Sudanese but included people from Darfur and from the east. The UNHCR, for its part, said that the majority were from southern Sudan and that they were there because they did not want to return to their country (after the peace agreements).[9]

It is generally agreed that the situation in southern Sudan was not secure at this point. In Darfur, in the west of Sudan, various armed groups were scattered throughout the region, increasingly less subject to control, and armed conflict with neighbouring Chad was deemed imminent. From the start of their occupation, in September 2005, the demonstrators of Mustapha Mahmoud Square had written on their placards (in both Arabic and English) that they did not want this so-called 'voluntary' repatriation, plans for which, however, still continued. This was a terrifying prospect both for those with refugee status and for those other Sudanese exiles viewed as 'illegal'. Refugees know that, everywhere in Africa, UNHCR announcements of repatriation lead first of all to a period of individual 'voluntary returns', then to one of 'collective returns' – which for them means the start of organized 'non-voluntary' returns. The representatives of the UN agency here are far removed from the cosy image that people in European countries have of the UNHCR.

The killing of these Sudanese demonstrators in the course of the brutal intervention by a regiment of 6,000 police on 30 December 2005 followed the regional representative of the UNHCR considering their file as 'closed' and asking the Egyptian government, on 22 December, to 'urgently take all appropriate measures to resolve this situation' – naturally 'by peaceful means'.[10]

Already a few weeks earlier, exasperated by a month of spontaneous camping outside its gates,[11] the representative of the UNHCR had written to the Egyptian government clearly explaining its refusal of responsibility: 'Although lacking precise information [sic], we have good reason for believing that the majority of the demonstrators are not refugees in possession of the UNHCR card . . . The majority are expellees who do not concern the UNHCR.' The letter concluded, 'The situation must not continue', and already called for the intervention of the Egyptian authorities, though requesting at the end a 'humane treatment' of the problem.[12]

On 27 December, seeing the situation deteriorate, UNHCR representatives agreed to negotiate with leaders of the demonstrators, and promised to re-open 'closed files'. Too late! Distrustful of declarations that did not guarantee any formal commitment on the part of the UNHCR, which they knew was their only genuine 'partner' in negotiations, the Sudanese remained where they were. The police assault, predicted and announced the day before by political and international milieus in the Egyptian capital, was anything but peaceful: 'The UNHCR said that the Egyptian government wanted to break the movement', Barbara Harrell-Bond protested; 'And this is the reason why I am quite distressed that Egypt is made responsible for everything, whereas it was the UNHCR that requested it. The police in Egypt are not trained to disperse people peacefully, as they are in other countries!'

It is clear that the Sudanese exiles – successively or alternatively viewed as 'refugees', 'asylum applicants' or 'expellees' – no longer existed as a problem of 'urban encumbrance' around the offices of the UNHCR.

This massacre, therefore, was not only one of individuals deprived of all their rights ('closed files', in the UNHCR's term), but also of people who considered themselves as stateless. This political dimension is indispensable to understanding the movement's development.

14

The event, in fact, shows that a 'citizens" protest did indeed exist (known rights, demands, public expression, negotiations). Its target was not the Egyptian government but the UNHCR – in other words, the higher expression of power in the perimeter of humanitarian government. The UNHCR is the sole interlocutor to which they felt a right to address themselves, but this UN institution chose to reject them, before reversing its position *in extremis* (but already too late), thus revealing, in the confusion and strategic fluctuations of the days before the massacre, the object of the disagreement: Is a politics of the stateless possible? Does a political right exist that includes the right to 'protection' outside the protection of a nation-state? Can citizenship be exercised by the stateless? Rejected de facto – in the sense that they were left to fend for themselves, receiving no response after weeks on Mustapha Mahmoud Square – the demonstrators demanded the application of their right to request asylum and resettlement, and, more generally, to ask the United Nations agency for refugees to protect them in lieu of their non-protection by an absent or failing state. Their action and the drama that followed are inscribed in a long story of the stateless, which raises for all of us the endlessly repeated question of the relationship of individuals to the state.

The stateless as urban encumbrance

The non-recognition of refugees and those asking for help produces, at the end of the day, people whose every right is 'rejected'; they stubbornly ask for a right to life, and find no state in which this minimal human right is extended to them. This empty place, i.e. this situation defined by the absence of one of the two terms necessary for the citizen relationship (the individual, the state), logically leads to action deemed 'illegal', this being nothing more than the search for a right to life in an amputated relationship, that of an individual without a state. We find here, therefore, the whole question of the stateless that Hannah Arendt showed, more than fifty years ago, is central for reconsidering citizenship and the nation-state, and to which the creation of the UNHCR in the early 1950s seemed to be a response. We must thus return here to this question of the stateless, before seeing how it is redefined in the present context.

In the very year that the UNHCR was established, Hannah Arendt characterized as follows the lot of those that she called the stateless:

15

'The nation-state, incapable of providing a law for those who had lost the protection of a national government, transferred the whole matter to the police.'[13] The political question of the meaning of withdrawal of state protection had been denied, from the 1930s onward, in the (seemingly technical and demographic) term 'displaced populations', still in use today. Moreover, internment camps, such as those for Spanish refugees in southern France, had been the systematic response to what was reduced to a mere problem of residence for these 'displaced populations'.

Submerged in the troubles of exile and the risks of anonymity, refugees made a common complaint that remained unheard: 'No one knows who I am.' By their flight, they had been forced to renounce their exercise of citizenship, the name of a double political relationship – both the recognition and protection of a state. In the world of exile, legislation on refugees (as individuals) or stateless minority peoples (as collectives) applied categories of identity that arose from the rejection that these individuals and groups experienced from the nation-state. The creation of the stateless meant recognizing the nation-state's inability to integrate these individuals and groups, from the double standpoint of protection (legal, security, social) and recognition (political right). Their existence thus ultimately forced a reconsideration of the definition of the nation itself.

Arendt showed that the question of the stateless could not be historically reduced simply to the Jewish question – even if this embodied the global and contemporary archetype of both exodus and genocide. She also showed in the early 1950s that the emergence of the Jewish state did not suppress the question of the stateless. And the half-century that followed these characteristic reflections has only confirmed them. It is true that over the course of history it is large de-territorialized minorities, or diasporas, that have most visibly raised the question of the state by that of their own autonomy, and thus their legitimate right to create a state of their own: the Jews, but also the Inuit, the Kabyls, the Somalians and the Palestinians have all encountered in their collective histories the problematic of a dispersed people in search of a state-territory.

Yet beyond this territorial aspect of the demand for recognition at the collective level, the same question of the state – and the stateless – arises as a 'mechanical' effect of the forced displacement of individuals, isolated or en masse, outside of any a priori ethnic or communal identity. Only a community of existence, based on shared experience and lived situation, can then unite these anonymous crowds in a history made up of violent disruptions, then an administrative category of identity ('refugees', 'displaced', 'illegals', 'asylum seekers'), and finally a special security and humanitarian treatment. Confined in spaces that are out-places, they see their political existence depends no longer (or not only) on their origins, but on local contexts of identification, and particularly on the camps in which they live. It is here that collective actions undertaken by these various categories acquire their political meaning, when the occupants of the camps intervene on the terrain that is allocated them, to demand social rights attaching to their present condition. Displacement, expulsion and action thus form the framework of a community of existence.[14] How is the tie between individuals, territory and the exercise of citizenship then woven? What is the political meaning of the 'neutrality' of these spaces without identity – the zones and camps that depend on administrative, police or humanitarian powers? How are their occupants identified, without state or identity, in the spaces of transit, in which they are confined for an indefinite duration?

'If I had to choose a single image to embody the present immigration policies, I would take that of the traffic policeman', wrote the philosopher Federica Sossi, after conducting a study in the detention camp for undocumented immigrants on the island of Lampedusa in Italy; 'or rather', she continued, 'in this age of so-called globalism, that of a whole body of traffic police trying to regulate the movements of human beings in the way that they do urban traffic'.[15] This image – which I could also use here for the meaning of the network of camps for refugees and displaced people in Africa, the waiting zones, transit centres and other 'way stations' – signals that a double development, both theoretical and practical, makes exile and the exiled a policing matter. The question of the stateless is not new, as we have seen, but it is resurfacing today in a different form: as a variant of the biopolitical conception of managing life it is transformed into a problem of urban encumbrance, i.e. of public order. By speaking only of circulations and flows, the management of entrants or the control of encumbrances, the question of the stateless is not just depoliticized, but dehumanized. The second is the consequence of the first, as the technical approach of maps, large numbers and flows contributes to de-subjectivizing the categories of population managed by this apparatus, according to a biopolitical principle.

An in-depth analysis of the work of Hannah Arendt undertaken by the philosopher Marie-Claire Caloz-Tschopp from the University of Geneva includes among the 'stateless' all those 'superfluous' individuals who in one way or another lose the protection of a state: refugees in camps or wandering, exiled minorities, internally displaced and expelled, i.e. the whole series of those who are today 'disconnected from any political system able to offer them a place and protect them'.[16] But statelessness is more broadly and deeply a premonition, even a preparation, for a complete 'human superfluity' in the sense in which total dehumanization (i.e. the suppression of life) is already historically and politically prepared by the suppression of rights.[17] Beyond the negative political figure of the stateless, there is thus more broadly another negative figure, in this case an anthropological one, as the basis for the special control, rejection and management of the undesirable.

There are a set of concepts inspired by Arendt that are employed today in this domain of study – this 'field', as Pierre Bourdieu would have put it, a thematic and pluridisciplinary one (philosophers, political scientists, jurists, sociologists, ethnologists, geographers, all exchange ideas) – summed up in the paradigmatic figure of the stateless in the broad sense, i.e. an individual with no exercise of citizenship, with no 'right to have rights'. There are other notions also in this set, which give nuance or complexity to the description of this superfluity, and justify the fact that the question we face today is that of the management of the undesirable on a planetary scale. The notions of 'supernumeraries' (Mike Davis), 'human refuse' (Zygmunt Bauman), 'bare life' (Walter Benjamin, Giorgio Agamben) or 'pariahs' (Eleni Varikas, Loïc Wacquant) are specifically used by these authors for describing a range of convergent present phenomena of sociological exclusion and spatial distancing. These convergences, and the various different studies, share in an anthropology of the contemporary production of undesirables, whether these are identified as pariahs, supernumeraries, or again as individuals and groups without the protection or recognition of a state, and without a territory of their own. This anthropology is in itself a political project of contemporary urgency. We need only ask what governing the stateless means today. This is simply a policing matter, which is being developed and perfected, and implies: (1) identifying the undesirable at a given point in time, in a given context, by giving them the names of specific populations; (2) 'containing' them by keeping them at a distance. These two operations keep those who are captured outside the legal and geographical borders of the common political order, whose surface is that much reduced. It is in this way, to echo Hannah Arendt's cry of alarm, that 'the desert is growing', and the 'common world' retreating as the sea leaves its shores and the very water disappears.[18]

It is a mere step from this to non-existence. And a step that can be crossed as soon as the political possibility is opened of letting people simply die, as witness a series of events in the border spaces over the last few years.

From refugee to rejected: accounts and identities

I shall turn my attention first of all to the production of categories of identity and numbers, then to the possibility of letting a section of the undesirables die off. The facts and analyses that precede have led us towards a necessary critical study of statistical 'truths', political announcements and strategies of communication concerning the present treatment of refugees and undesirable foreigners throughout the world. The production and use of large numbers on the one hand, control and differentiation of targeted populations on the other, are both among the means that humanitarian government applies to manage the undesirable and rejectable part of the world. We shall go on to look at the spaces and functions of this global mechanism.[19] I shall describe here its means, in particular those bearing on the production of figures and categories of 'populations' counted.

Around 50 million persons are qualified by the UNHCR as 'victims of forced displacement'.[20] Among these, between 10 and 18 million, depending on the year in question, are registered as refugees in the strict sense, i.e. living outside their home country. Massively concentrated in Asia and Africa, these refugees are on top of the 4 million Palestinians who left their land as refugees from the 1940s to 1960s and live in various Middle East countries (Lebanon, Jordan, Syria and the Palestinian Territories).[21] Something over 3 million persons, however, are viewed by the UNHCR as 'returnees', i.e. persons 'in the course of repatriation' to their country of origin. And finally, something between 25 and 30 million, according to different estimates, are internally displaced persons (IDPs).[22]

All these figures are very approximate, and change from year to year; they are controversial, and constantly challenged. They do not include a considerable (but nevertheless uncountable) number of exiles who have not declared themselves refugees and are considered as illegal. These include, for example, the 130,000 supposedly 'invisible' Afghan refugees resulting from the American attack of October–November 2001, whom the UNHCR managed to get the Pakistani government to recognize officially *in extremis*, so that it could place them in emergency camps that it established along the

Afghan frontier. They also include a section of Somalian, Ethiopian and Rwandan refugees in neighbouring countries, referred to as 'self-settled': some because they prefer to try their luck illegally in the informal economy rather than being shut up in the camps; others still wandering because their status as refugees has not been officially recognized. And again, for example, the 9,000 people who reached the Canary Isles clandestinely from sub-Saharan Africa between January and May 2006 after a perilous voyage on makeshift rafts (*pateras*) from the coasts of Mauritania and Morocco, not to mention those who reached the Spanish or Italian mainland; all these left behind them, in the sea, hundreds of 'brothers' who died during the crossing.

At the beginning of 2006, according to the report published on the UNHCR website, there were only 9.5 million refugees in the world. By and large, commentators took their lead from the UN High Commissioner for Refugees, António Guterres, and did not express any real satisfaction. A certain incredulity was inevitable towards such highly political announcements of a decline in warfare – announcements whose function basically aims at glorifying the policing strategy led today by the USA and its various allies against the indistinct and inexhaustible bloc of 'rogue states'. In actual fact, this military strategy has rather led to a transformation of war, a social and spatial dissemination of militia violence, and the establishment of social and economic chaos in contexts of crisis or those that have rather too swiftly been proclaimed as 'post-war' (Iraq, Afghanistan, Liberia, Sierra Leone, Sudan, Angola, etc.). This decline, we should remember, only concerns refugees in the strict sense, those properly registered, whose official number (which leaves out the 4 million Palestinian refugees) passed 15 million in the early 1990s, reaching 18 million in the middle of that decade, before falling to 12 million by the turn of the millennium and finally to 9.5 million according to the announcement at the start of 2006.

This number rose again in 2007 to over 11 million, particularly including the 2 million Iraqis outside their country's borders, who for the most part are not recognized as conventional refugees (in terms of the Geneva Convention of 1951). In October 2007, for example, there were between 500,000 and 750,000 Iraqi exiles in Jordan, a country of 6 million inhabitants. Only 49,000 (around 7 per cent) had been registered as asylum seekers. The great majority of Iraqi exiles were thus without papers.[23] At the start of 2008, according to the International Organization for Migration, Iraq was still faced with a 'serious humanitarian crisis': out of 26 million inhabitants, more than 2.4 million Iraqis were displaced within the country and 2 million had fled, chiefly to neighbouring Syria and Jordan.[24] But these two states do not offer refugee status, and restrict the possibilities of residence. According to a report from the Coordination Française pour le Droit d'Asile (CFDA), the length of authorized stay for Iraqis in Syria was extended to three months in 2006, but since 2007 has been no more than one month when the visa is delivered at the border. In Jordan, Iraqis now only receive transit visas of two days, and are thus almost immediately illegal and expellable. Lebanon, finally, has totally closed its doors to Iraqis. And Europe has granted refugee status to 20,000 Iraqis (in Sweden, the Netherlands and Germany), or less than 1 per cent of the total number of Iraqi exiles since 2003, whilst also restricting legal possibilities for acceding to refugee status or 'resettlement' through the UNHCR. If the European Commission, the United States, Germany and France did indeed come up with significant funds, at the conference on the question of Iraqi refugees organized in Geneva in April 2007 by the UNHCR, these were allocated exclusively to 'externalization', i.e. assistance with looking after Iraqis in countries adjacent, and even the solutions proposed were marked by a certain fragility. Thus the UNHCR itself signed agreements with Syria, Jordan and Lebanon, providing that these countries would limit their recognition of refugee status to a term of one year, after which these people would be liable to imprisonment or forced return to Iraq, unless they benefited from an improbable 'resettlement in a third country'.[25]

The present treatment of Iraqi exiles, of which I have given just a summary 'snapshot' for the period 2006–8, illustrates what has happened to wars marked by a protracted climate of violence and chaos. And yet, while being actors in this new form of war, conceived as a police operation on a world scale, the Western countries have made use of this novelty in order to reverse the rights of refugees. A Swedish court, for example, held that 'there is not really armed conflict in Iraq'. Such an assertion has immediate effects on the provision of refugee status. The questioning of conventional refugee status (as defined by the Geneva Convention of 1951) and the production of temporary and limited statuses, each with a national character and not subject to international rules, very rapidly leading to situations of 'illegality' and the expulsion of foreigners, is the dominant tendency in the world today. In a more general fashion, the decline (observed since the early 2000s) in the official figure for persons coming under the category of 'refugees' corresponds to an actual increase in other categories: IDPs and such substitute categories as 'territorial asylum', 'humanitarian asylum', 'temporary protection', etc. Thus in the European Union in 1999, only a quarter of refugees were 'statutory' or 'conventional', i.e. coming under the Geneva Convention, while others enjoyed only 'temporary asylum'. In France, the share of acceptance of so-called 'conventional' asylum applications fell from 80 per cent in 1981 to 20 per cent in 1999,[26] and to less than 10 per cent in 2007. More or less the same development can be found in all European countries for this period, certain of these reducing the share of conventional refugees to a quite insignificant proportion (1 per cent in Greece, for example).

In the worlds of exile – particularly among public authorities, international agencies and NGOs working in this sector – there is a notable propensity to extend the terminology of categories. Refugees, displaced, disaster victims, evacuees, migrants, asylum seekers, rejected, expelled, repatriated, returned . . . This list has grown ever longer in recent years. According to country or continent, one or other of these categories seems to be taken for granted, despite appearing strange in another country. Thus Poland, until its entry into the European Union in November 2007, classified Chechen asylum seekers who were refused the title of statutory refugee as 'tolerated': the situation in Chechnya was considered dangerous, and they were not expelled from Poland. But though officially 'tolerated', they were in fact interned in some fifteen centres for asylum seekers. In France, the wind of protest that swept the centres of administrative detention (CRAs) in the first half of 2008 – against the bad living conditions and the draft European law that allowed the period of detention to be increased to eighteen months, for the closing of the detention centres themselves and for the regularization of the *sans-papiers* – made a broad public familiar with the term *retenus*,[27] which does not correspond to any precise legal category.

We thus see a proliferation of categories that makes the management of flows of people more complex, and the real figures more opaque, as well as the conditions of life of all those who come under these categories. The invention of specific criteria also makes it possible to 'de-internationalize' the statuses and rights granted to exiles, even those for whom the risk of persecution in a context of war or generalized violence leaves no doubt, as is the case with the Chechen and Iraqi exiles, who need have no hesitation in claiming the status of refugee as defined by the Geneva Convention. As we have seen in the case of the Iraqis, the categories of 'temporary', 'humanitarian' or 'subsidiary' asylum and assistance make it possible to remove the individuals thus designated from the international legal framework, and give more room for manoeuvre to national or inter-governmental policies (especially European) regarding the duration attaching to this category (generally reduced to a year) and the scope of rights accorded. At the same time as the freedom of movement for foreigners is restricted, the legal and material means for expelling them and keeping them out have expanded. If expulsions of undocumented foreigners in France have for several years now had an annual target of 25,000, this measure can be blamed on the European Parliament's passing a directive in spring 2008 that allowed an extension to eighteen months of the detention period for such foreigners in closed centres. The two measures share a single objective: to create laws and spaces of exception for an indistinct set of undesirables.[28]

Recent studies of the legal technique and material procedure of examination of asylum applications, bearing more precisely on France and Europe, show the expeditive and inquisitorial character of relations between the representatives of the institution and the exiles: the logic of suspicion, the extremely limited time for face-to-face interview with the asylum applicant, incomprehension due to translation and cultural gaps, all ensure that 'the account of exile is crushed and flattened',[29] and thus explain, almost technically, how arbitrary the categorizations are. The toughening of this procedure is also promoted by a more strategic factor: it is well known how the agents of OFPRA[30] in France have personal quotas of rejections to attain, in the absence of which they risk the non-renewal of their one-year contract! But this constraint is not a local specificity or merely anecdotal. It actually generalizes the reversal of procedural logic that has taken place: on the one hand, arbitrary rates of rejection of asylum requests can be seen in many other countries, European and American;[31] on the other hand, whatever the particular case, the procedure consists in 'an examination taking between a few minutes and a few hours . . . by officials who have only local means of investigation, most often with scant resources in the way of documentation and up-to-date data on the countries in question'.[32] Jérôme Valluy, a political scientist who spent several years as a judge on the Commission des Recours des Réfugiés (CRR), notes, in a commentary corroborated by several confidential testimonies from OFPRA agents on their interventions at the Roissy airport, how even the explanation of a hasty departure can refer to an experience that goes back several years:

> either because the situation of the exile insidiously deteriorated to the point at which an inhibiting fear was subjectively perceived, or because the triggering factor, even if quite sudden, did not spare the exile the

23

further suffering of going far back in time to explain, to himself first and then to others, this strange capsizing of his life; and finally because the chaotic society that presses people to exile displays a complexity that is equally hard to master in both biographical narrative and socio-logical analysis.[33]

But the procedure aims at constructing a specific reality: not the res-titution of the personal biography of this or that exile, but the justi-fication of a statistical result of the treatment of asylum applications: the rate of rejection is thus essentially 'tribute to the choices of public policy'.[34]

In 2007, the rejection rate of asylum applications in France, as in Europe generally, rose above 90 per cent, at which point it is legiti-mate to believe that the Geneva Convention of 1951 that defined the status of refugee has today been challenged by the facts on the ground, opening the way to future political and institutional chal-lenges, the rumours of which are growing in parallel with technical improvements in the management of population movements.[35]

The abandoned: living and dying as a pariah

The strategies of control, stoppage and rejection may extend not only to territorial quarantine, even expulsion, but also, at the end of the day – though this still remains exceptional in quantitative terms – to the death of the 'encumbrances'.

Let us take the second half of 2005, which ended with the Cairo massacre which I discussed at the start of this chapter. The weeks and months that preceded this saw an exacerbation of threats to the life of certain refugees, exiles and asylum seekers in a general context of pursuing the undesirables.

In Kabul, early in October the same year, ten hunger strikers were demanding their regularization by the UNHCR, which partially con-ceded to them when the media began to take an interest in the affair. Nearly two months later, two of their number set fire to themselves outside the UN office, after the UNHCR had stopped its support and refused to grant them 'resettlement'.

On the night of 28 September 2005, eleven rejected and 'illegal' asylum seekers died on the high fences that form the border between Morocco and the Spanish enclave of Ceuta (where a barrier 3 metres high has been erected), killed by the Spanish and Moroccan police who 'took the right' to fire on the crowd who were attempting to cross. According to various voluntary organizations, other individuals have been transported and left in the south Moroccan desert, others again near the Algerian frontier, where they died.

Expelled from Morocco to Algeria in August 2005, a group of 535 African migrants (from Cameroon, Congo, Mali, the Central African Republic, Nigeria, Liberia, etc.) were deported by five Algerian trucks into the desert near the frontier with Mali, by the oasis of Tinzaoutine. Located some 300 kilometres from the first Malian town, and 400 kilometres from Tamanrasset, Tinzaoutine is 'a place where God does not exist', as one survivor put it, 'where there is all the suffering on earth'. Survivors described their walk for a week through the desert until they reached the first Malian posts, and their survival thanks to the milk given them by some nomads that they occasionally passed.[36]

Let us now go back a couple of years. In Guinea, between August and October 2003, at the Boreah refugee camp in the Forest Region, I met a group of men and women from Sierra Leone and Liberia who had been forced to take refuge there a few weeks before, after living in the Guinean capital of Conakry for several months (in certain cases years), or at least surviving there by means of informal trade, fishing and the sale of fish.[37] They explained to me the troubles that had forced them into the camp.

In June of that year, in Conakry, a number of exiles from Sierra Leone and Liberia demanded, in a street demonstration whose target was the UNHCR, to be recognized as refugees and helped by the UN agency. The response of the UNHCR at the time gave satisfaction to the Guinean government, which required the question to be settled as a problem of public order – the refugees had to move to camps in the Forest Region, 600 kilometres away, otherwise they would be deemed illegal: 'after the transfer date [to the camps], those refugees who remained at Conakry ran the risk of being forcibly seized in round-ups [by the Guinean police]', said the official note of the UNHCR, which at the same time de facto abandoned responsibility for their protection.[38]

The exemplary character of these exceptional situations, showing both the limits of life and the limits of politics, appears just as much in the actions, resistance tactics and declarations made in several countries by asylum seekers, displaced persons or refugees asking for specific help (the right to work, help with housing, support for establishing themselves in towns, etc.), as we shall see below from a series of examples. These actions find an echo in those emerging, for example, in France, where *sans-papiers* and those whose asylum applications have been rejected often find themselves side by side in making themselves heard (via squats, occupations of churches or local administrative buildings, hunger strikes in detention centres, etc.), creating a new type of political struggle without any recognition of their citizenship being a precondition for this.

In Bogotá in December 1999, nearly 200 Colombian *desplazados* (displaced by the war within their country) occupied the offices of the International Committee of the Red Cross (ICRC), relying on the diplomatic protection of the site so as to make their voice heard more clearly outside the country, and not to be expelled. Soon over 1,000 were demanding access to *certificación*,[39] and claiming financial support for 'productive projects' in the city, with some three-quarters of the occupiers wanting not to return 'home' and to be allowed to settle in Bogotá. The police responded by closing off access to the street leading to the building. Although the movement obtained some satisfaction after several months of struggle, certain *desplazados* decided to remain and squat the building, which had been abandoned by the ICRC staff: at the end of 2002, twenty-six families were still living in these offices, the Colombian authorities not having the legal means to evict them since this was a 'neutral' and protected site. Since 1997, the year that the Colombian parliament passed a law recognizing the status of *desplazado* as a 'humanitarian problem', several invasions and occupations of various institutions had taken place in the country: ministries and town halls, but particularly churches, embassies, and the offices of international organizations. There was an ongoing debate between government bodies and human rights associations as to the criteria for granting a *desplazado* card, the length of this recognition (three months, renewable once), and consequently the number of internally displaced in the country: 3 million according to the voluntary associations, only half this number according to government sources.

At Luanda, in early November 2002, some fifty 'refugees' representatives' from different countries (Rwanda, Sudan, Congo-Brazzaville and the Democratic Republic of Congo) demonstrated at the Angolan parliament to demand decent living conditions. These refugees had occupied the offices of the UNHCR, in the centre of the city, since the previous August, as a protest against their mistreatment. Expelled from the parliament building by the police, they demonstrated in the streets of Luanda, and sent a letter to Agence France Presse accusing the UNHCR of not providing them with minimal support: drinking water and shelters. They also demanded not to be repatriated to their countries of origin, and claimed application of the Geneva Convention in order to obtain resettlement in an African third country.

'Not in the Pas-de-Calais', said a senior official of this French *département* in October 2002. The barring of new arrivals from the Red Cross reception centre at Sangatte did not interrupt the influx of refugees to the region and the town of Calais. The security strategy of considering every refugee as a policing problem removed any hope of citizenship and reduced them to a stigmatized identity that was reinforced by every police act of rejection. Did this Pas-de-Calais official seeking to seal off his *département* know that he was paraphrasing the American expression 'Not in my back yard' that gave rise to the NIMBY symbol for denoting the privatized and sealed quarters of the white middle class in Los Angeles?[40] He also paraphrased the statements made a year earlier by a representative of the Australian government in September 2001, at the time of the *Tampa* affair.

In August of that year, the Norwegian cargo boat *Tampa* had picked up over 400 Afghan refugees from the Indian Ocean, near the Australian possession of Christmas Island. Refusing them entry into its territorial waters, the Australian government was faced with a hunger strike by the refugees. It placed the ship under surveillance by an elite commando unit, mobilized its special air force and prevented the ship from entering its national territory. This placed it, legally, against the principle of non-return inscribed in the 1951 Geneva Convention (an illegal immigrant cannot be returned to his country of origin before the examination of his asylum application), which forced it to revise its position somewhat. The refugees then suspended their hunger strike and were eventually transferred to neighbouring territories, in New Zealand and the minuscule island of Nauru, an independent Pacific state of 11,000 inhabitants linked closely with Australia. In the course of the Australian government's altercations with the UN and international legal agencies, a senior official of the Australian ministry of justice publicly declared that the refugees from the *Tampa* 'were free to go wherever they wanted outside of Australia'.[41]

Other Afghans and Iraqis who were refugees in Australia awaiting the response to their asylum applications were held for several months in six detention camps, including one at Woomera, built in 1999 in the South Australian desert. Hunger strikes, riots, street demonstrations, destruction of barbed-wire fences, confrontations with the police, escapes, as well as suicides and self-mutilations were among the forms of resistance with which these refugees without status confronted the 'Australian model', which militarized the country's relationship to refugees and undisguisedly assimilated the humanitarian camp to a military camp.[42] A few years later, in December 2005, a new detention centre for asylum seekers was constructed on Christmas Island.

The situation of refugees, displaced persons and asylum seekers in the world today has a double particularity: it represents an extreme relegation, and provokes the emergence of political subjects in equally extreme forms. There is an intensification of the limit at which socially and politically rejected people find themselves, just as there is a redundancy of exceptionality in the historical and contemporary figures of the pariah. Concluding her investigation of pariahs, Eleni Varikas mentions this de-centring that permits us here to doubt the false evidence produced by the state about norms and the abnormal, the inside and the outside, the line of frontiers, etc. I shall quote a lengthy extract, as this describes very well the 'against the grain' approach that I see as necessary in order to remove any normative bias from the study:

> By locating at the heart of politics experiences that were – and still are – stigmatized as minoritarian and exceptional, the stories of pariahs open a field of questioning in which the vicissitudes of historical democracy can be revisited and re-assessed from the standpoint of their failures: barbarisms made thinkable and possible by a system of legitimization in which domination, unable to speak its name, is obliged to resort to categorizations that still today exclude whole populations from the right to have rights, even from the very concept of humanity. By placing in relief what remains present and threatening in the pariah condition, such questioning against the grain makes it possible to resist the devastating logic of such categorizations by recalling how much violence was required for them to acquire their indisputable self-evidence.[43]

It is this crossing of the limit that raises the problem, a crossing produced by a combination of political and intellectual relegation, creating the theoretical space occupied by those persons and groups who are – at the cognitive level if not yet physically – excluded 'from the concept of humanity'.

By de-centring and reflecting on politics on the basis of this double exception – as a series of special categories in spatial, social and legal terms, and as the expression of a specific political inequality and 'minority' – it is possible to render more visible the violent production, by the state, of norms and the abnormal, categories and pariahs, territories and the extra-territorial, the counted and those left out of account. And it is starting from this 'perimeter' with its many criteria, defined by public policies (national, inter-governmental, UN), that we can grasp the new forms of politics that are being born within it, i.e. at the limit.

The end of refugees? The connections between immigration and asylum

The image of the refugee has profoundly changed since the period of the 1930s to 1950s. Fifty or sixty-five years ago, the intellectual and political dimensions of exile were validated and gave rise to strong partisan solidarities with the waves of Spanish, Jewish, Hungarian, Russian and other refugees, who did indeed find refuge in camps, but also in families or with political or intellectual friends in both Europe and the United States. At the other end of this trajectory of the refugee we have the 1980s, and above all the 1990s, after the fall of the Berlin wall: the years of 'population displacements', massive and depersonalized crowds walking along roads with bundles of clothes on their heads and a child on the back, or heaped in immense makeshift camps, chiefly in Africa or Asia. Frontier crossings by anonymous hordes fleeing in confusion: this new situation justified the collective emergency attribution of refugee status, in what is known as prima facie procedure.[44] In this context, political solidarity gradually gave way to the anxieties aroused by these wandering masses in movement, certainly perceived as masses of 'victims', but just as often as supernumerary and undesirable populations.

The figure of the 'internally displaced person' (IDP) appeared in the discourse of the major international organizations in the 1990s, at the same time as the management of refugees outside their country of origin was entering a critical period, especially in Africa. Since then, the number of IDPs has not stopped growing. At the end of the decade, however, the concept of 'internal asylum' was also introduced into European policy discussion of immigration control. This responded particularly to NGO researchers and actors who were already familiar in Africa or South America with camps for the 'internally displaced'.[45] The concept of internal asylum appeared when the European states and UN agencies were discussing strategies for externalizing the asylum procedure, i.e. aiming to contain asylum seekers outside the European borders, in regions of Asia or the Mediterranean, or else in Africa. This strategy of promoting 'internal asylum' clearly

29

echoed the experience of camps for the internally displaced in the countries of the South: these camps are managed or created by national and international NGOs. They 'collect' those who can be called 'refugees *intra muros*'. Hoping to return home when the situation settles down, or blocked at their country's border for a variety of reasons (lack of funds to pay for transport, lack of security at the border crossing, refusal of entry by the neighbouring country, etc.), these people become 'internally displaced'. Their number in the world, according to different estimates, ranges from 25 million to 30 million; the figure is hard to verify since they are not all housed in camps. The countries best known for holding internally displaced persons in camps are Liberia, Sudan and Angola. Colombia, which counted close to 3 million *desplazados* in 2007, does not have any officially open camps, but several informal and permanent gathering sites have come into being (in sports halls, for example), and certain NGOs have tried in vain to create spaces of 'neutrality' respected by both the guerrilla forces and the paramilitaries. These spaces are designed to receive displaced persons from rural areas – peasants in Colombia being the first 'hostages' of the armed conflict between guerrilla forces, army and paramilitaries. This strategy of internal asylum in neutral spaces met with dramatic setbacks, as shown by the well-known examples of San José de Apartado and San Francisco de Asís,[46] whose representatives were massacred a few months after being awarded various honorary titles and prizes for their initiatives by human rights organizations in Europe and the United States. The project continues, but has recently taken the new form of an attempt to create neutral spaces known as 'humanitarian zones'. The leaders of these zones then speak a language close to the humanitarian discourse of justification: the image of the victim then comes to the fore in place of a more political discourse on peasant movements, internal war or human rights.[47]

In the perspective defined by European inter-governmental policy, internal asylum is ideal as it places the undesirables at a double distance: firstly, in camps, and secondly, far from the European borders – chiefly, indeed, in African countries. A number of NGOs have thus seen their 'protection' strategies for the internally displaced revised, reinterpreted and completely reversed by European policies with quite different ends.

In the same way, the European governments' mechanism aiming to give a special role to so-called 'buffer states', particularly in North Africa, in enclosing and filtering foreigners, is based on the same principle of keeping out and enclosing undesirables, while getting the voluntary humanitarian organizations to contribute in 'managing' flows and refuges.[48] There is now military and police cooperation between European and African countries for handling population flows. In the wake of Morocco, other African countries were also annexed to the security policies of European governments: Libya opened camps and signed agreements with Italy for readmitting expellees, while Spain collaborated with Morocco and then Mauritania in establishing camps in which expellees would be placed, and Senegal cooperated profitably with Spain and France against 'illegal immigration'. We have seen above how the European countries and the United States, with the collaboration of the UNHCR, supported Middle Eastern countries financially with a view to 'externalizing' their temporary responsibility for Iraqi refugees, likely to be rejected and expelled after one year of recognition.

Over the last few decades, the dominant image of the exile has thus been transformed. It initially took the form of the refugee, itself devalued over the years until it could be explicitly challenged – for example, in European governmental spheres that seek to 'globalize' control of population movements without distinguishing between 'conventional' refugees and other individuals who have left their country.[49]

It was then the figures of the internally displaced that came to the fore, two or three times more numerous today than those of the statutory refugees. The internally displaced and the institutional response to them in the concept of 'internal asylum' have been in constant flux, since the extreme distance that they embody (leaving potential refugees imprisoned in their own country) makes the refugee question invisible . . . and thus makes possible the silent collapse of international solidarity towards them.

It is now the figure of the 'rejected' that is emerging and tending to supplant the increasingly less visible problematic of the refugees and internally displaced: the rejected are no longer exiles, and held to be illegal – often equated in France with the category of *sans-papiers*, more generally redefined and stigmatized as illegal immigrant. This generic term criminalizes in an indistinct fashion any displacement of individuals who are undesirable under one heading or another.

But if refugees, displaced and rejected represent three successively dominant categories of exile, from the 1950s through to today, these classifications can also be assumed by the same individual in the space of a few years or even a few months, in the course of their movements. Certain lives cross over these identities, assigned according to the principle of communicating vessels between categories and regions of the world. For example, a Liberian *displaced person* who lived in 2002–3 (at the height of the civil war between Charles Taylor and the LURD[50] rebels) in a camp for the internally displaced, on the outskirts of Monrovia, became a *refugee* in 2003 if he then fled to a UNHCR camp in the Forest Region of Guinea and was given this qualification, then an *illegal* if he left in 2005 to seek work in Conakry, where he would come across many compatriots living in the Liberian quarter of the Guinean capital. Then, after spending days at the bottom of the hold of a cargo boat, he might try to enter Europe, ending up in one of the hundred or so ZAPIs ('waiting zones for persons under review') at the French ports and airports. He will now be officially considered a *detainee*, before he can be registered as an *asylum applicant*, with a 90 per cent chance of being *rejected*, his demand being classified by the OFPRA agent as 'manifestly unfounded'. He will then be taken to the frontier and *expelled* from France, or else *held* in a CRA while waiting for the administrative procedures necessary for his expulsion to be finalized (which may take weeks or months), or again left at liberty in the situation of a 'non-expellable irregular'. He then becomes a *sans-papiers*, a status somewhat close to that of *tolerated*, which is given in Poland to persons in a situation similar to his own – generally, in that case, to Chechens. If he makes a further request for asylum, he runs a heavy risk of being rejected again, as Liberia is no longer considered a dangerous country since the peace agreement of 2004 and the surrender of Taylor. How can the staff of OFPRA or the CRR be made to understand that the situation of Liberia in 2007 is chaotic, that the former militias have become armed gangs ready to undertake any kind of 'contract', that the presence of the UN armed forces represents a fragile safety-valve, and that their departure, envisaged since 2006 but postponed every six months, risks provoking a return of violence?

One fact thus stands out today: the management of undesirables is becoming ever more complex and diversified, in terms of the terminology and statistics of identifying categories and the spaces associated with them. It draws on at least two combined forces, humanitarian and police, as can be seen in the treatment of 'sub-Saharans' in Morocco, and more generally in North Africa, where voluntary organizations and NGOs have responded to appeals from the European governments and the European Commission for offers to take charge of the detention of sub-Saharan 'illegals', or to come to their aid in the context of such detention – which is certainly not the same thing, but forms part, whether they like it or not, of the same mechanism of control, simply attenuated somewhat by a 'humane treatment of the problem'. Humanitarian action thus increasingly finds itself, if not systematically 'trapped', at least included a priori in the control strategies of migratory flows of all kinds.

Some people may find it surprising that this chapter devoted to figures and the different categories of 'displaced persons' in the world has drawn so little on demography, or quantitative data, however crude or relative. Such data, we may note, are abundantly widespread, and readily available in reports by UN agencies and on their websites – especially the reports of the UNHCR, which are not sparing on tables, graphs and visuals.[51] But we have seen how these quantitative data have been produced 'on the ground' before being passed through the cogs of a statistical production able to produce truth effects that are seemingly beyond discussion!

By choosing instead to base myself on facts, conflicts and cases of aggression drawn from field studies or attested information of events of the last few years, and presenting the categories and principles of classification of individuals, I have sought to show that these principles produce, at the same time as figures, different modalities of recognition, responsibility or rejection. My purpose is thus clear: every act of naming and classifying is a political act. It is based on simple tautologies, i.e. on closed circuits of reasoning in which figures can only confirm the arbitrary definitions given a priori in specific political contexts according to 'the devastating logic of categorizations'.[52] Definitions of this kind are not based on any universal and fixed scientific framework, they have only the appearance of scientific rigour.

For example, as we saw above, a hastily negotiated agreement between the UNHCR and the Pakistani government in November 2001 led to 130,000 Afghans who were living 'illegally' in Pakistan being granted, overnight, the status of 'refugees', with the sole object of having them occupy the camps set up by the UNHCR, against the background of strong media propaganda, which had so far remained almost empty. Similarly, the 'regularizations' of 'illegal immigrants' that European governments have sometimes effected demonstrate how categories can be manipulated and statistics modified in record time.[53]

What is particularly arbitrary in Europe, in the present controversies over asylum seekers, or in the classifications of 'refugees', 'bogus refugees', 'illegals', etc., is also echoed in Guinea, Angola and

Australia. There is nowhere in the world that can serve as a standard for proper classification: all categorizations of 'refugee', all asylum policies, are fluctuating realities in history and space. From near or far, they basically depend on the attitude of the dominant powers towards those countries that are dependent on them – politically, militarily or economically.

These facts are not totally new. Gérard Noiriel has shown very well the connection between public policies of population control, the economic situation of the host country, and the development of the right of asylum.[54] Evoking the 'globalization of interdependencies' that became apparent in the 1970s and was reflected in the challenging of the principle of the right of asylum (the text of the 1951 Geneva Convention), Noiriel goes on to emphasize how 'until the mid 1970s . . . a large number of foreign workers *who could have claimed refugee status* did not bother to request this favour, certain that they would find work in the industrialized countries'.[55] As a consequence, if economics is indeed present in the question of the right of asylum, this is because the present economic crisis lays bare the assignment of identity to foreign workers who are the first to lose their jobs. They thus find themselves without any other social attribute than their foreignness, their biography, and the history of their relationship to the host country.[56] The only human rights that these properties – reducing them to the unique status of foreigner – are capable of founding are in the end those arising from the right of asylum. When this is now called into question, the category of 'rejected' and/or 'illegal immigrant' is then produced – two names for the same story.

There is thus a contemporary way in which economic crisis and ideological retreat in the face of a global culture make exile into a criminal experience, no longer valued as it has been at other points in history.[57] At the dawn of the twenty-first century, xenophobic and identitarian attitudes are developing more or less everywhere, and form a public pressure that tends to restrict the right of asylum and promote the building of walls and camps.

The political question of the stateless is more current today than at any previous time, even if the terms have changed a great deal since the creation of the UNHCR and the 1951 Geneva Convention. Still today, whatever the legal and identity categories ascribed to them on the path of exile, those women and men labelled 'refugees', 'internally displaced', 'expelled' or 'illegal' are still referred to the essential question of their citizenship, which alone opens for them the way to the 'right to have rights'. In this context, conventional refugee status becomes more rare – which does not mean that the real causes of its attribution have disappeared, those pertaining to violence and chaos in the country of origin, as is shown by the case of the 2.5 million Iraqis living outside their country, the majority of whom do not have the title of refugee. What has changed is the migration policies of the countries of the North, and the control that they exert over those of the South (in Africa, Latin America, the Middle East and Asia), and over those individuals hailing from them, no matter what the situations of violence, chaos or distress that provoked their departure.

— 2 —

Encampment Today:
An Attempted Inventory

Along with population displacements, frontier spaces and camps form a reality that is not only in spatial movement, but also quite 'liquid' in its substance – in the sense in which Zygmunt Bauman speaks of a 'liquid modernity', unstable and uncertain, in the world of today.[1] Camps and frontier zones are exemplary to the point of excess of this liquidity, even a certain 'plasticity' if we keep to the strict sense of the prevailing material in the building of camps: tents, covers, boxes, etc., made out of plastic sheeting. They are spaces of mobility. Airlock, sorting zone, park, refuge, enclosure, camp: what role do these play in regulating the flow of persons? If the sites opened and managed by the UNHCR and the major NGOs – camps for refugees and displaced persons, camps to house returnees, transit zones – form the principal matter of the present study, they have to be placed in a broader ensemble of confinement and circulation.

The numbers involved

Official statistics give only a very partial picture of the concentration of refugees, displaced persons and asylum seekers in camps. In 2002, the UNHCR counted some 4.5 million refugees, in the strict sense, in the camps under its authority. Almost half of these were in Africa (47 per cent), with 38 per cent in Asia and 14 per cent in Europe.[2] The accommodation of refugees in camps, according to Luc Cambrezy, a geographer at the Institut de Recherche pour le Développement (IRD), is 'the speciality of poor countries': in Africa in 2002, these camps sheltered 83.2 per cent of refugees assisted by the UNHCR, and in Asia 95.9 per cent, as against 14.3 per cent in Europe.[3] These rates, if they are applied to the number of refugees registered with the UNHCR in 2007, give a total somewhat higher than the 6.5 million statutory refugees housed in camps throughout the world. Even if we have to be satisfied with statistical approximations, we can maintain that camps are indeed the fourth solution of the UNHCR for resolving the refugee 'problem' – a massive and lasting solution, and clearly the preferred one in Africa and Asia, to the detriment of the three other official solutions: repatriation, integration in the land of asylum, and resettlement in a third country. They are also a shameful solution, as is the permanent existence of camps in general, for the institutions that establish and manage them: no specific mention is made of them in the documents published to present the action of the UNHCR to the world.[4]

On top of this, 1.5 million Palestinian refugees – out of the 4 million counted by UNRWA – still live in sixty or so camps set up between the late 1940s and the 1960s in Lebanon, Syria, Jordan and the Palestinian territories of the West Bank and Gaza. More recently, Sudanese and Iraqi exiles, not counted among the 'refugees' officially adopted, have settled around these camps, increasing their population informally while confirming the potential for camps to be properly urbanized – in which respect the Palestinian camps, in their very excess and their long history, are exemplary rather than exceptional.

The figures for refugee camps proper have to be supplemented by those for camps for the internally displaced, in particular in Sudan. There are camps around Khartoum in which over a million Sudanese from the south of the country have been settled and urbanized since the 1980s; in the same country, 2.3 million people from Darfur have been displaced since 2003, with nearly 2 million of them living in camps: Darfur province alone had at least sixty-five of these camps at the end of 2007, the largest – at Gereida – housing 120,000. These figures come from an Amnesty International study of 2007 on the displaced of Darfur, which stated:

Others are not living in camps but sheltering in towns in Darfur, squatting in shacks or living with relatives or others who have offered them a corner of their house. In addition, hundreds of others, mostly newly displaced, are sheltering in the bush, where they survive precariously on wild fruits and cereals or with help from local people whose villages have been spared. Thousands more Dafuris escaped to towns elsewhere in Sudan, mostly in neighbouring Kordofan state. Some reached eastern Sudan, where many people from Darfur have lived for years working on economic projects, and some fled to Khartoum. About 240,000 people from Darfur are known to be living in twelve refugee camps in eastern Chad.[5]

There are also older situations – in certain countries that had very large numbers of internally displaced (Angola, Liberia, Afghanistan) – where the return of such people has been only partly counted and, when departures from the camps did take place, the paths of return did not lead the displaced back to their region of origin (or that of their parents) but very often to capital cities or larger towns close to their original rural zones. This was the case in Liberia, where half a million IDPs were housed in camps during the war, with 240,000 still in this situation at the end of 2004, and between 30,000 and 50,000 at the end of 2006. In 2007, in the rural zones, a large proportion of 'missings' was noted, people who, it was supposed, were still in Monrovia. In Angola, camps for the displaced received over a million occupants between 1970 and 2002 (on top of several hundred thousand actual refugees), and the 'returns' of displaced people that began in 2002 failed to repopulate the rural zones. On the contrary, the displaced, and especially their children, remained overwhelmingly in or near the towns where the camps were located.

Finally, we must mention the uncertain future of people who were displaced and now find themselves in contexts defined officially as 'post-war' but which are still chaotic, as in Afghanistan, where camps for displaced persons received several hundred thousand people between 2001 and 2005. On top of this, tens of thousands of internally displaced were provisionally received in new camps in late 2007 and early 2008 in the east of the Democratic Republic of Congo and in Kenya.

If we try to give a snapshot of the approximate number of camp residents at a moment in time, taking into account the available but heterogeneous figures that we have just cited for the period from 2002 to 2007, with adjustment and update to the lowest likely level for 2007–8, the population of official camps – those of the UNHCR and UNRWA, and those for the internally displaced – may be estimated today at some 12 million. This number does not include so-called 'self-settled' camps (land that villagers have allowed homeless refugees to settle on), nor the detention centres and waiting zones in Europe and North Africa (several tens of thousands of 'detainees').

Camps, transit zones, reception centres, camps for the displaced or 'villages' of refugees – the situations vary greatly and are always in flux. The UNHCR's classifications distinguish different conditions of reception and management. We can start by considering four major types of gathering spaces, as these are seen by UN, humanitarian, and policing agencies: 'cross-border points' in the UNHCR's official terminology; 'transit centres'; 'refugee camps' or 'refugee settlements'; and camps for 'internally displaced persons'.

I shall present the broad features of these four types of spaces, drawing chiefly on African examples, since these correspond to the different spaces that I have visited and studied. Comparing them to other examples, in particular European, North African or Middle Eastern, we shall see that certain parallels are possible in terms of the role played by these spaces in the movement of individuals and the removal of the most undesirable, on a scale that is no longer local or regional, but very largely globalized. This will lead us to reclassify these types of site according to the function that they occupy in a wider mechanism of survival, control and distancing. We shall thus be able to expand our approach and successively introduce the spaces that correspond to four major constellations of function and mode of management. I list these below, using my own terms for an analytical and generic designation, while indicating in parentheses the terms by which they are currently known:

- self-organized refuges ('cross-border points', informal campgrounds, 'jungles', 'ghettos', 'grey zones', 'squats');
- sorting centres (transit centres, 'way stations', 'holding centres', camps for foreigners, waiting zones);
- spaces of confinement (refugee camps, UNHCR rural settlements).
- unprotected reserves (camps for internally displaced persons).

We shall now go into more detail on each of these four groupings.

Self-organized refuges

'I took refuge here' is the expression that establishes these limit situations, the most 'borderline' of sites. In effect, this first set of spaces can be identified by the fact that they are composed of refuges in the primary sense of the term – places where people have found refuge. They are hiding-places or provisional shelters in the forest or in town (squats), sites of rest or waiting between two border posts, where people stop for a while, always ready to leave. They are characteristically extremely precarious as well as informal, invisible or even illegal.

In the zone of conflict on the Mano River (Liberia, Sierra Leone, the Forest Region of Guinea, between 1989 and 2004), what the UNHCR defines as cross-border points are spaces that humanitarian organizations sometimes refer to as 'grey zones', on account of their being hard to access and almost invisible. Tents are provided by an NGO, sometimes food distribution in case of emergency, possibly rare visits by health workers from a medical organization a few hours each week or fortnight. One example will give the measure of the precariousness and invisibility of these refugees.

At the time of a visit in October 2003 to the 'cross-border point' of Thuo, a village on the Guinean border with Liberia, which the Médicins Sans Frontières vehicle reached several kilometres beyond the final 'transit centre' of Bossou (in Guinea), 100 refugees were housed in two large tents. They were living in extremely precarious conditions: damp, mud, lack of food. The MSF mobile team visited once a week. These are spaces of desolation. There are police posts a few dozen metres from the tents, one at the point of entry to Liberia, the other likewise to Guinea. There is no food distribution, so that refugees are forced to rely on the local villagers, a practice that the UNHCR adduces to justify not taking responsibility for these people ('African solidarity'). There are young women with children and young men who escaped forced recruitment by the armed gangs and want to reach a camp in Guinea because they seek physical safety or dream of continuing an education that has been interrupted several times since the start of the war. On the whole, these are single people or small groups, elements of families dispersed after their last flight a few months before – or in some cases years. The few adult men present with their families stand out as exceptions. They take charge of the fate of others, seemingly more fragile, who are exhausted. They become 'tent heads' and are the interlocutors of the UNHCR and NGO agents when they come to Thuo.

The individuals that we spoke to had been there for one or two weeks; they were waiting for UNHCR lorries to arrive and take them to the transit centres and refugee camps of Lainé or Kola, located to the north around Nzérékoré, the capital of Guinea's Forest Region. In actual fact, there was a game of hide-and-seek between the UNHCR and certain refugees who did not want to be registered immediately and taken to a camp. Some of these were exploring the surroundings, to assess the possibility of remaining in the villages and finding help there in exchange for labour that they could offer at a very low price. Others had certain family members registered with the UNHCR and taken to a camp, while trying for their own part to find a place

40

locally, possibly benefiting from the monthly ration of the World Food Programme, which they would go and collect from the camp on the day of its monthly distribution.

This form of cross-border point, with a low 'visibility' from the viewpoint of the UN and humanitarian organizations, has parallels with other forms of gathering, in particular so-called 'self-settled' campsites where exiles congregate before being in any way recognized or controlled by the UNHCR. This is the case, for example, with the self-settled camp outside the village of Buedu in Sierra Leone, some 15 kilometres from the Liberian border. A large number of Liberian refugees arrived in the region in 2001, at the time when the fighting in that country was starting up again in Lofa county, after several years of relative calm.[6] More than 35,000 Liberians, from towns and villages situated just on the other side of the border, arrived in the district of Buedu alone. Even though they came from places that were not far away, and belonged to kindred lineages,[7] their arrival saturated the villagers' available housing stock and largely exhausted their food supply. The inhabitants then asked their refugee 'relatives' to settle on some unused land outside the village. This occupation became a self-settled camp in 2001. It gathered up to 4,000 people before the UNHCR forcibly closed it the following year, arguing that it was too close to the border, and brought all the refugees into its own camps in the centre of the country (the Bô–Kenema axis). The refugees in the Buedu encampment had a rigorous organization, with a 'chairman' and secretary who kept a precise count of the arrivals and departures of Liberians, both in the camp itself and more generally for the district of which Buedu was the centre.

Other forms of informal gathering show parallels with this modality of self-organized refuges, which, as the case of the Liberians here illustrates, involves exiles not yet recognized under an institutional category (neither refugees nor immigrants, nor asylum seekers, nor even 'undocumented'), i.e. literally stateless as we have defined this in chapter 1. Largely invisible and unclassifiable from the standpoint of both national and international organizations, they are relatively well organized as communities formed in their present precarious – and, they believe, provisional – situation. They survive thanks to contact with the local population, often being allowed patches of land to cultivate or some job to do (after the model of the Liberians in Sierra Leone or Guinea), as well as food or covering donated by voluntary associations. The many small camps of illegal immigrants established in the wood at Dubrulle near Calais, just a kilometre from the port used by lorries crossing to England, are an illustration of this (in particular as regards the aid of voluntary associations). This is also the case with the camps that African exiles have established in Morocco: waiting to attempt the crossing into Spanish territory, they take refuge in the forests of Belyounech (near the Spanish enclave of Ceuta) and Gourougou (on the heights above Melilla, the other Spanish enclave).

The sociologist Smaïn Laacher has made a study of these camps, their conditions of survival and their internal organization.[8] At Dubrulle, outside Calais, 'you come across small encampments grouped by national and ethnic community. These are makeshift shelters made out of tarpaulins and plastic for the walls and branches covered by a piece of cloth for the roof, which the rain and cold easily penetrate.'[9] The camps are formed by family or tribal affinity, or by nationality (Somalians, Sudanese, Eritreans, Ethiopians, Iraqis, Afghans). The occupants of these sites have given their refuges the name of 'jungle'. Those in the self-settled encampments in the Belyounech forest call their camps 'ghettos'. Based on the stories of African exiles who had spent several months in these encampments, Smaïn Laacher has described the complex political organization of the forest occupants. In both places this came into being gradually, introducing an internal order into the 'ghetto'. This order made possible a detailed collective organization of attempts at crossing the border fences (a route known as the 'fence trip'),[10] the provision of water and food (by searching refuse bins), emergency organization to cope with police raids, etc. These are communities formed on the spot at the moment of meeting, according to nationality – fourteen communities are installed in the Belyounech forest: from Ivory Coast, Gambia, Guinea, Senegal, Congo, Mali, Chad, Sierra Leone, etc. The community 'chairmen' are re-elected monthly, if their own fence crossings have not succeeded. There are also a second and a third chairman, an elected council with its head, a judge, police, a treasurer, as well as individuals responsible for relations between the different communities (the 'African Union', made up of the various community chairmen, known as the 'blue helmets'). The turnover is substantial, although certain individuals may remain in place for several months – in exceptional cases even years[11] – but the functions that keep the organization going are maintained. The point, as Smaïn Laacher notes, is to 'transform this space so as not to succumb to it'.[12] In the woods around Calais, as in the camps of the Moroccan forest, such sites make it possible for their occupants to remain out of sight of the local population and the police: 'Everyone knows they are there, but the most important thing for everybody is to preserve their invisibility.' The Moroccan forest camps represent a 'space of fixation close to the border',[13] comparable in this respect with the 'jungle' shelters around Calais or the self-settled camps of Liberians in Sierra Leone, or again the tents that other Liberians occupy on the border ground between Guinea and Liberia.

Finally, the same invisibility and illegality, the same marginal situation, characterize those unadopted displaced persons and refugees who take refuge in urban squats. More than three years after the official end of the war in Liberia, Monrovia in 2007 was still, people said, a veritable 'displaced persons' camp'. The expression designates on the one hand the rapid rise in population of the poorest and most marginal quarters of the capital after the official closing of the camps for displaced people on the edge of the city;[14] on the other hand, and still more explicitly, to say that Monrovia is a vast 'displaced persons' camp' is to allude to the abundance of squats established in the city in former hotels, buildings under construction, abandoned houses and those half-destroyed by the war.

In January 2007, along with two workers from Médecins Sans Frontières, I visited a squat in an unfinished building in the district of Congo Town. The occupants were displaced persons from several of the Liberian counties most touched by the war, including Nimba, Bony and Lofa. This squat was led by a 'chairman' who had been there since it was first established in 1991, less than two years after the start of the first war in Liberia. We were told that he was elected, and people called him 'the boss'. His wife ran the largest shop on the ground floor of the building, where a small market in foodstuffs and everyday needs was permanently held. The squat's occupants did not have work, but some made a living by breaking up stones and selling them by the roadside.

At the other end of the city, a squat in a former hotel has been occupied by displaced persons since 2003. The building had previously been used by the army of president Charles Taylor. It has seven storeys, and is located on a small hill at the end of the main avenue from the city centre. There were around 2,500 inhabitants according to the local 'chairman'. He was himself a former employee of the hotel, who remained after it was requisitioned by the army and was recognized by the soldiers as the authority for the place, then by the displaced persons who arrived later. It is him that they go and see on their arrival to obtain authorization to stay. He has been there for years, hoping that after everything is over the hotel will be repaired and open again, and that he will get back his old job.[15]

We can continue this list of self-organized refuges and steadily widen their characteristics. In Liberia again, for example, certain internally displaced people from the north of the country have settled in the disused building of a former radio station situated close to a displaced persons' camp.[16] At that time, early in 2007, the majority of the internally displaced evacuated the camp on the orders of the UNHCR, but, as well as those who did not leave, it was informally occupied by new arrivals. There were then between 4,000 and 5,000 occupants, half of them refugees from Sierra Leone who refused to return to their country and half displaced persons from Liberia itself.

The building of the old Voice of America station is a squat without water or electricity. Several small rooms and a few large communal halls have been very basically equipped: a mattress, a chair, a brazier for cooking. Among the occupants, all Liberians, some have not been registered as IDPs, others have been registered but say they are waiting for assistance with resettlement – supposed to pay the cost of their return trip and contribute to covering their expenses on arrival.

There is a similar confusion of civilian populations (refugees, internally displaced, returnees) in the Kailahun region of Sierra Leone close to the borders with Guinea and Liberia. The 'illegals' are numerous here, simply because the UNHCR and the local political authorities 'decided' in 2003 that there were no more Liberian refugees in the town and its district. The reality was very different. Kailahun town had been a stronghold of the RUF[17] rebels until the end of 2001. Late in 2003 it had a strong military presence: that of the Sierra Leone armed forces (who had their camp at the edge of the town), that of the 'Pak Bat' (the Pakistani battalion of the UN blue helmets), as well as various foreign experts from 'Mil-Obs' (military observers of UNAMSIL, the United Nations Mission in Sierra Leone). As well as this military presence, there was that of NGO and UNHCR officials, also recent and substantial. Although no census or official assessment of the population had been carried out, everyone agrees that there were around 1,000 inhabitants in the town during the war (1991–2002), as against 15,000 before the war and nearly 8,000 in 2003, over a year after the return of peace. In December 2003 I carried out a check on the entries concerning people hospitalized at the MSF clinic in Kailahun.[18] We learn from this register that the town and its surroundings only counted at that time 20 per cent 'residents' (i.e. individuals who had remained in the district throughout), as against 73 per cent 'returnees' – the latter breaking down into 13 per cent who had been internally displaced, 37 per cent who had been refugees

44

in Guinea, and 23 per cent refugees in Liberia – and finally 7 per cent Liberian refugees, i.e. nearly 600 Liberians at that date in the small town of Kailahun. Informal districts acquired a stable identity, including 'Kula Camp'. There you could find Liberian refugees and Sierra Leonese 'returnees' whom the UNHCR had brought back from Guinea.

More generally, zones squatted by displaced people and refugees exist in many African towns, particularly in capitals such as Khartoum or Conakry. In the Guinean capital, an unfinished hotel building serves as a squat where Guinean soldiers live alongside Sierra Leonese refugees, 100 or so occupants in all.

All these situations are marked by an extreme material precariousness, and the feeling that those people who settle there will remain only for a short period. If this is indeed the general case, these zones are also transition points with a long life expectancy, and sometimes sites of urban stabilization.

This incomplete picture of the 'grey zones' is the ground floor in the great edifice of camps in the world today. But it leads to two paths of research that must be briefly mentioned before we continue our inventory. On the one hand, these different camps and their occupants are linked by a continuity of meaning and function. A space of self-established refuges can be marked out as follows: it reaches from the big tents on the Guinea–Liberia border to the peripheral districts of African and Asian cities, by way of the forest encampments and certain squats in European cities. These refuges are border spaces, or more precisely spaces between borders. They are extreme cases of 'out-places', the most distant, the least visible and the least integrated. They take conceptions of locality to the limit, in both a spatial and a political sense. Indeed, with the precarious form of tents, encampments, 'invasions' and urban wastelands, we can associate the figures of threshold and interstice, in a relationship to space and the state well evoked by the French word *banlieue* – the physically and legally uncertain territory of the 'ban', on the margin of society but still under the hold of the state that keeps the power to control and abandon it. Maintaining this paradoxical relationship at the limit of physical and social life is perfectly rendered by the ambivalence of the word 'ban': the expression of law (a solemn proclamation or interdiction), but also with the sense of outlawry. The *ban-lieu*, however, is not strictly speaking a place, rather a relationship that connects the public power – generally represented by the state, but also, as we have shown, by the 'international community' – and the shores of precarious life, whether this precariousness is

45

expressed in terms of habitat and urbanism, employment and income, civil right or social context. A global *ban-lieu* is today being increasingly formed, neither strictly urban nor rural, but peripheral to each of these sectors, an intermediate or *liminal* position that epitomizes its physical and political classification.[19]

On the other hand, as we have seen from the majority of the above examples, these refuges are not simply self-settled but also self-organized. Hierarchies re-emerge in the context of emergency survival, minimal relations of power that assure the establishment of an order in the disorder of events or the 'jungle'. In the face of situations of extreme relegation, a crisis or an emergency, provisional communities are formed in the context of flight, illegal existence or disaster, whenever the individuals who come together in such a situation share a minimum in the way of moral and political rules. What then are these rules that serve as the foundation of a shared meaning in an emergency situation? Even if in the cases mentioned here the social contexts observed largely refer to a common basis, the shadow of this reference is a broad one, stretching from the family to the nation, and only rarely translates the reproduction of milieus of mutual acquaintance or pre-existing social networks. We can at least note that, if the groups formed in this emergency situation share from the start some common values or languages, they are not based on a recognition of identity but far more on the situation, space and event that are shared.[20] The survival communities may all be different, but they tend towards the formation of *communities without identity*. The 'jungle', the 'ghetto' or the 'camp' (when this term is used to refer to a district of a town) are symbols formed on the basis of common place-names, indeed among the most globalized of this kind; they have no identity markings. The gatherings are situational, and in this sense exemplary of a social modernity that includes and goes beyond the case of self-settled refuges that we have just described.[21] In a general fashion, indeed, this kind of gathering, created in the dynamism of a particular situation, allows us to question the realism and social efficacy of identitarian assertions and the divisions of the world that their ideologies sustain.

On the border: the sorting centres

Transit centres, waiting zones, holding and detention centres – all these spaces occupy the same functional position in the edifice of the camps today, a function that can be generally designated as that of

46

'sorting centre'. As distinct from self-organized refuges, these are under the direct control of national administrations (ministry of the interior or a ministry in charge of immigration), police institutions, UN agencies and/or humanitarian NGOs.

Whatever the continent on which they are found, these transit spaces are generally associated with practices of selection, expulsion or admission, and with contexts of 'flow management' that imply for those in movement a more or less prolonged moment of immobility, waiting and multiple constraints. Here again, there is a proximity between the space of intervention and the language and actions of UN, humanitarian and police institutions, which can lead to overlapping, voluntary or involuntary, complicity, even the 'obscure arrangements' denounced by the lawyer Guglielmo Verdirame and the anthropologist Barbara Harrell-Bond in the African countries.[22]

In all these places, individuals are recorded on files, cards or registers, they are passed through the mill of medical examinations, called 'screenings' in humanitarian terminology, and equally through the mill of biographical 'screenings'. On arrival and on departure, selection and redistribution assigns them different identity categories. In Europe, the centres of reception, holding and detention are designed for asylum seekers, foreigners 'in an irregular situation' intercepted at the border or on the national territory, individuals held in waiting for an expulsion decision or a response to an asylum application – a right that is only granted today to a minority of applicants.

These camps of foreigners on the margins of Europe have, for Claire Rodier and Emmanuel Blanchard, a purpose that is not that of expulsion or imprisonment, but rather that of an 'airlock'; the question is to brake or reorient the trajectories of immigrants, basically to control them more closely, rather than make them absolutely impossible:

> Comparison with an airlock . . . allows us to discern the function of the camps fairly well. They are places for organizing the transit between two countries, a latency period in which the desires, expectations and dispositions of the candidates for acceptance are remodelled. This is also a privileged moment of socialization into the police and administrative practices that the life of the immigrants will have to be organized around.[23]

An ephemeral social universe is formed at the same time as it is discovered by those who pass through it and sometimes even settle there despite themselves. According to an investigation made at the initiative of the European Parliament in 2007, the length of detention in

47

these closed centres 'is sometimes not limited by law and in practice in some countries it can be extended by several years'.[24]

The majority of (open) reception shelters and (closed) detention centres in Europe use recycled old buildings: former military barracks (in Austria and Poland, for example), disused warehouses, hangars (the Sangatte 'hangar' of 1999–2002, or that of Zapi 3 at the Roissy/Charles-de-Gaulle airport since 2001).[25] Finally, the same report stresses 'the grim, and sometimes dehumanizing appearance of the facilities . . . (e.g. use of cages and containers in Italy, a former floating platform in the Netherlands)'.[26]

Whether more or less open or closed, these places are transit zones, waiting areas, centres for the reception and detention of foreigners without the right to stay and asylum seekers. They are generally hard of access, either because they are controlled by public or private police services, or on account of their remoteness and isolation. Let us dwell for a moment on one of the countries studied by the European Parliament inquiry – Poland. This country counted in 2007 some seventeen 'reception centres' for asylum seekers and thirteen 'holding centres' for foreigners without residence permits. The reception centres were exclusively reserved for asylum seekers, 90 per cent of whom were either Chechen or from the northern Caucasus (Daghestan, Ingushetia). The holding centres, for their part, took in foreigners in an irregular situation (who had entered without a visa, or had outstayed the conditions of their temporary visa). Asylum seekers are also often sent to holding centres if they are deemed to be in an irregular situation. The foreigners detained are of various nationalities, but come mainly from Vietnam, China, Armenia and Georgia, as well as Chechnya, Moldavia, Mongolia, Iraq and Sri Lanka.

The holding centre at Lezslowola is a former military base renovated in 1996 (as is also the case with several of the reception centres for asylum seekers):

> Surrounded by high double fences topped with barbed wire and an electric system, this is made up of three buildings (one for single women and families, with three to six beds in a room; one for single men, with dormitories designed for ten persons but which can hold up to thirteen detainees . . . ; one for the administration). . . . The distribution into cells is either by family or, for single people (the majority), by nationality, ethnic group, common language: there is the 'Armenian' room, the 'Vietnamese' room which often also contains Chinese, etc.[27]

In Poland as in several other European countries, there is a certain de facto lack of differentiation among foreigners held, detained or

48

'received' in these centres, even if the notions of 'open' and 'closed' centres keep their meaning in terms of the object of this passage through a waiting and sorting zone (a wait for expulsion in some cases, possible integration in others). Asylum applicants and the undocumented are there simply because, being in an irregular situation and/or awaiting regularization, 'removal' or admission, the authorities do not know what to do with them or where to put them; only the imperative of control, more or less 'humanized' by the action of humanitarian and human rights NGOs, guides the application of migration policies by the police.

In this relative imprecision of statuses and fates, the clearest and most stable index of the identity of those confined in this way is the space outside of the place in which they end up. In effect, according to a current procedure of reversing cause and effect, their removal appears to be the empirical basis of a xenophobic attitude towards them ('if they are kept apart, there must be a reason . . .'), which tends to 'criminalize' them morally and thus favour their imprisonment. According to a doctor who works at the Lezslowola detention centre, the greatest problem at the centre is that of the detainees' lack of information about their rights, and the fact that they do not understand why they are detained for so long: 'Individuals are sent here initially for three months, their detention is extended, they are not well informed about their rights . . . the presence of foreigners in this centre is not justified, the very existence of the centres is meaningless, it has no use and is unacceptable.'[28]

In another Polish detention centre, the 'centre of arrest and deportation' at Okęcie, the inquiry described the trajectory of a young Nigerian – after reaching Poland six months before, he recently went to ask for help in a church:

> From the church he was directed to the Caritas association; a Caritas member advised him to go and make an asylum application at the office of the repatriation bureau, where he was arrested by the police while depositing his application. He was taken directly to this centre. Since he has been here (a month), no one has really explained his situation to him, he has just understood that he has been put here for thirty days. He does not really know why, he does not know that his detention may be extended every three months, up to a year: 'The hardest thing here, the problem, is the lack of air, it's that the door [of his cell] is always locked . . . the air doesn't come in.'[29]

A more structural reversal redefines the very conception of the border, on the basis of the legal function of removal. For the anthropologist Chowra Makaremi, who conducted research with the ANAFÉ[30] organization into the Zapi waiting zone at Charles-de-Gaulle airport, it is the exceptional legal status of the 'person in question' that colours the legal classification of the space: a foreigner 'who is not yet on the national territory' must find a correspondingly extra-territorial space, even if this other space has to be artificially invented. Thus the Zapi 2 was located for a few years on the first floor of the Ibis hotel at Roissy. By government decree this space was defined as a non-national border zone, whereas the ground floor and second storey of the same building remained under French national jurisdiction.[31]

Frontier spaces and even 'temporary extra-territorial residence' are thus needed for the application of this strategy of categorization and special treatment of undesirable foreigners. These spaces no longer follow – at least not only – the lines of the geographical territories of nation-states. The border is everywhere that an undesirable is identified and must be kept apart, 'detained' and then 'expelled'. The space that connects the undesirable individual with the border is the camp in the form of airlock or sorting centre. Before any other quali-fication, this form of confinement defines the camp as the stationing space on the border and on the margins. In this tension, inherent to a space that is both inside (physically) and outside (legally and politi-cally), there is expressed very intensely 'a kind of obsession with the border, which, while making this ever more invisible and impossible to locate, makes it radiate everywhere that there is a movement of individuals who are not free to cross it; this produces countless forms of confinement, ending up by coinciding with individuals'.[32] The border that 'radiates' through to the individuals affected is part of a general process that also sees the camp being miniaturized, so that it can be ever more rapidly dismantled and shifted, even in the case of the 'heavy' camps where prima facie[33] refugees are placed in Africa, as we shall see below.

The majority of these spaces of transit, waiting and sorting are managed in Europe by police or border guards, regional or municipal administrations, but also by private security companies and by certain NGOs, such as the Red Cross at Sangatte, which gives a formal par-allel with the African situations in which transit zones managed by the UNHCR or certain (inter)governmental NGOs are generally air-locks to the actual camps.

In Africa, 'transit centres' are situated at the entrance to all UNHCR sites, in order to receive, register and verify the physical state of the refugees who have just arrived and to channel them appropriately.

50

They can expect emergency aid for a period of a week to a month. Once all the checks have been carried out, they find a place in a tent or shelter already existing within the refugee camp. There are also transit centres close to the borders, such as the three hangars at Baala in the Forest Region of Guinea, 2 kilometres from the Liberian border. In the second half of 2003, Baala received huge waves of Liberian refugees. In October of that year, 752 of these were assembled in the three hangars before being transferred in two convoys to the refugee camp at Lainé, some 120 kilometres further north. Other transit centres serve as 'way stations' on the roads from the border to the camps.

In every case these are tents, huts made out of boards and plastic sheets, or hangars. They are better equipped and maintained than the tents of the 'cross-border points' which we discussed above. In principle refugees here are supposed to receive regular hot meals, but there are often disruptions, particularly in the more remote transit zones. When they are settled in the camp, they receive food aid in the form of basic products (rice, bulgur wheat, etc.), and prepare their own meals.

UNHCR sites can present intermediate situations between 'transit centre' and 'refugee camp', as is the case with the Ivory Coast refugees placed in the 'transit camp' at Nonah in Guinea from the second half of 2002, following major confrontations in their native country. This camp was viewed by the UNHCR as a transit centre, but by the end of 2003 its residents had been there for over a year. They were receiving food aid under the World Food Programme and medical support from Médecins Sans Frontières, but forced to remain in large collective tents housing from 50 to 100 persons. They did not have the right to build family huts, did not benefit from social programmes, etc. As the months passed, an internal improvement of the tents developed, permitting a division into apartments with the help of covers, plastic sheets, sacking, mats, etc. The protests of the Ivorian refugees were continuous, as soon as they understood that they had no possibility of settlement in a camp as 'regular' refugees.

This protest shows very well the intolerable paradox of being held in a waiting zone with no possibility of exit, which generates major tensions within such spaces. These tensions are particularly acute in the camps for foreigners in Europe, faced as they are with the waiting and incomprehensible sorting conducted there. It is true that this waiting is characteristic of all forms of camp where people on the move stop and often end up living. But it is probably in these transit and sorting situations that the waiting is least supportable, since no

51

infrastructure is provided to kill the time, the possibilities of going out are zero or limited, and finally the outcome and its explanatory logic remain very largely incomprehensible to the detainees.

There is likewise a sharp social tension in the reception and detention centres for foreigners in Europe. On the one hand, there are acts of revolt: riots and fires as a protest against the conditions of detention – in Luxemburg, for example, in January 2006, in the UK in November of that year, in France in the first half of 2008; there have regularly been hunger strikes in these centres, in virtually all European countries. On the other hand, the report of the European Parliament previously mentioned notes 'acts of despair': suicides and attempted suicides in the majority of countries visited, at open centres as well as closed ones, have become increasingly frequent.[34] Finally, the detainees are subject to violence on the part of those in charge of them (physical violence and assault, sexual abuse, verbal violence), and there is also internal violence of similar kinds between the residents themselves.

In these transit spaces, hierarchical relations and the violence with which these are expressed are intensified. Thus when abuses of power were noted at the UNHCR establishment at Maheba in Zambia,[35] it was specifically in the camp's transit centre that these took place. Other factors also promote tension and violence within these spaces. To list them briefly: the moral obloquy that seems always to be cast on exiles who have just emerged from violent and chaotic situations; the moral criminalization of their identity by people who see them being placed in quarantine; the feeling of rejection among people who see themselves explicitly treated as supernumerary; the contrast between the distress felt by the transitory occupants and the absolute power over their lives held by representatives of the managing agencies (a power expressed, for example, in amounts of soap bars, coverings and food); finally, the poor visibility of these zones of arrival and waiting. These factors together explain the readiness to commit violence with impunity, and underpin a general climate of exceptionality.[36] Protest has no proper place in these sites, and itself takes exceptional and exacerbated forms, before being rapidly and violently repressed.

Imprisoned outdoors: the refugee camps

The third face of the contemporary edifice of camps is the refugee camps in the stricter sense; these also generally take the most stan-

52

dardized, planned and official form. Though visited from time to time by representatives of UN agencies or journalists, and often photographed for their dramatic aesthetic qualities, refugee camps are not completely visible in their everyday life, since they are generally in out-of-the-way locations and access to them is supervised. Besides, nothing fundamental seems to happen there.

The sites established by the UNHCR vary considerably in size. They may shelter fewer than 2,000 people in settlements that form a kind of village; this is the case, for example, with the camps for Mauritanians in Senegal. But they may have as many as 200,000 residents, as was the case in the Goma region of the Democratic Republic of Congo between 1994 and 1996.[37] In the Great Lakes or the region of Dadaab in north-east Kenya, there are similar situations in which several camps are scattered around a single humanitarian base. All this forms a material and human apparatus that is both gigantic and precarious, sheltering tens or even hundreds of thousands of refugees.

The refugee camps are always hybrid organisms, not reproducing any socio-spatial form that already exists; they are new experiences for the locality in which they are established, if only for the permanent paradox that their existence expresses, between an indefinite temporality and a space that is transformed because its occupants necessarily appropriate it in order to be able to live in it. Conceived originally with no other project than that of simple survival, or the provisional stationing of a displaced and controlled population, these camps have been transformed over time and with the multiple uses that their occupants have made for themselves of the resource that humanitarian assistance represents. The formation of camp-cities or large urban districts, the Palestinian camps today representing the most developed model of these, is the culmination of a logical development of refugee installations. We shall return to this urban dynamic of the camps in greater detail on the basis of a case study undertaken in Kenya.[38]

But the existence of refugees has also been marked in part by a different form, particularly in Africa – that of rural settlements and refugee villages. The geographer Véronique Lassailly-Jacob has shown the large scale that the UNHCR policy of rural settlements took between the 1960s and 1990s, especially in eastern and southern Africa (Tanzania, Uganda, Zambia, etc.), as well as in Malaysia and Mexico (Guatemalan refugees in the 1980s and 1990s), before it was finally abandoned.[39] This type of settlement was seen as a solution for the 'local assimilation' of refugees,[40] but also as a means of filling up underpopulated or impoverished rural zones, which might directly be of interest to the host country. Conceived as sites of agricultural production, these installations were even supposed to attain self-government after a period of four years, at the end of which the UNHCR would withdraw. But, both in the cases studied by Véronique Lassailly-Jacob and in that of the rural settlement of Maheba in Zambia that we shall study below, the reality was quite different, agricultural self-sufficiency was never achieved, and 'the majority of these sites did not attain their objectives of economic viability and integration into the host region';[41] several NGOs and UN agencies also remained aloof from the operation of these sites. The Maheba camp in Zambia has existed since 1971, and its different 'zones' have gradually taken on the appearance of a string of village concentrations along a track of 40 kilometres. Each sector corresponds to a distinct arrival period of refugees, often with distinct geographical origins or territorial and political affiliations, and finally with different conditions of life and access to resources: the more recent arrivals live in transit tents, unequipped and exhausted, while those who have been there since the 1970s stand out, as in a village organization, as the holders of power over the land or resources of the site.[42]

A solution close to this, in village form but without the agricultural settlement projected by the UNHCR, has prevailed for the Mauritanian refugees in Senegal. In 1989, some 70,000 Black Mauritanians from the south of the country were deported to Senegal. Assisted in an initial phase by the Senegal Red Cross, various NGOs and the local population (largely related to the refugees), they were subsequently viewed by the UNHCR and the Senegalese state as prima facie refugees (a title given collectively, as we have seen, without individual refugee cards being granted), and divided between 280 UNHCR sites of varying size, accommodating between 50 and 2,000 people. Even if material aid from UN agencies declined from the late 1990s, the Mauritanian 'villages' that these sites became were still in existence in 2006, and have become a resource for the economic mobility and strategy of the refugees there.[43]

As a general rule, camps are established on virgin land like a sudden and sometimes violent incursion into the local environment. After first being installed in large tents, the refugees go on to construct around these collective tents huts and cabins out of mud-brick and wood, with roofs of thatch or plastified cloth, the material being generally provided by NGOs. Individual or family habitations of one or two rooms surround the central tent, which is taken away when all the cabins have been constructed. At the same time, in a few months or anything up to a year, there is a gradual improvement of dirt roads, systems of water supply (wells, cisterns, pipe networks and standpipes), latrines, septic tanks, as well as some public buildings (clinic, school, camp administration).

In parallel with the material construction of the camp, an original social formation arises. The distribution of American maize or bulgur wheat, oil and salt is made monthly by NGOs under contract with the UN World Food Programme; 'sector leaders' appear from among the initial tent heads; churches or video shops are built out of mudbrick and covered with plastic sheets from the UNHCR or NGOs; market places and football pitches are improvised, etc. Even if it is understood that the camp does not have a planned duration, everyone builds a living space that may be precarious but is relatively habitable.

At first sight, the camps always present certain strange 'lacks' in relation to the squalid towns or peripheral districts that they often end up resembling. The Kakuma camp, for example, located at the border with Kenya and Sudan, opened in 1991 and counting over 60,000 inhabitants today, particularly accommodated in the late 1990s young men and boys who had fled the war-torn Sudan in order to avoid forced recruitment or the devastating effects of the conflict. One of the strange features of this camp was its demographic imbalance: the sex ratio there in 1998 was 166 men to 100 women, rising to 270 men per 100 women in the 15–29 age group.[44]

Elsewhere in Kenya, near the Somalian border, the three Dadaab camps opened in 1990–1 had a population of around 160,000 in 2007, most of these being refugees (or children of refugees) from neighbouring Somalia. As was also the case with the Goma camps in the Democratic Republic of Congo (where 700,000 Rwandans were housed for two years, between 1994 and 1996, on the border with their country), the ban on working and more generally the absence of rights outside the camp in the host country often led the refugees to inactivity, apathy and dependence on humanitarian care and assistance, or alternatively towards local networks of work and commerce, informal and inevitably 'illegal'.

The techniques of management and control are always being improved. In the last few years, the UNHCR and the governments of the host countries have been seeking to build camps of a more reduced size than previously. Because of concerns about controlling their populations, the camps opened most recently (in the 2000s) in Africa typically shelter between 5,000 and 10,000 people. Even if they are grouped together – as in Sierra Leone where until 2005 eight camps were established on a space 60 kilometres long between the towns of Bô and Kenema – these camps are managed separately (in general by NGOs that subcontract the function of 'governing' the camps from the UNHCR), while being placed under the inspection of a regional administration of the UN agency. This arrangement makes it possible to avoid explosive situations and uncontrollable chains of events.

In effect, while developing in material terms, and to a degree also economically, the refugee camps form themselves into social and political milieus. This is often perceived only a posteriori, when they have become over time something like projected but abandoned towns, with conflict around their management and the representation of the refugees.[45] Finally, the more general issue in the refugee camps – as soon as their existence persists beyond the moment of emergency and is established for a longer duration – is that of their transformation into spaces of identification, relationships and even memory for those women and men who live there (albeit waiting for a possible 'return home') for years or decades, or who have been born and marry there, have buried their dead and established a range of relationships with the local population.

Unprotected reservations: the displaced persons' camps

To bring this inventory to an end, we must mention the camps for 'internally displaced persons'. Though these resemble to a degree the refugee camps, the constant fluctuations and controversies, at both world and local levels, around the organism charged with creating and managing them, makes their situation particularly fragile for their occupants. From the data presented at the start of this chapter, we can estimate that between 4 and 5 million internally displaced people are today living in camps across the world.

If the United Nations has taken an interest in the question of the internally displaced since the early 1990s – as in Bosnia, Iraq or Rwanda – this was initially to avoid a refugee 'problem' elsewhere. This amounted to promoting the confinement of potential refugees within their own country by providing a minimum humanitarian assistance, without, however, guaranteeing any protection to compensate for the failure to escape from their country and the constancy of danger. Populations in flight were detained, but effective protection of life was not ensured. The political scientist Cécile Dubernet speaks in this connection of 'resounding defeats, not only the fall of the Bosniac security zones but also the attack on the Kibeho camp in Rwanda in April 1995'.[46] In the same way, after the war in Darfur flared up again in 2003, UN agencies had to recognize their inability to protect the fundamental rights of the internally displaced Sudanese, the great majority of whom – around 2 million – were housed in camps. The image of the mousetrap is an apt one to describe these camps.

This situation remains a concern today, practically identical despite the developments of the last few years within the UN – in particular, the indirect attribution of responsibility for IDPs to the UNHCR, after it had been for a while under the control of the UN's Office for the Coordination of Humanitarian Affairs.[47] Since 2006, in fact, in the context of a strategy of improved operational coordination on the ground between UN agencies (the policy of the so-called 'cluster system'), the UNHCR is responsible for three fields of activity: the management and coordination of camps, of emergency shelters and of protection – these include civilians displaced by conflict, without their being explicitly mentioned.

It is the NGOs, in fact, both local and international, that remain the real managers of the displaced persons' camps. At the end of the day, care is minimal: a food ration that does not cover the needs of families is distributed monthly by the World Food Programme, placing these people in a very singular situation, as has been observed in the six camps at Bong in Liberia, which in August 2004 housed over 80,000 internally displaced people. This is the situation of a dense and heterogeneous agglomeration of people without resources, who left their goods, land and employment several years ago, hundreds of kilometres away. Though totally available and ready for any kind of activity that could revivify them as simple citizens, their social fragility is as great as that of the refugees abroad, even if the fact of not having left their country makes them a bit less 'foreigners' in relationship to the camp environment.

Apart from problems of simple physical security in a violent context, the absence of legal and social protection transforms the displaced persons' camps into regular unprotected reserves of labour power, both docile and strong. The camp demography, in effect, is sometimes as particularly attractive for potential employers as is the social docility of the displaced. Thus, in one of the camps in Liberia's Bong county, the Salala camp, lorries fill up every fortnight with around forty young men (between fifteen and thirty years of age, in general vigorous 'ex-fighters'), who are taken to work on the rubber plantations of the Firestone company for 50 US cents a day. They stay for two or three weeks in a forest encampment on the 'greatest rubber plantation in the world', where they carry out unskilled agricultural work such as clearing, weeding, etc., before being returned to their camp, where they receive their share of the World Food Programme ration. The camp 'chairman' (himself a displaced person, who has already performed similar functions in other camps) acts as intermediary between the Firestone foremen and the IDPs, the agro-industrial company paying him a 'tax' for each worker recruited. Finally, the main characteristic of the displaced persons' camp at Salala is that it concentrates nearly 4,000 potential workers between thirteen and forty years old,[48] readily available, defenceless and subject to the patriarchal power of the head of the camp, who sells their labour-power to the highest bidder. This is done with the full knowledge of the representatives of the Liberian administration in charge of the displaced persons, and of the local NGO charged with managing the camp in the absence of the UNHCR. The Firestone company is the main beneficiary of this proximity of cheap labour-power, but some local landowners also employ the displaced persons on their properties close to the camps.

In offering this attempt at an inventory, I have not sought to produce a typology, nor indeed to list all the empirically possible cases. I have focused on the African situation, and, in part, also that in Europe. The case of the Palestinian camps deserves special attention in relation to their singular urbanization, both within and around them. As for the material aspect of the camps, there are several situations that I have not mentioned here: for example, the Turkish camps that between 1988 and 1993 housed several thousand Kurdish refugees from Iraq in apartment blocks, with groups of twelve to thirty people in dwellings of 60 square metres.[49] I have tried, however, to include the spectrum of contemporary forms of placing in camp, or 'encampment' in Barbara Harrell-Bond's sense.[50] I have brought out the major characteristic(s) of each social–spatial–administrative form, as this is experienced. This is why a breakdown into four models still seems to be the most pertinent. I shall now sum this up with some final comments, as follows.

The spontaneous urban or forest camps, the self-settled and self-organized refuges, represent in my view the most essential and universal form of refuge as such. This is the place that each displaced person seeks to recompose, with the shelter as condition of survival. We shall return to these refuges at the end of our investigation, since they also represent the principle according to which it is possible to conceive a social refoundation on the basis of mobility and chaos. If the idea of refuge could only be separated from the camp, then refuges could be considered as towns in the making.

Meanwhile, waiting zones such as transit centres and camps for foreigners are today the way that borders are both populated and redrawn. What defines the reality of national borders today is no longer the geographical outlines of states but rather the sum of corridors, airlocks and sorting centres that virtually draws a 'map of camps' as state borders.[51] The women and men who pass through them before being expelled or accepted are 'tolerated' for the period of waiting, and this tolerance, as simply keeping alive, can last for a long while. The report of the European Parliament previously mentioned cites a 'record' wait of ten years in a reception centre for asylum applicants.

If the refugee camps in the strict sense appear in this context as privileged sites, out-places where a sense of other people and a sense of locality are reconstructed over time, thus creating a new social polarity, they are also sites of other kinds of violence, as we shall see in the following case studies. Finally, camps for accommodating internally displaced persons represent today the most precarious and uncertain forms of this 'encampment', and everything indicates that this 'solution' is set to expand, as one of the likely effects of the promotion of 'internal asylum' and the externalization of the management of migratory flows. The regular announcements in recent years of a steady increase in the number of internally displaced people in the world (now between 25 and 30 million) prefigure the invention of new spaces.

Part Two

Everyday Life in the Twenty-First Century's Refugee Camps

— 3 —

An Ethnologist in the Refugee Camps

The prehistory of the world is at an end, its history is beginning. Anthropologists have always been, unbeknownst to themselves, specialists in beginnings, even if the beginnings that they studied gave off a scent of death: abolishing at one blow the actuality of what went before, they opened up the future only by arousing immediate nostalgia. It could then happen that, despite the attention that they claimed to pay to the 'total social fact', anthropologists were more sensitive to the beauty of what was vanishing than to the scope of what was coming into being.[1]

My project of an extended study of refugee camps was born in Colombia in 1999, and with it there matured the ambition of understanding 'the scope of what was coming into being'. At Cali and the rural regions of the Pacific coast, I discovered 'migrations'[2] that were scarcely ever the result of personal choice or a freely made family strategy, but arose rather in the context of a mobile 'dirty war' between guerrillas, paramilitary groups and government forces, in a diffuse climate of terror. Moving to towns, whether medium or large in size, gave the displaced populations a sense of relative protection. At Bogotá the following year, during the occupation of the International Red Cross offices by hundreds of *desplazados*, I witnessed violent acts of revolt, surprising also for the social stigmatization that the rebels were protesting against, in the city and institutionally.[3] But what shocked me most was the level of precariousness and danger of the *desplazados'* existence. How was it possible to live in such a state of destitution, not just material but also social and literally physical, a total absence of recognition that brought purely and simply the risk of death? This is what the international agencies and human rights organizations call 'protection'. Some groups of displaced persons in Colombia tried (and are still trying with the help of the church and certain NGOs) to form spaces to protect themselves from the civil war, rural territories initially known in the late 1990s as 'communities of peace', and from 2005 called 'humanitarian zones'. But they have experienced sharp defeats, since, as the conflict developed, the people gathered there, lacking armed defence, could be ransomed, wounded or murdered by the armed groups in the region, generally the paramilitaries.

Is a camp better than nothing?

On my return to France, full of this experience and all the questions it raised, I wanted to continue and deepen this study in comparable situations, initially in Africa, where I was already familiar with certain sites, and where the 'material' for such research was not lacking. I set out with a question that was very simple, perhaps somewhat naive: What difference does it make to be in a camp? Is a camp better than nothing? True, this question echoes the 'protection problem', as this is called by the UN agencies. But it also resembles, as soon as it is raised, the purely existential question: is something better than nothing? There is indeed in this project on the camps, and beyond, a topicality that is ever more pressing, a research that is not just contemporary, but anthropological in the sense in which our task in all circumstances is to describe the processes of life, death and transformations of societies and culture – to describe beginnings, for example, as Marc Augé invites us to do in the epigraph to this chapter, rather than nostalgically scrutinizing once more the past beauty of what is disappearing; we have to study the contexts and spaces where new social worlds are being born, even if this is within a context of chaos and violence – something that is in no way original today, if we consider the political and economic situation on a global scale. The question 'Is a camp better than nothing?' therefore contains the project of discovering how life is reborn in a history of death. What this study brings out is the swing from life to death, from chaos to social creation, that is observed in the history of individuals at the same time as it takes place in the history of societies – given that we are speaking of individuals and societies brutally transformed by war, exile and the discovery of new social and spatial mechanisms created by the 'international community'.

The case studies presented in this second part are an exploration of everyday life in the camps. Far from being satisfied with establishing the existence of a biopolitical mechanism – the confinement at a distance (at least provisionally) of all kinds of undesirables, and the power of life and death exercised over them by humanitarian government – we shall also observe the different modalities in which the spaces of confinement are transformed and become, after a certain length of time, sites of a possible public space. The discussion here will be based on the description and analysis of situations in which a redefinition of the sites themselves, a collective action or speaking out, takes place – not because refugees spend their time demonstrating or having meetings (far from it) but because, regardless of whether they are a rarity, acts of refusal, confrontation or revolt denote the moment at which reality swings, when disorder makes its appearance in the face of the order of the camps for which humanitarian government is responsible, and brings the refugees out of their anonymity as 'victims', supposedly without a voice or subjectivity, to become subjects freed from this assignment of identity, authors as well as actors in their speech, initiatives and space.

Besides, it is the specific property of the camps that they exist, not identically, but according to the same underlying principles in many parts of the planet at the same point in time. They are thus constitutive of a reality that goes beyond the local existence of each particular one, and that is developing as a global reality. Each camp is born as a local or national 'solution', but also as part of a global mechanism. Each camp, in this respect, shares in the beginning of the history of the world as a world.

Refugees, ethnologists and the international community

This global dimension very concretely determines the possibilities of access to the field, always an unavoidable problem in ethnography. To be able to start conducting my studies of refugee camps, I needed authorization and introductions from an international organization. In the present case, I had also to obtain the simple right of entry. In concrete terms, the decision whether I could cross the gate of a camp in Zambia or Kenya was made in Paris, Brussels or Geneva. I tried in vain to find an entry via the UNHCR. The length of the procedure needed to obtain agreement to a study programme (nearly two years, I was told!), the fact that this programme had to meet precise requirements formulated by the UNHCR administration (in the event, an interest in the refugees' informal economy that was certainly not innocent), the timing envisaged for the study, which had more in common with the rapid study of an 'expert' than basic research with its inevitable hesitations, were some of the reasons that led me to seek other approaches than that of the UNHCR, despite this being the central interlocutor for any initiative in the refugee camps. This is why I turned to the NGO Médecins Sans Frontières (MSF-France), thanks to a colleague who was situated, as I am now myself, both in the world of research and in that of humanitarian organizations. Since 2000, therefore, it has been with the MSF teams on the ground that I have had access to the camps, moving about in them almost freely and making contact with the camp administrations, whether those of the UNHCR or of other organizations working for it.

Having approached MSF, I did not find myself in the situation of having to respond to a commission. But what was this organization's 'request' in exchange for the facility of access that I had been granted? I met first of all with individuals who were sincerely excited by the idea of self-criticism. If this had only been effectively practised by a few of their number, it was also an indispensable element both for their public image and for the internal operation of the organization as a whole. Critical evaluation, therefore, is always demanded after any operation on the ground – from individual debriefing to collective 'case conference'. The operational officials and the organization's own researchers[4] are always on the lookout for a better understanding of ongoing themes: post-conflict violence, situations of military occupation, the question of protection. As far as the refugee camps were concerned, I understood at the moment of starting my project that MSF had an operational appreciation of the camps – there is nothing more practical than a camp for carrying out a medical screening or a vaccination campaign. Bound up with this technical or logistic representation, the camps also represented a marvellous 'display' of humanitarian intervention. One of the MSF travelling exhibitions,[5] moreover, reproduced a camp in miniature by showing the supposed trajectories of refugees from one structure of support to another, ending particularly with aid from MSF. Finally, to be really complete, we have to say that several individuals were sensitive to the questions that this situation raises in terms of the confinement of the 'beneficiaries' and the long duration of their isolation, which they participate in even if they did not create it.

And yet the fact that sincere interest was shown in a critical study of the camps, without this involving in any way a commission of operational expertise that would have 'framed' the possible responses in advance, does not remove anything from the complexity and novelty represented by a field of investigation that is uncommon in ethnological research. It is by starting from the sites themselves, therefore, that I shall now tackle a problem that is both ethical and theoretical – the two aspects being closely bound up in as much as the place of the ethnologist on the ground largely determines the construction of his or her object of research. In anthropology, the relationship of investigation is customarily defined as a dual relationship between investigator and investigated. From this point of view, all anthropology is 'dialogical'.[6]

In the refugee camps, however, we regularly encounter another actor that seems at first dependent on the 'good' dialogical relationship of the ethnographer. This is the case with the UNHCR, in charge of the administration and more generally the control of the camps, or else one or other of the NGOs active in them. Rather than a single third party, this is in a general fashion the diffuse presence of representatives of the 'international community'. The dialogical relationship that underpins the ethnologist's knowledge becomes, one might say, a three-way dialogue.

As distinct from the social mediations that are customarily met with on the ground – embodied in the figures of the village headman, the council of elders, the 'land chief', the head of the neighbourhood or ethnic group, the leader of religious or voluntary associations, themselves a part of the milieu being studied – the mediator in the camps is of external provenance just like the ethnologist, but is none the less omnipresent. This mediator, moreover, bears a strong symbolic and moral charge in relation to the field in question. There is thus a very real difference in relation to what we already know. These mediators who come from outside but are omnipresent inside view themselves as foreigners in the midst of a study to which they themselves permit access, when they do not just annex the researcher completely, transforming him or her in this way into an expert or adviser to whom they feel close, belonging to the same social world – the world of 'expatriates', 'UN staff', the 'international community'.

This triangulation of research may seem at first no more than a practical problem – a 'field problem' of the kind often discussed. Very often it simply arises as a new set of constraints on access to the field, in the sense, for example, that you actually enter the camps only in a vehicle authorized to do so, whether belonging to the police, the UNHCR, a UN agency or an NGO. Except for when the organization that 'took on' the researcher itself has offices in the camps, the 'timing' of the study must follow that of the daily work of the NGO, and the ethnologist has to leave the field before nightfall. Finally, I have often found it hard to get my intermediaries in the humanitarian organization to understand and accept that I did not want to parade around the camp in a four-wheel-drive vehicle with driver, armed with a walkie-talkie permanently switched on and a white MSF vest, even if I could well understand that this strange get-up responded to the standardized requirements of a certain level of security! But it seemed to me that this constraint goes further, and well beyond just the organization that you arrive with. The triangulation I refer to here means that you have, in the field itself, the simultaneous presence of the observer, the observed, and a third element represented by one or several external parties whose action and gaze are determinant. They themselves conceived and directed the manufacture of this space (in other words the camps and their logistics), they manage it and control the persons present even while assisting them; they will decide one day to close the camp – meaning in some sense the end of the field for the ethnologist.

The intervention of this third element in the ethnographic field introduces moral values, principles and terms that come from the institutional and doctrinal world of the interveners – humanitarian, security, social, the UN, etc. – and that qualify the world they have created: the space, milieu and individuals among whom they intervene. This leads to strategies of adaptation, negotiations, translations or misunderstandings on the part of those individuals who live on their space of intervention and enter into relationship with them.

What can the ethnologist do in this context? Taking 'refugees' as the object of research (likewise 'prisoners', 'the homeless', etc.) would mean confusing the object of research with that of the intervener who creates this space and this category. There is a viewpoint, a morality and a politics of humanitarian action – the human universal and its degraded, tainted obverse in the dramatic figure of the victim, the sight of whom moves, disturbs and frightens.[7] To recognize this category as a true one, a reality given in advance that must simply be accepted in order to 'understand better', is to accept by the same token the indisputable evidence of this situation, which authorizes an exceptional and extraterritorial social, material and political organization – that of the camp. To take the category of refugees as the object of research would thus mean leaving out of the field of vision the humanitarian government that establishes, defines, controls and fixes the space of life of the categories that it simultaneously recognizes and creates. Their existences, however, are indissociable.

68

What then is the ethnologist to do? Espouse a priori the universalistic morality of humanitarianism, and ask whether the victims respond to these interventions as expected? 'They are misguided'; 'What is their culture?'; 'Are they ready to receive this aid?' – these are remarks and questions often addressed to anthropologists working in this field. Or rather, as I maintain in this study, should we take into consideration the situation as a whole, the sum total of discourse and practice presented, and observe their confrontation? Since all humanitarian intervention creates its own space, we have constantly to shift our point of view in order to grasp the space as a whole within which relationships and hierarchies appear, along with confrontations, disagreements, misunderstandings, cultural changes, political forms, and so on.

Between the institution of humanitarian assistance and control on the one hand, and the anthropologist on the other, there is a transparency that is implicitly accepted as soon as the anthropologist takes the category produced ('refugees', 'displaced') as natural and self-evident; and this transparency makes possible the production of the 'useful' discourse that is expected, for example, from the UNHCR expert. And then, without wanting this and possibly against his or her own convictions, the anthropologist is logically led to identifying and naming 'cheats', 'gatecrashers', 'false refugees', etc. – in other words to contributing to the biopolitical work of population management. On the other hand, if they grasp the whole series of viewpoints that confront one another within the humanitarian space, they must include the producers and verifiers of categories in their description. They thus remove themselves from the biopolitical science that they would share in if they were to concentrate, with an enthusiasm that is initially humanist, on the category of refugees. To render the totality of the situation while being present within it requires consideration of the whole series of viewpoints on the social and political chessboard that these humanitarian spaces represent, surveying it in its totality in order to grasp its diversity, even heterogeneity. It is this overall configuration at a particular moment in time that then becomes the object of study, and not 'the refugees'.

It consequently seemed to me that in order to give an account of this fieldwork I had definitely to adopt the form of case studies, seeking to restore each time the ensemble of an observed situation. I shall do this by emphasizing the question that dominates each situation in a pragmatic fashion, i.e. by taking the viewpoint of the subjects who face one another in the situation being studied.

We shall seek first of all to understand the paradoxical foundation of the camps: each new arrival discovers here the problem of an undefinable temporality (an endless emergency), and an exceptional situation that has become regularized and everyday (chapter 4). We shall go on to see how a particular cultural experience gradually takes shape in the trajectories of the refugees, their traffic and tactics between the marginal border zones, villages, towns and the heart of the humanitarian mechanism that they enter at a given moment: if there is such a thing as a refugee culture, as I do indeed believe, its description leads us in quite a different direction from the received ideas about the passive culture of 'assisted' victims (chapter 5). Analysis of other fields will then show us certain aspects of the resocialization of refugees, making camps into sites of a possible local identification, either on the broad spaces of the rural zone where occupation is differentiated according to generations of refugees and period of arrival (chapter 6), or in the massive and dense forms of camp-towns (chapter 7). The study continues by describing certain collective mobilizations in the context of which groups of refugees take as targets and interlocutors the various 'branches' of humanitarian government (UN agencies, NGOs, national departments in charge of refugees) (chapter 8). Finally, with respect to these actions or in the context of the study itself – taken up and 'appropriated' by the refugees as a moment of self-presentation that swings between justification and protest – I inquire into speaking out and controversies among individuals who are generally reduced to the condition of 'victims', more or less 'vulnerable' and voiceless: what will concern us here is the formation and transformation of the victim as witness into a subject of speech (chapter 9).

— 4 —

The Interminable Insomnia of Exile:
The Camp as an Ordinary Exceptionalism

Two problems that arise in all studies of this subject make the reality of the camps immediately paradoxical. They determine right away the strangeness of these places. The first problem relates to the temporality of the camps. It is only the emergency situation and its exceptional character that justify these spaces, but at the same time these factors tend to reproduce themselves, to spread and establish themselves over the long term. This permanent precariousness is the first fact that strikes you when you arrive in a camp. The second question relates to the status of the space, which always boils down to the self-evident fact of its extra territoriality: a camp does not belong to the national space on which it is established, hence the rite of passage of gateways, identity checks, etc., on entry, symbolizing the transition not into a prison, but rather into a different regime of government and rights. Within this 'extra-territorial' space, the exceptional situation that the refugees encounter becomes the ordinary texture of their existence. It seems to me important to tackle these two questions right away, as they are the ones that force themselves on you when you penetrate into a refugee camp.

Waiting and absence: notes on the Palestinian camps

In general, if ethnologists are to find a meaning for their observations, these have to be inscribed in a temporality that goes beyond the present event alone. In all circumstances, their reading of social facts is focused both on the present and on the event, which have to be grasped 'from life', but at the same time is attentive to the processes that make and unmake these on a timescale that is a priori open. The

71

reality of contemporary terrains, whatever they are, can no longer be definitively confused with the illusion of atemporality on which the use of a mode of description known as the 'ethnographic present' was formerly based – an absolute present of a supposedly eternal culture of peoples kept at a distance from history, on whom the ethnologist was in a sense the accredited specialist. The need to reintroduce temporality into anthropological analysis, and beyond this also the historicity of the facts observed, and thus to question constantly the configuration and the effects of time on the present that ethnologists share with the peoples they study, has already been very well argued in recent anthropological works.[1]

It is at this precise point that temporality proves to be a problem in the constitution of the facts of the present – because the new approach of anthropology is more attentive to it, but also because the reality itself has changed. In the face of lives and situations that are precarious from every point of view, a sensitive measurement of reality takes as its main criterion the possibility of duration. From this point of view, we can say that the life of refugees and the situation of the camps are models of uncertainty. They are spaces and populations administered in the mode of emergency and exception, where time seems to have been stopped for an undetermined period. A camp is an emergency intervention that has been on 'stand-by' for months or years: five to ten years, or even more, for the camps in Sudan, Liberia, Guinea; more than fifteen years now for the Somalian refugees in Kenya; over thirty years for the Sahrawi refugees in Algeria; thirty years again for the Angolan refugees who were in Zambia from the early 1970s to 2002 and beyond; over fifty years for the Palestinian refugees living in the various countries of the Middle East, in camp-towns on whose margins other refugees, Iraqi or Sudanese, have now come to settle. Wars keep going, and the 'inhabitants' of the camps also establish themselves for the duration. Waiting becomes an eternity, an endless present. The common term for all these spaces could well be that of 'waiting room'.

There are two opposite models of thought about the temporality of refugee camps. The first of these holds that the refugees are awaiting return. Their whole exile bears the strange and heavy sensation of an interminable insomnia.[2] Time seems configured by the waiting to return: back to the lost place that the exiles keep alive in their memory, back to a time that biography itself renders unreal . . . by waiting, what they experience here, in the camp where they have ended up, has no meaning, no legible existence, if not to justify the demand for return by the suffering that this interminable insomnia provokes – the personal complaint becoming a component of collective demands; the latter, in fact, calls forth the former. This is embodied in the figure of the Palestinian refugee remembering the Naqba (the 'catastrophe' of forced exile in 1948), the primacy of the 'native land' over the 'land of exile', and the unacceptable present conceived as the absence of the Elsewhere and the wait for the Great Return. It is this figure of the 'refugee Absent' that the historian and essayist Elias Sanbar describes: 'The refugee is characterized by unease. Unease at seeing absence prevail and departure confirmed. Unease at never again seeing the swallowed-up land. Unease at finding the homeland unrecognizable and irretrievable.'[3] Waiting and absence are the lot of the imaginary refugee, although paradoxically everything happens in the camp and in the present, and this is where this painful perception of time as waiting and absence is elaborated.

On the West Bank, the present of the refugee camps, within which this representation of absence and waiting is constructed, is formed by a double enclosure, by two frontiers – that separating the West Bank from Israel, and that separating the refugee camps from the West Bank itself: two walls. The small Palestinian town of Kalkilyia is on the border between Israel and the West Bank. It is hemmed in on all sides by 13 kilometres of the 'barrier' that separates the two territories. This is a complex system that the word 'wall' is inadequate to describe, as Éric Hazan notes. On the one hand, it follows a complicated course, seemingly incomprehensible, but enclosing the Palestinians in its links and sealing them into unliveable enclaves; on the other hand, the technology of the 'barrier' is the object of particular attention on the part of the Israeli authorities:

The wall that encloses Kalkilyia is made up of concrete sections with watchtowers and surveillance cameras, as shown to the whole world in photographs and films. When you go out of the town, a further mechanism continues the encirclement. An asphalted track is designed for the movement of patrol vehicles. On both sides (though in parts only on one side) there is an electronic but not electrified barrier; an electric one would not be a serious obstacle, as it would only need to be broken at one point to be ineffective, but the least contact with the electronic barrier sets off an alarm, the surveillance cameras placed every fifty metres focus on and visualize the intruder, and jeeps arrive within minutes. The two barriers bordering the track are doubled on the outward side by a wide and deep ditch, and by a triple set of barbed-wire rolls. On each side, this ensemble is hedged by a 'buffer zone' cleared by bulldozer, in some places hundreds of metres wide. The system may be called a "wall", as it is just as unbridgeable as concrete.[4]

The geography and technology of the wall show the essential role of this frontier for the Israeli administration: the West Bank 'wall' is gradually making this 'borderline' not into a territorial limit between equals, but rather into an organized space of stoppage and 'imprisonment outside' of the other as undesirable. Despite condemnation by the International Court of Justice, this wall isolates from the world, and from the green lawns of Israel, the dried-up Palestinian Territories that are no more liveable today than the South African Bantustans were yesterday. But within this immense camp of undesirables that Gaza and the West Bank have become, other camps reinforce the suffering: the Palestinian refugee camps kept apart on Palestinian territory. In fact, the West Bank space is not entirely placed under the Palestinian Authority. 'Zoned' into distinct statuses, it is divided up into towns and villages under the control of the Palestinian government in Ramallah, roads and agricultural 'colonies' controlled by the Israeli army, and refugee camps under the control of UNRWA, the UN agency responsible for the Palestinian refugees. Israeli army checkpoints mark the crossings from one 'zone' to another.

It is understandable how, in this context of constant oppression and threat, a dense 'interior' has been formed over the years, and a largely 'ghettoized' one, still more so in the camps than in the Palestinian Territories that surround them. The refugee camps on Palestinian territory are ghettos within the ghetto, camps within the camp.[5] Under this constraint, many people break holes in the wall and move from one side to the other. The historian and sociologist Sylvaine Bulle observes that an increasingly urban everyday life is beginning to modify the symbolism of Palestinian identity.[6] At the same time, this is centrally based on the institutional enclosure of the camp and on the status of refugee. This tension and paradox is expressed in the life of the camps today.

Every study of a Palestinian camp begins with the inevitable guided tour, an almost identical ritual, which I experienced on the West Bank in 2005 in the three camps at Nablus, and in those of Jenin and Tulkarem. I reproduce here some notes and impressions from this visit to the Nablus camps.

Guided tour of the Palestinian camps at Nablus

Nablus, Askar camp, 6 July 2005. After the Beit Ilma camp (a.k.a. Camp no. 1) two days ago, and the New Askar camp yesterday, today's visit to the Old Askar camp follows the same lines.

A guided tour indeed, but, above all, in each of the three cases, a very 'politicized' visit to a terrain that itself seems already over-politicized. In the image of Palestine, refugees play a central role. Their suffering is the point of departure: it is symbolically recalled, during the visit to the camps, by meetings with the 'old people'. Each man and woman giving their personal version, all these old people (the first generation of Palestinian refugees) tell their true stories, what they experienced, starting from the 'catastrophe' of 1948 . . . their lost land, the invasion of Israeli soldiers, the flight of the peasants, the certainty that they would return to their lands, their settlement under tents in the camps (Ramallah, Tulkarem, Askar, Balata, etc.), the years spent in tents still believing they were going to return . . . A few years later (1956, 1958), UNRWA gave them one or two rooms built of rubble – proof of this past can still be seen in Old Askar, a camp opened in 1952, with some of its units built in the years immediately after and not modified, allowing 12 to 15 square metres per family.

The visit to the New Askar camp (constructed in 1964 as an extension of Old Askar 2 kilometres away) was also exemplary in its fashion. As distinct from the other Nablus camps, this was neither recognized nor assisted by UNRWA, and has no hospital, school or social services. You have to go to Old Askar for this care. At New Askar, the UN organization was held responsible for the duplication of suffering – this word having become the broad and loose signifier that is filled with quite different contents from one camp to another. What you 'visit' in going to the camps is a suffering with two anchorage points: the memory of the lost land, maintained by the repeated testimonies of the old, and the confinement of the refugees in the 'out-places' that are the camps. These camps, for their part, have to keep intact the symbol of waiting to return, i.e. immobility and non-existence. This suffering seems to follow a continuous line, from the war and exile of 1948 to the present moment.

Visits are organized by second- or third-generation refugees, now in their forties and playing a political role in the camp (refugee committees, Fatah leaders, those in charge of the social centre, etc.). They give the commentary on the visit. They transform suffering into politics. After the testimonies of the old people, the visit continues with the families of martyrs (*shahid*),[7] and a commented walk through streets which bear on the walls of houses either old or recent traces of bullets or shells from the

Israeli army's violent incursions, often at night and often deadly, which are still part of everyday life in the camps. This continuous sequence always leads up to the idea of 'return' to the lost lands (in houses in the camps, families keep 'the key' of their house of origin, which for refugees in Nablus is generally in the Jaffa region).[8] Return as a solution to suffering is the Palestinian political leitmotiv (the 'right of return'), but it is contradicted by the actual modes of life of the second and third generations in the camps of the West Bank towns. What you see at Nablus is that, as in the French *banlieues* or working-class quarters, certain refugees leave the camp and settle in a district of the town once their finances permit this. To be a refugee in the Balata camp does indeed mean living in the largest refugee camp on the West Bank (25,000 inhabitants), but it also means living in Nablus in an inferior condition rather than being literally excluded. 'Refugee' is the inferior status of the Palestinian urban condition.[9] There is a dualism, and sometimes a sharp cleavage, between this urban reality of the camps and the politics of suffering bound up with the symbolic place of the camps in Palestinian identity. Suffering and the figure of the victim are the basis of Palestinian politics, if today stripped of the revolutionary projects that brought a convergence in the 1970s between the Palestinian *fedayeen* and the Cuban or Vietnamese revolutionaries. The only political story today is the singular histories brought together in a great common history of suffering that combines the absence of the lost Elsewhere with the expectation of return – and between the two a long and unliveable parenthesis.[10] This is literally the politics of suffering and victimhood, and seems to be the only way of existing, with one's biography, in the present of the Palestinian camps in the occupied territories.

There is an objective and inescapable connivance between this politics of suffering and the 'cause of victims' that underlies the discourse of those humanitarian NGOs that seek to give a meaning to their action.[11] For it is notable how the 'Palestinian cause' as put forward today and the humanitarian 'cause of victims' share the same interpretative logic.

Nablus, Balata camp, 23 July 2005. It is this 'self-evident' connivance between the humanitarian cause and the Palestinian cause that a Fatah official and his five militiamen from the Al-Aqsa brigades sought to press home to me, when they turned up by chance while I was at Balata camp putting questions to an old notable on the camp's history and social organization. The old man had been telling me the story of his exile since 1948, his arrival at the Balata camp in 1957–8, and his very political desire to remain at Balata despite certain offers to relocate elsewhere (particularly from 'a representative of the British government'): 'Once you leave the camp, you lose your 1948 rights of return; the three leading families of the Balata camp decided to stay in the camp so as to remain refugees.' Then, apropos of his sons, he was more pragmatic: 'They do not refuse to go elsewhere and live in other districts, but they need this address: "Palestinian Refugee Camp"'. . . . The questions that the Fatah leader put to me after brusquely interrupting this interview aimed solely to check that the organization Médecins Sans Frontières (the rubric under which I was introduced in the camp) had adjusted its political position (that the land is Palestinian) to its practice of relieving the suffering of the victims . . . I agreed without too much beating about the bush.

Waiting and absence thus may constitute the very essence of the present, a doubly painful one. This can be noted from the other emblematic figure of the refugee camp provided by the Sahrawis.[12] The conception of time becomes completely political – this being the way in which it is really *actual*, and this actuality makes it ambivalent: the present is fully lived, even though it is perceived as a state of waiting. The four refugee camps established since 1976 in the Tindouf region of southern Algeria housed some 50,000 refugees in their first year, rising to 155,000 in 2002 and over 200,000 in 2008. Recent research shows the transparency between the space of the camps, that of a society in suspense, and the territory of an exiled state. It is waiting, above all, that gives meaning to the suspension of time in everyday life that everyone experiences – suspension also of the historical time of the refugee identity. The wait for humanitarian assistance confirms Waiting in general:

> Everyday life remains dependent on the chances of arrival of humanitarian aid, and often gas, food . . . and water are also awaited . . . The whole of life is thus organized as a function of waiting, and this at every level: waiting for food, waiting for news of one's family . . . waiting for a possible change in the political situation of the SADR[13] and thus of that of the refugees, etc.[14]

Even if the habitat has been transformed, and buildings of sand brick constructed in the 1990s 'on account of the Sahrawis' realization that they would be settled in the camps for a prolonged period',[15] the tent remains the symbol kept up by each family to signal their identity as refugee, the temporary inscription in the camp and the perspective of return. Both absence and waiting are established as a political principle as well as the foundation of identity. This is why the social and political organization of the camps[16] is conceived as a displaced double of this eternal Elsewhere of the refugees: the land from which they have been expelled and from which they are now absent. It refers to this in two ways. On the one hand, it is presented as a reproduction of Western Sahara, the land that has been lost and is claimed – reproduction, for example, in the toponymic transposition of places and institutions of the land of origin into those of the camps. And, on the other hand, conversely, it is a 'territorial experiment' that, though applied to the space of the camps today, is intended, in the political ideology of the Sahrawi liberation movement, to be reproduced in Western Sahara when this is regained.[17] Rather than a state in exile, the space of the camps becomes 'the territory of a refugee Sahrawi state'.[18] The logic is reversed, and at this precise moment it is notable how the camp itself, here and now, produces and maintains the political demand for a Sahrawi state. In the same way, and beyond the particular political situation of the Middle East, it could be said that 'the camp produces the Palestinian'.[19]

As these two limiting cases show, the Palestinian and the Sahrawi, from the point of view of the (non-)becoming of the camps and their role as the site for constructing a political project of return, the attitude that consists in conceiving the temporality of refugee camps as an absence and a waiting for return is paradoxically fuelled by a presence and a long socialization in the space of the camps themselves – since 1948, the mid-1950s and 1967 for the more than a million and a half inhabitants of the Palestinian camps, and since 1976 for the Sahrawi camps. This lays the basis for a second series of questions regarding the temporality of the camps, in an opposite direction to the first, but ultimately capable of helping to discover the present meaning of these camps that seem to be defined only by absence and the waiting to return.

The African camps: a present that never ends

There is thus a second fact of the camp's temporality, after that of the waiting associated with the absence of the native land which we have just described. In a very pragmatic fashion, the exiles live, survive, have encounters, organize their existence. A real time is established when the present is extended. But it is still nothing more than an enduring present. In the actual space of the camps, what meaning is associated with the possibility of describing the place itself in duration? The camp is the manifestation of an immediate present, since it excludes both past and future. It excludes them by excluding itself from all history, for past and present are only conceived, ultimately, in the Elsewhere of the lost land and the hypothetical future of return, as we have just seen. It also excludes them because, here and now, it is only the emergency regime that governs its particular existence. This is certainly a presence that is self-evidently defined in opposition to the imaginary of the absence experienced in exile, but a presence that for all that has no spatiotemporal reference of its own: what is this space over time? No collective memory of the 'site' can legitimately be formed when one is deemed to be waiting only to leave it; no particular history of it has ever been written. No 'ruin' is kept and treasured; on the contrary, the camps of today are an exemplary terrain of those ephemeral buildings that are increasingly constructed out of lightweight materials, taken down as quickly as they are put up, and moved elsewhere. The emergency regime that establishes them as a precarious material reality is nothing more than the expression of a 'presentism' driven to excess. This presentism is today a general organizational principle of social and political representation, which tends to dominate our world; in particular, it denies the function and meaning that spaces themselves acquire in the long term and which they transmit in the memory of their inhabitants.[20]

This desert of meaning is felt still more – and the observer is that much more touched by it – when nothing comes to fill it, not even this full idea of exile – existential for the exiles themselves, political for the nationalist leaders – when waiting is an absence of the Elsewhere, an absence within which the present is preparing a return. I did not find this in the camps of Zambia, Kenya or the Mano River. There is no instance here of the comforting oxymoron that the feeling of absence is after all the foundation of a presence-in-the-world.

On these terrains, time itself has thus become the most critical parameter of reality. Does this exist? Is it going to produce sediment, acquire a patina, marks of historicity? It is indeed the formation of a temporal reality in a context that is provisional by definition, of a signifying reality in a simple logistic artefact, that lies at the centre of the anthropological problematic of the camps.

In the African camps where I conducted my research, I found the pure constraint of an enduring present, the imposed temporality of confinement and adaptation to a space that its inhabitants transform in the course of the long parenthesis of their life in the camp. It is within this parenthesis that ethnologists can establish themselves and meet refugees, moving around in the camps from case to case, in collective or individual tents, in the MSF's bush clinics or the stores of the World Food Programme. It was on these occasions that I sometimes discovered a 'fault',[21] the possibility of escape, something unexpected in a present that seems to be the sole beginning and end of time in the waiting zones: shelters over which time is taken to improve them into almost pretty huts; stalls that are set up every day on a rudimentary market place; families who converge from one camp to another, finally joining up again; conversations that become critical expression against confinement, against 'the UNs' in the camps,[22] and are sometimes transformed into written lists of demands, demonstrations by refugees. Tales of the past, the organization of the present and predictions for the near future make it possible for the refugees to consolidate their presence in these spaces. If they endure, if they spread, then it is appropriate to conceive them beyond the apparent and immediate function assigned to them by the humanitarian language of emergency.

And so it is not war, population displacement or the building of a wall or camp that in themselves solicit the attention of the researcher, as they do that of the emergency doctors who come to the aid of a population in danger, or the journalist who has a few hours or days to write a 'paper' on a current topic. It is indeed these events, but only in so far as they are constitutive of a lasting reality.

To speak of the camps today – which is the essential purpose of this study, and in a certain fashion its most political goal – is to contribute to bringing them out of non-existence and non-temporality, socializing them as themselves milieus that are deeply hybrid and alive – speaking of them to say that their de facto duration has social and cultural repercussions, even if the habitat, the economy, the matrimonial or political life that we observe there has hardly any other possibility of developing other than provisionally, discreetly or illegally.

The camp as space of exception

The second constitutive problem of the very reality of the camps concerns the status of the space. Once the checkpoints and gates have been crossed, refugees find inside the camps a situation of exception that is the new routine of their existence. Since in principle they have no right to move freely or work in the countries where the UNHCR sites that have taken them in are located, those who leave the camps do so either by special and temporary derogation, or illegally.[23] They have no de facto citizenship (neither that of the country they have left, nor that of the country receiving them), and no other 'right' than that decreed by the individuals who hold power over their lives in the camps. This situation of exception may sometimes have beneficial effects, for which the local population envy the refugees: humanitarian organizations develop programmes for women's health, against sexual abuse and rape in and around the camps, against intra-familial violence; they conduct programmes of peace education, establish post-traumatic dialogue groups, etc. Above all, the camps exert a very real attraction on the surrounding population, who seek to benefit from the aid that is offered – especially in terms of medical attention and food.

In some of the camps, however, or in sectors of a camp, other individuals or organizations may decree other rules that are specific to these locations, and thus exert exceptional domination. Everyday life in the camps is often marked by this form of socialization, an internal violence additional to that of the warfare and social violence at the origin of the forced displacement.

It is well known that prostitution and the sexual abuse of under-age refugees have been the object of 'scandalous revelations' and moral denunciations, particularly in 2002 when a report by the Save the Children Fund was released to the media on the subject of 'sexual exploitation and violence on refugee children in Liberia, Guinea and Sierra Leone'. These practices of male and generational domination take advantage not only of material destitution, but also of the profound deterioration in the social entourage of the great majority of refugees on their arrival in the camps. The loss of parents killed at the place of departure or along the way, the dispersal of families in flight, hunger and disease, all attack and diminish every refugee physically and socially, and especially women and children who are often isolated survivors of massacres. This destructuring in advance (before family units are recomposed over months and years) reinforces the absolute power held in the camps by whoever has a bit of money or food. In such cases there is neither 'rape' nor harassment, nor explicit pressure. The context itself makes any 'illegal' action unnecessary on the part of the 'big man'.[24]

A few months before the Save the Children report was released on the internet, I found myself in a camp that could well have been one of those investigated. On the Maheba site in Zambia, the UNHCR delegated its powers to the national section of a large denominational NGO, the Lutheran World Federation. This employed agents who were Zambian nationals, in some cases local, as well as refugees themselves; they were accustomed to working in the camp and possibly moving from one NGO to another. One of them was particularly responsible for transit centres: he was a refugee who had arrived in the camp twenty years previously. The transit centres are the sites where new refugees arrive from the border, exhausted, hungry and often sick. These centres represent one extremity of the humanitarian chain, a critical site for checking its efficacy, but they are also the 'terrain' which this man from the NGO administering the camp is the only person to visit regularly. In the transit centre, moving between the tents, the NGO representative distributes small quantities of soap bars, kitchen utensils, and very occasionally also coverings; the new refugees may have to wait for two days or even a week for their food distribution. The NGO agent knocks some people over, insults others, treats one person as a 'liar' and another as a 'thief' because she asks for a plastic sheet that he says he already gave her the day before. The assignment of places on which the new arrivals can install four posts and a plastic sheet stamped 'UNHCR' is the responsibility of the same man who distributes, divides, gathers or separates refugees by pointing to them with his finger, and shouting at those who complain. They have been in the transit tents for a month, but already he seems to know them well; he threatens one young man whom he suspects of being a delinquent and thief, kisses a young woman, is embraced by another young man, enters and remains in the tents as he sees fit. The abuse of power, possibly sexual, if it takes place at that point, is inscribed in a deep social misery that is reinforced by the political exceptionalism, a male and generational domination that is an integral part of a situation of 'power over life': the UNHCR delegates to the NGO, which delegates to a single man 'land' where he applies his law. . . and thus practises one of the forms of a wide-ranging exceptional regime.

The refugee camps are not zones of 'non-right', but rather zones of exceptional rights and power, where everything seems possible for those in control. In the same camp, by way of reaction to the malfunctioning administration, several volunteers from international NGOs, including Médecins Sans Frontières and the Jesuit Refugee Service, protested to the UNHCR. Five employees of the camp administration had been unofficially recognized as responsible for the misappropriation of food or funds, and for sexual abuse, including the person in charge of distributing food to the 25,000 refugees on the site who benefited from food aid. Although no legal action was taken against them, they were dismissed and had to leave the camp. As for the 'man on the ground' mentioned above, he himself resigned and beat a hasty retreat, though not without denouncing in writing the many practices of embezzlement of money and material that he had observed within the NGO that employed him and administered the camp.

If refugee camps are, on paper, in the official texts, governed by international law, humanitarian law and other human rights, assaults on these rights are an everyday occurrence. No one can have any doubt about this if they spend any time in a camp – this is certainly no kind of scoop. I have just given the example of a situation that can be called ordinary exceptionality, which I observed in one of the camps where I conducted my study, in Zambia in 2002.[25] Barbara Harrell-Bond and Guglielmo Verdirame, who conducted a long study in the late 1990s on conditions for the protection of refugees in Kenya and Uganda, reported similar findings to my own, and drew particularly severe conclusions as regards the NGOs and the UNHCR. Their diagnosis is all the more significant in that these are researchers linked to the Refugee Studies Centre and the University of Oxford, the first centre to be established in 1982 (by Harrell-Bond herself) for the specific issue of refugees and forced migrations. The Refugee Studies Centre works in close collaboration with the major humanitarian NGOs and several UN agencies that finance its activities, including Christian Aid, Save the Children UK, the Norwegian Refugee Council, the International Rescue Committee, as well as ECHO, UNICEF, UNDP and the UNHCR itself.[26] Their findings and the positions they adopted are thus strategically important, as they explain the point of view of various experts and the policy of the institutions. It seems important to me to dwell for a moment on the main conclusions of their study.[27]

Barbara Harrell-Bond and Guglielmo Verdirame show the pivotal role of the UNHCR. Noting the 'astonishing duplicity' of the NGOs and the UNHCR, they speak of a 'Janus-faced humanitarianism'. A 'public face' corresponds to the image of 'compassionate cosmopolitans driven by ideals and values, and committed to helping refugees', the image that the humanitarian organizations and UN agencies seek to present. The public image is what is seen in the countries of the developed world, particularly in the course of fund-raising campaigns. In stark contrast to this, they maintain, is the 'private face' of humanitarianism as the refugees see it, 'often callous, sometimes cruel, and – nearly always – ineffectual'.[28] The anthropologist and lawyer insist on the 'pose' that the NGOs take up as 'representatives of civil society', and the UNHCR as 'a member of the UN family and representative of the "international community"'. The refugees, for their part, whether they are in camps or in the big cities, have 'discovered that power exercised under a humanitarian guise was not so different from power in other guises'.[29]

In both Kenya and Uganda they have noted failings in humanitarian action, and still more so the shady arrangements between UNHCR agents and certain NGOs to organize expulsions to the border and the 'screening' of asylum seekers according to procedures that any legal evaluation at all would deem unacceptable. As in other African countries, the aid to refugees is strictly conditional on their segregation in the camps, which is contrary to the text of the 1951 Geneva convention on refugees, as they emphasize, their study being particularly attentive to the legal dimension of exile. Segregation in the camps in fact prevents the realization of the three principles that officially guide the action of the UNHCR to bring refugees out of the precariousness in which they find themselves: integration in the host country, resettlement in a third country or repatriation. As we have seen above, repatriation is generally the 'preferable' solution supported by the UNHCR, even against the desire of the refugees themselves, which leads the UNHCR and the organizations it contracts with to organize 'collective repatriations' that are in fact forced returns. However, for want of the power to realize these returns, whether for political, economic or organizational reasons, the UNHCR keeps the refugees in camps, and this 'temporary' situation can become eternal. In point of fact, in Africa the UNHCR's refugees are always kept apart, a practice vigorously and angrily denounced by Harrell-Bond and Verdirame. Neither repatriation, nor integration, nor resettlement; for them, 'encampment' really is the UNHCR's 'fourth solution' – not admitted, but systematically preferred to the two others.

Without even talking about the 'worst kind of camp' – those experienced, for example, by the Rwandans in Tanzania and the Congo in the 1990s (on the lines of the famous Goma camps of 1994–6) – but focusing simply on the camps that have served as 'models' in terms of assistance and protection (such as those in Uganda in the same period), the authors note that 'the full catalogue of human rights – both civil and political, and economic, social and cultural – were violated'.[30] This is the main conclusion of their study: if a sovereign power is transferred from states to international and humanitarian organizations, and if no control over the effects of this power can be exercised at the local level, then this power will never be threatened. On this basis, 'violations of human rights in the camps can be perpetrated with full impunity'. Finally, the verdict matches the findings presented: there is a contradiction between keeping people in camps and respect for human rights, since the camp 'constitutes a unique setting for the arbitrary exercise of power'.[31] Everything that these authors note in the framework of what is called 'protection' then takes its place in a broader 'ethnography of injustice'.[32]

Some immediate comments are needed after reading *Rights in Exile*. The importance and courage of this well-argued list of failures of humanitarian intervention have to be admitted. I would add that their critique could be continued on a deeper basis, starting from a different point of view. Once you go into detail on the long-term daily life in the camps, and follow the 'ethnography of injustice' that Harrell-Bond and Verdirame profess, then their contexts, in the concrete situation, present several practices that can be classed as 'perversion', 'misappropriation' or 'defeat' of the humanitarian effort. How are we to describe and interpret these?

It is true that a moral effect of deception or betrayal is sometimes felt by an outside observer or by the actors themselves, but this is not always the case – far from it – and I have very often myself felt the paradox between the imagined scope of the official rescue enterprise (the grandeur, as it were, of the 'public face' of humanitarianism) and the relative inefficacy of the operations on the ground (the 'private face') in relation to such proclamations. This gap, which is sometimes considerable, is not necessarily expressed concretely in perversion, abuse or misapplication for which responsibility is always simply individual and local. It is more often expressed in double language, misunderstandings, tensions and conflicts. On the ground, in the refugee camps, operations are often limited to patching-up work that brings a bit of assistance to a few people, but also, naturally enough, 'bulks up the figures', shifts supplies and spends a programmed budget. Every day, criteria are used, always difficult and always debatable, to determine a selection of beneficiaries. Injustice comes into the power mechanism that humanitarian intervention immediately produces, all the more so when it is combined, as is generally the case in Africa and Asia, with the deprivation of freedom to move around and to work on account of confinement in the camps, and the long duration of this settlement apart.

It is rather the myopia of certain humanitarian operators in relation to the immediate or global context of their intervention that has often shocked me. This is far more frequent, even commonplace, than the misappropriation and manipulation that is sometimes condemned without taking account of the social realities into which these practices are inserted. For example, to mention a very well-known practice in the humanitarian world, we can ask to what extent the resale of the food ration distributed free by the World Food Programme is an adaptive strategy for the refugees in a context of profound nutritional insufficiency, rather than a 'manipulation' or 'misappropriation' of the humanitarian effort. How should we understand the repeated findings of injustice that the authors of *Rights in Exile* relate, and how should we analyse the duplication of violence experienced by those women and men who undergo the obligation of encampment, when they have just emerged from the phase of war, exodus and survival?

Should we speak, at the end of the day, of failure, or rather of an ordinary exceptionalism, as the basis of a particular government, i.e. humanitarian government? It is this latter reply that I argue for here. For in the context in which it is deployed, the humanitarian apparatus itself is this ambiguous power. Its intervention seems justified by an almost divine 'authorization', universalistic and supernatural, that is deployed whenever it finds a favourable terrain in a sudden exceptional situation – that created, for example, by an emergency, a catastrophe, a state of war, the massive arrival of a population in distress, but also by the expulsion of undesirable groups, the 'hunt' for illegals by police forces, the confinement or detention of asylum seekers, etc.

This exceptional situation rapidly ceases to surprise and is transformed into an exceptional space when humanitarianism establishes and consolidates its own spaces and its own mode of government – for months, years, even decades.[33]

The fact that all these spaces, despite their apparent extraterritoriality, can be effectively located, facilitates the observation of the terrain and makes it possible to understand, by way of the ethnographic study, the experience that is lived, to describe it and grasp the power of transformation that arises from it. Beyond the legal and political exceptionality, real life is constructed in the camps as a social life that is largely resilient and, in its own way, also transformative.

— 5 —

Experiences of Wandering, Borders and Camps: Liberia, Sierra Leone, Guinea

A strip some 200 metres wide, which the international workers call the 'grey zone', runs between the border posts of Liberia and Guinea, and it is here that Liberians wait in tents for the UNHCR to register them and transport them to the refugee camps in Guinée Forestière, the forest region of Guinea. The people here are visible enough, but they have lost all right to national citizenship without yet being 'refugees'. If they do not want to enter the camps (which are a synonym for security, but also for enclosure, assignment to a strictly limited space, a form of ghetto), they can hide themselves when the UNHCR lorries arrive. Little by little, people learn to develop survival strategies that include a lasting if precarious relationship with the humanitarian apparatus: multiple registration, double residence (in the camp and in town), work on the black, the purchase of food-ration cards, etc. What we see here is a dense experience akin to what is sometimes called a 'refugee culture', but which is nonetheless quite contrary to the passive and resigned image of the assisted that is generally understood by this term.

I spent five months, in 2003–4 and then in 2007, visiting the quarters and camps inhabited by refugees and displaced persons from the Mano River conflict, which affected Liberia, Sierra Leone and Guinea. I started by plotting the initial empirical foundations that enabled me, via comparison and convergence with other situations, to attempt an inventory of the possible kinds of camp, as elaborated above in chapter 2. Most of all, however, I drew from this the conviction (and, I believe, some data to support it) that these spaces have been sites of profound cultural change. Without exhausting the full range of information and impressions gathered in the course of this study, I believe that it is useful and important to bring together here as much data as possible on the culture that is born in these places of flight, violence and refuge, in transit zones, borders and camps. At the end of this discussion, I shall be deliberately provocative, and say that, like the 'cultural areas' of ethnologists of a former time, we can describe here a new cultural air, neither ethnic nor linguistic, nor even strictly geographical, but corresponding to what war, humanitarian aid, and the wanderings of refugees and displaced persons from the Mano River region have brought into being.

The Mano River conflict

The Lofa region, in north-western Liberia, was the most intense focus of the so-called 'Mano River' war, waged from December 1989 to August 2003 on the frontier between Liberia and Sierra Leone, and bordering on the Forest Region of Guinea to the north. What is known in Liberia as the 'first war' ran from 1990 to 1996, when the forces led by Charles Taylor were on the offensive, until his seizure of power was consolidated by an election in 1997. The 'second war' (1999–2003) saw the attacks by the rebel group Liberians United for Reconciliation and Democracy (LURD)[1] against Taylor's government forces. By 2004 Liberia and Sierra Leone were both under the control of UN forces, several thousand strong.[2] But the conflict maintains its regional character, and certain chain reactions of destabilization have been provoked by the displacement of armed groups of rebels and militia inclined to intervene under contract in neighbouring countries – such as western Ivory Coast and Guinée Forestière.

At least half a million Sierra Leonese (out of a population of 4.5 million) were displaced by the conflict, either within their own country or in adjacent lands (Liberia and Guinea), and nearly 900,000 Liberians out of a population of 3 million. There are 400,000 Liberian refugees in Guinea, Sierra Leone and Ivory Coast, as well as a total of 500,000 displaced persons internally, 260,000 of whom were living in camps in May 2004. Almost 10 per cent of the population in Sierra Leone, and nearly a third in Liberia, have thus had personal experience of war, flight and refuge, with social and cultural effects that have still to be understood.

A whole series of questions arises from these various experiences. What spaces were formed on the margin between war and ordinary life? What new modes of life are learned in the spaces of flight and refuge? What lasting cultural changes have been generated by the refugees' experience in the web of assistance and control?

The space of war and flight, of informal refuge (in the forest or in town) and the humanitarian camps, has formed an unprecedented framework of experience, even if not all movement was into totally unknown terrain. In part, though only in part, the refugees moved in a space that was relatively unified both linguistically and in terms of lineage and religion, apart from the more remote places of exile (Ghana, Ivory Coast, let alone Europe). But we still have to grasp the full lessons of this experience, study the unity of modes of life, the efficacy of networks of mutual recognition, the changing context of solidarities, the redefinition of family frameworks, as well as the meaning of the encounter with the world of the international humanitarian organizations. To unravel this complexity, we shall proceed in stages.

A Sunday at Kissidougou

Kissidougou is a small town in the Forest Region of Guinea, near to which three refugee camps were established in 2003: Boreah, Kountaya and Telikoro, with a total of more than 32,000 refugees, Liberian and Sierra Leonese. It is also where the offices and housing of the NGOs operating in the camps are located.

On Sunday afternoons, some expatriate volunteers from the town's several NGOs get together in the grounds of Enfants Réfugiés du Monde to play volleyball six a side. In one team, there are two people from ERM, three from the International Red Cross and one from the UNHCR; in the other team, two from MSF, two from ACF, one from the UNHCR and one from Première Urgence. The same individuals, along with a few others, also meet up on Saturday evenings to celebrate an arrival or departure, or for a 'themed fête': either 'at ACF', 'at MSF' or 'at Première Urgence'. These meetings, and the connections rapidly made, have formed a fairly large expatriate community in the small town of Kissidougou. Two restaurants with international cuisine, and a few rare food shops, profit from European-type consumption. The mayor of the town appreciates the presence of the NGOs, who mostly assist the local population as well as supplying aid to the refugees.

These are generally young volunteers, around thirty years old; they are European, American or Australian, and they have various motivations: religious compassion, solidarity with the most vulnerable, the desire for a rumbustious life, *altermondialiste* political commitment. They spend the week dealing with the concrete problems bound up

89

with the realization of their humanitarian mission (logistical problems, personnel management, organization of meetings for 'sensitization'). The action within the relatively stabilized camps is rather repetitive and routine, which disturbs some of the volunteers who were expecting a more adventurous experience. Such experiences do indeed happen, but they are more rare and in different contexts, such as 'outreach' tours at the reception centres on the border.

On Sundays, too, everyone tries as far as possible to make closer personal connections with the Guineans who work for the NGOs. Some expatriates are asked to eat with them and get to know their families. They may be invited to the christening of the child of an NGO worker, or spend the afternoon in their yard; others go with the local inhabitants to mass at the Catholic church (the town has nearly as many Catholics as Muslims).

They all know, however, that they are not there for very long. Three months, six months, very exceptionally a whole year. (This turnover is general NGO practice, either because the volunteers go back to their activities in their own country after this humanitarian interlude, or because the organizations consider that conditions of life and work in the field are difficult and so missions should not be too long.) However attracted they may be to 'meeting the people', they remain marked by the humanitarian function that brought them there, a function of assistance that is by its very nature distant, because 'biopolitical' – a treatment of others viewed as victims, and implying no distinction between the beneficiaries in terms of assistance, preference or relationships. It is because these people are 'victims' that the humanitarians are there. In this West African country that was formerly a French colony, humanitarian deployment is a component of the post-colonial situation.[3] The relationship between Whites and Blacks that is played out here is no longer that which obtained between a France that was initially imperial and colonial, later 'cooperative', and an Africa tied in various ways into close relationships, especially political, with at least a part of the colonizing country. The interdependence was a strong one, less that of the notorious 'Françafrique' business deals (which continue) than that of a bilateral political commitment around movements of decolonization and African independence.[4]

Let us be clear here. This assertion in no way means nostalgia for a time that was also marked by the despoiling of major natural resources, extreme forms of exploitation of colonized labour, political violence and racial brutality. It does though seek to emphasize that this political and social interlocking also contained within it, in principle, a certain 'responsibility', even if the actual application of this principle, particularly after independence (cooperation, development), left more in the way of frustration than success. The continuation of this history, the disengagement that followed the end of the Cold War, the 'structural adjustments' of the 1990s, were perceived by many Africans as a brutal abandonment, comparable if not equal to the despoliation and domination of the past. At least part of the meaning of humanitarian commitment comes from this context, i.e. from the fact that it has been the substitute for an internal domination – in the sense that the Empire was formerly the political unit of reference within which different types of socialities were developed: violent, authoritarian, paternalist, but also supportive.

Humanitarianism thus experienced a strange moment of glory in Africa in the 1980s and especially the 1990s. Its rising power was contemporary with this abandonment by the former colonial empires, and even one of its logical consequences. This had its repercussions for the individuals committed to humanitarianism, who sought to bring an emergency response to its disastrous effects, prepared for the feeling of being a drop of survival in an ocean of chaos. There were consequences too for the global meaning of humanitarian intervention in Africa, fundamentally associated with the White presence and the depoliticizing of relationships between the First (White) World and Africa. Locally, in Africa, humanitarians initially took over from colonists and colonial officials, then from cooperators and developers, to embody the new modality of White presence and domination. Beyond the emotions and ideologies involved here, we may well ask where the continuities and breaks lie.

Let us return to Kissidougou on a Sunday, the day of rest for the humanitarians. Even if they regret this, they will not manage to speak the local language, not having sufficient time to learn it, but above all because it is not useful to them in carrying out their mission. They will not know 'the people' because they are not required to do this either. The Sundays stretch out; they end up preferring the ephemeral intimacy of 'fêtes' and volleyball. On Monday morning, the procession of white four-wheel drives with their respective logos will take them back to the everyday life of the camps.

In the Guinean camps

Among the three camps close to Kissidougou, Boreah is located some 30 kilometres from the town, a little over an hour by dirt road.

91

The Boreah camp (Kissidougou district, Guinée Forestière) sheltered 7,500 refugees in September 2003, with at least twelve international organizations present: the World Food Programme supplied and stored food products; the UNHCR was the overall coordinating organization; the International Rescue Committee, from the USA, ran primary schools; the Belgian section of Médecins Sans Frontières operated two health posts; Enfants Réfugiés du Monde, from France, organized leisure activities, recreation and dialogue for children; Action Contre la Faim, also French, ran agricultural projects; Première Urgence, French again, was responsible for the distribution of food and for raising chickens; the Guinean Red Cross was involved in the management of the camp, with particular concern for 'social division', and distributed plastic sheeting for the roofs of huts; the American Refugee Committee offered loans of money in support of 'economic projects', and was also involved in dealing with sexual or 'gender-based' violence; the Center for Victims of Torture handled mental health care; Action by Churches Together, also American, offered psychiatric support; the German public agency for technical cooperation (GTZ) was involved in the construction of the camp and in running a centre for occupational training; also present were the UK Save the Children, the Canadian Centre d'Études et de Coopération Internationale, a Guinean NGO which handled food aid to the most vulnerable (REPC), and the Relief Activities of Detraumatization and Improvement of Refugees (RADIR), an NGO established by some refugees with a view to developing sport and dramatic activities, role-playing games, etc. The Bureau de Coordination des Réfugiés (BCR), representing the Guinean government, had an office there, in charge of a 'mobile security brigade' from the Guinean police, as well as some forty-three 'security assistants' recruited from among the refugees. Finally, a 'refugee committee' was established under the supervision of the UNHCR and the BCR.

This excessive framework is at first perplexing. It is a very visible presence, but less effective than it might seem from reading the weekly or monthly reports of the NGOs, the incalculable number of 'inter-agency' coordinating meetings, meetings for 'sensitization', the big signboards and flags of the UN agencies and NGOs that decorate the camp landscape, let alone the fleet of white four-wheel drives that circulate in the fenced-in space. For the refugees, however, this presence is just one part of the context of their lives, the part that views them as victims, as individuals with the right to an assistance that they do not control, and in the face of which they can only be spectators, demanders or plaintiffs in the best of cases, if not troublemakers, 'cheats', 'manipulators', or 'taking advantage of the system', to use some of the many phrases that describe them as refugees.

This tremendous international presence, in fact, suddenly becomes less central to understanding that world once you start to get into the stories of the individuals living in the camps, which acquaint us with the other contexts of their existence. This history also enables us to restore and account for the unforeseen behaviour in the camps, such as the list of demands from the refugee committee in the Boreah camp; the movement of women who blocked the main road to the camp; the gesture of the Liberian refugee who attacked the UNHCR delegate in his car at Conakry; the cries of a Sierra Leonese refugee woman prostituting herself in West Point, a very poor district of Monrovia, for less than half a US dollar, who shouted: 'Stop doing investigations, give us something to eat!'

The stories of refugees that are summarized very briefly in the pages that follow, two from Sierra Leone and two from Liberia (all of whom I met in the Boreah camp in 2003), and the references to some other experiences, will enable us to describe certain aspects of the many personal ways in which war, flight and the camps have been experienced. These people speak of a near past marked by violence, anxiety and forced displacement, as well as a gathering that is sometimes also forced. They do this because I asked them the question: 'What happened to you? How did you come here to the camp?' Other people said nothing or expressed themselves differently.[5]

Abou D., a Sierra Leonese refugee in Guinea (Boreah camp), fifty-three years old. Abou used to work in a cigarette factory in Freetown, and was organizational secretary to his local branch of the Sierra Leone People's Party, then in power. On 11 January 1999, when the RUF rebels invaded Freetown and overthrew the government, Abou was at home with his wife and four children. There was a knock at the door and he heard: 'We've come to see Mister D., you're one of the people against the RUF.' Then they broke down the door: 'I was in bed with my wife, the children were in their room, one of them in the sitting room. When they knocked, I climbed up on the roof through a skylight.' Abou continues his tale: one of his children was seized, the rebels said they were not going to kill him but mutilate him. 'They took him out of the house and cut his leg off. Then they set fire to the house and left.' Abou got out of the house by crossing the flames, his arms and face were burned. He then lost sight of his children. He fled by sea, then by road, and reached the small town of Kambia, still in Sierra Leone. There he found a friend who took him to hospital.

Over a year after the killing and the burning of his house, a friend brought him three of his children whom he had seen in Freetown. They had only just reached Kambia when the RUF attacked the town. Abou escaped to Guinea with the three children, crossing at Pamalap on the border with southern Guinea. 'In the camp I met several fighters', he says, 'fighters with the RUF. It was a hell again.'

They were transferred to another camp: 'Helicopter gunships dropped bombs on the camp. My three children disappeared. I was taken and put in prison for two weeks because the Guinean police believed I was one of the rebels. Many people were killed. The UNHCR came and told the Guineans that we were not rebels but refugees.'

In May 2001, along with other people from the camp, he was transferred to the Sembakounya camp (near Dabola) in Guinée Forestière. Here he discovered a nephew, who was still with him two and a half years later. On 20 June 2003, he says, to finish the list of this string of camps that has marked his life for more than four years, those Sembakounya refugees who did not return to Sierra Leone were transferred again to the Boreah camp, where I met him.

Abou does not want to return to Sierra Leone. He has lost his wife, and only has left one of his four children, the one with the amputated leg. The others are 'missing' – a word I would later hear repeatedly in the Lofa villages of northern Liberia. When he was in the Sembakounya camp in 2001 he was interviewed by someone from the UNHCR, to fill in the form to request 'resettlement in a third country'. He did not specify which country he wanted to go to. Rumours circulate: people say that refugees have been resettled in Norway, the United States, Australia and Canada. He would not receive a response. Previously, in the year 2000, at Forecariah on the border between Sierra Leone and Guinea, he had already been interviewed by someone from the 'protection' department of the UNHCR. Save the Children had also interviewed his son, 'to hear about his amputation', he says. Here in the camp, his nephew prepares his food for him. He lives with him and the invalid son. He says: 'The Sierra Leonese don't want to talk much about what happened, otherwise they start crying. It's very bad.' He misses the Sembakounya camp 'which was much better' than that of

Boreah where he is now: 'There were things to do.' His nephew worked as a teacher, which brought in a bit of money. The houses were made of brick, whereas here they are mud and very damp. 'At Sembakounya I wasn't well, I'd lost my children, my mind was confused, I had some medicines, tranquilizers. Not here.' He strikes me in fact as very beaten down, never moving, rather depressed I believe.

Ibrahim K., Sierra Leonese refugee in Guinea (Boreah camp), thrity-two years old. Ibrahim had been living in the Boreah camp for over a year when I met him. He was born near Freetown, the capital of Sierra Leone, where he lived with his parents, brothers and sisters.

In 1998 he left Freetown for Kono, a town in the Diamond district where he planned to ask his uncle for money to help him to continue his studies (he was then twenty-seven and in the 11th class, the penultimate year of secondary school). One Saturday morning, 26 February 1998, at 6 o'clock, the 'jointers'[6] attacked the town: 'We were bombed, everyone left, I followed the people who were running. I couldn't return to Freetown as the roads were blocked.' He tried to cross over to Guinea at Kombahélé and Kamiendo. He was arrested by the 'jointers', who held him and his family for two weeks. At this point in the tale, this is what Ibrahim told me, just as I wrote it down:

> Our clothes were ruined, I'd taken two pairs of trousers and three shirts with me. They were all torn. They said to me: 'We're going to give you clothes; do you want shirts with short sleeves or long sleeves.' I said 'long sleeves', to protect me better when I walked in the forest. I waited. They called people, and afterward you didn't see them any more. A woman came to warn me; she was the girlfriend of one of the leaders of the soldiers. She took me behind to show me what they did: they cut off the arms, either at the wrist or above the elbow. The woman showed me how to get away. I walked for three days in the bush.

After arriving at another village in Sierra Leone, he stopped to work there and find something to eat. After three weeks, the same 'jointers' sent a message that they were going to attack the village. Ibrahim fled once again. This time he reached the Guinean border. From there he went in successive stages to the

Massakoundou camp in Guinea where he was registered as a refugee. But after a month he left to go and work in a diamond-producing zone. The UNHCR wanted all the refugees to stay in camp; Ibrahim then returned to Massakoundou, but left again very quickly. He was arrested by Guinean soldiers who sent him along with other people to the UNHCR camp at Sembakounya. There he found work as a security volunteer with the UNHCR. Finally, on 3 June 2002, he was transferred from the Sembakounya camp to the one at Boreah, where I met him in September 2003.

He lost his wife in the Sembakounya camp in 2001. She died suddenly from an illness: 'In the morning she wasn't well, she told me that she had something to say to me, and in the evening I found her in the hospital, she was dead. But I know what it was.' When they were arrested at Kamiendo in 1998 by the 'jointers', his wife disappeared, and he did not see her for a week. He was told that people said she had been raped by the 'jointers'. 'That's what killed her', he assures me. He entrusted his five-year-old daughter to a friend's family in the Sembakounya camp, who would be arriving here at Boreah in a few days' time.

When I met Ibrahim, he had been working for four months as a security assistant in the camp. 'The problems', he said, 'are mainly theft because people don't have work, and the guards don't have lamps to survey the camp at night: doors and plastic sheeting are stolen'. Ibrahim complains that the NGOs in the camp don't provide work for the Sierra Leonese, the jobs are all for Liberians, 'because they say that the Sierra Leonese have to leave and go back to Sierra Leone'. Two years later, starting in 2005, it would be the turn of the Liberians to be forcibly spurred to return to their home region; in 2007, again, thousands were transported collectively in lorries back to Lofa in northern Liberia.

Like Abou, Ibrahim requested 'resettlement in a third country'. He has not received a reply. He has a map of Freetown on his bedroom wall, the only room in his hut. He shows me where he used to live in the State House quarter, which was all destroyed. Ibrahim is very well organized and methodical: an imitation clock on his door informs the potential visitor where he is at different times of day. He is involved in a sports association in the camp, as well as his work as a security assistant. Throughout his travels since 1998 he has made notes. Hence this precision with dates and episodes – even macabre ones – that serve as reference points in a story that was experienced above all as a prolonged wandering, to which his notes and words try to give a meaning. He also shows me an album with photos of his late wife, and his five-year-old daughter now in the Sembakounya camp, also friends that he met in the camps he passed through. The notebook, the photo album, the 'clock' with its daily diary, the map of Freetown – all these are reference points that enable Ibrahim to construct a personal resistance to the profound desocialization that the accumulated fears, the endless transfers, the cruelties suffered by his loved ones, and their violent death might logically have provoked.

When the Sierra Leonese were invited to leave in the last quarter of 2003 (organized collective repatriations followed a few months later), the Liberians had been arriving for one or two years, but Boreah was not the first camp that they encountered. The majority of Liberian refugees, in fact, had gone through a whole chain of camps since 1990, in Liberia, Sierra Leone and Guinea.

Some of their number, such as Bobo N'K., a Liberian born in 1974 at Lofa Bridge (close to the Liberian–Guinean border), undertook a lengthy journey through the camps while they were children or adolescents. Bobo, very nervous, remembers in minute detail the stages of his life (what he lost, what he escaped), and the sufferings endured for fourteen years.

Bobo N'K., Liberian refugee in Guinea (Boreah camp), twenty-nine years old in 2003. One day in September 1990, 'at four in the morning, the NPFL [National Patriotic Front of Liberia] forces of Charles Taylor arrived in the town. They settled in, people heard shooting and fled.' Before this attack, knowing that Taylor's rebel forces would be arriving soon, Bobo's father had taken two of his brothers with him to Macenta in Guinea. 'He is Malinké', Bobo explains, 'an ethnic group targeted by Taylor'. His mother, of Loma ethnicity, remained behind, as 'her identity was not targeted'. She is now at Macenta in another camp, the one at Kuankan.

Many people, including Bobo, fled after the attack on Lofa Bridge by the rebels. They crossed the border and made for the town of Zimmi, in south-eastern Sierra Leone.

On 21 March 1991, he remembers precisely, the RUF attacked the zone where they were – Kuendou, near Zimmi. They fled in the direction of Kouma, farther from the Liberian border.

On 24 March 1991, the RUF attacked Kouma. They fled again.

On 3 April 1991, the RUF attacked on all sides. Bobo and others in flight headed for the town of Bô in central Sierra Leone. The Bô region had a number of camps that were used throughout the 1990s both for internally displaced persons (Sierra Leonese) and for Liberian refugees. Bobo then spent seven months in one of the camps close to Bô, the Gondama camp (then occupied by refugees and IDPs). After this everyone was transferred a few kilometres away, to Taiama, a camp that was at the time a transit zone (Taiama would become a refugee camp a few years later). The UNHCR took people from this transit zone, including Bobo, and brought them to the Waterloo camp (a camp for IDPs and refugees) near Freetown. He remained in this camp from 1992 to 1995, and left at the age of twenty-one, the day it was attacked by the RUF. At that point the camp's occupants went to a further camp, that of Jui, just a few kilometres from Waterloo. Bobo spent two years there.

On 25 August 1997, he again remembers precisely, the Jui camp was in its turn attacked by the RUF. That was when Bobo fled in the direction of Guinea, and thus crossed a second border. He entered through the Pamalap border post, came to the town of Forecariah in Guinea, but was then sent to the transit camp of Farmoyera, back closer to the Liberian border. He left this transit camp by himself and made for Guinée Forestière, over 500 kilometres away, meeting up with his family in the Macenta district. His father, mother and brothers were there, no one was missing. His father was working in the diamond mines between Macenta and Guékédou. Bobo then resumed his education and finished secondary school. He was twenty-six years old.

It was at this point that he decided in 2000 to go to the Massakoundou refugee camp near the small town of Kissidougou to look for work. First of all he found a job as an event organizer with Handicap International. Then on 6 September 2000 the whole 'Guékédou salient' (a part of Guinea surrounded by Sierra Leone) was attacked by the Sierra Leonese rebels of the RUF. The war lasted until December that year, with the Sierra Leonese RUF and Taylor's Liberian forces attacking Kissidougou in Guinea. 'On Sunday, 13 December 2000 at three o'clock in the morning', Bobo continues with the same precision about dates and times, 'the Massakoundou camp was attacked'. The 27,000 refugees in the camp decided to leave that same day, but the Guineans blocked off the road to prevent them leaving and going into the forest. This episode is one of the many incursions of the

Mano River war into the Guinée Forestière, but the reverse incursion (into Liberia, by armed forces organized and trained in Guinea – ULIMO[7] and then LURD, in particular) was also significant. Three days later, the prefect of Kissidougou intervened to permit the Liberians to leave the camp. But 'as we were prevented from going to Conakry', he says, they headed for the forest around the village of Niafrando. Two days later, a team from Médecins Sans Frontières arrived and gave them tents, water and medical aid. Bobo only remained there for a few weeks, before leaving with a group of eighty people for the Kountaya camp (one of the three camps in the Kissidougou zone) in order to work in a factory producing latrines for the MSF. On the way back to Niafrando, when passing through Kissidougou, the group was arrested and taken to the military barracks. There they were stripped completely and searched one by one. Eleven of them were beaten and tortured. The soldiers accused them of carrying drugs, which Bobo denies. They were kept tied up in prison for twenty-five days. The prisoners' relatives asked MSF for help, and the organization approached the UNHCR which obtained their release – against money paid to the Guinean soldiers. The group of Liberians was then brought back to the Niafrando camp, where MSF gave them a little money (some 10 euros each) and a cover. Bobo was then recruited to work for a few weeks as a 'health activist' for MSF. On 26 April 2001, he was relocated in a new camp close to Dabola, the Sembakounya camp (his eighth in ten years). Two years later, on 3 July 2003, he was transferred with the majority of its occupants to the Boreah camp. A month later, he again found work with the MSF team in the camp, filling in the entry and exit records at the MSF clinic.

This is where I met him. He was very nervous and found it hard to follow a long conversation, a difficulty expressed in nervous tics, worried looks, putting his hands in front of his face or rubbing it vigorously, as if he was washing himself before each sentence.

His father was a military adviser for ULIMO – the first force in Liberia to oppose the advance of Taylor in that country and the RUF in Sierra Leone. In 1997 he tried to return to Liberia, but he was recognized and arrested, possibly killed. His mother is now in Conakry. Bobo fears for his own safety. He has put in an application with the UNHCR for 'resettlement in a third country'. But the local official replied that he had to produce a 'recommendation' from an NGO. This strategy on the part of the UNHCR aims to discharge the organization from responsibility for triage among the thousands of refugees who, given their experiences, would no doubt all be entitled to international 'protection' as this is defined in the Geneva convention of 1951 on the right of asylum for refugees. To introduce an additional criterion of a 'humanitarian' nature is illegal from the standpoint of conventional asylum practice, given that the protection these exiles request falls solely under the competence of the UNHCR. To ask the NGOs operating in the camps to make an initial triage and forward to the UNHCR only those cases viewed as appropriate from a humanitarian point of view amounts to a camouflaged denial of protection for the great majority, who are not recognized as 'victims' or 'vulnerable' – or only to a lesser and insufficient degree.

In the Boreah camp where he lives, Bobo has with him two children of seven and nine. His wife fell ill and died after giving birth to their second child in the Jui camp. He also has with him three younger brothers (attending school in the Boreah camp) and a sister with two of her children. It is this family of nine that Bobo is managing to support thanks to an income (called an 'incentive' and not a 'wage') from the Belgian MSF and the food ration of the World Food Programme.

Other Liberians in the camp have had similar journeys, as witness these little notes left on the table in the MSF office at the health post:

> Monsieur Whaye B., zone B, house 27, Krahn ethnicity. Liberian nationality. Refugee card (WFP) no. . . . ; beneficiaries: 5. Entered Sierra Leone 1990, Waterloo camp;[8] entered Guinea 1997, Forecariah camp, relocated Sembakounya camp in 2001, then Borea camp in 2003.

> Madame Béatrice T., zone B7, house 29. Krahn ethnicity. Liberian nationality. Refugee card (WFP) no. . . . ; beneficiaries: 3. Left Liberia in 1990. Waterloo camp in Sierra Leone. Entered Guinea 1997, Forecariah camp, then Sembakounya camp. Subsequently relocated 2003 in Boreah camp.

> Monsieur Sidiki M. K., zone C2, house 23. Liberian nationality. Mandingo ethnicity. Refugee card no . . . Beneficiaries: 6. Entered Sierra Leone 1990, Waterloo camp. 1995 in Jui camp. Entered Guinea 2007, Forecariah camp, relocated 2001 in Sembakounya camp, subsequently relocated 2003 in Boreah camp.

Etc.

Some of the farmers in the Lofa region in the 1990s did not want to move too far away during the war. Their journeys were therefore generally different from those that we have just mentioned. That was the case with Monsieur Abu M.

Abu M., Liberian refugee in Guinea (Boreah camp), aged sixty. Abu comes from the Kolahun region, in the Lofa county of northern Liberia. He explains that he did not leave Liberia in the 1990s. People moved into the bush when there was fighting. A group then came to tell them to return home. This continued until 1996, which was followed by a period of relative peace (1996–9) corresponding to Charles Taylor's taking power by force and this then being confirmed in a vote.

In 1999 Abu was at home with his whole family. This was after the general election of 1997; there was no more war, they were told. They stayed peacefully at home. But news of war came from Voinjama (a town to the north-east of Kolahun, near the Guinean border). The government forces passed their way en route to fight at Voinjama. A rebel armed faction entered the villages. 'They began to shoot and fire shells, the towns were attacked. Then another faction arrived, they had very powerful weapons and attacked the government forces. These people told us their name: LURD. The rebels seemed like city people. Then the government forces attacked the towns, saying that the people were supporters of the LURD.' Coming from Voinjama, 'the rebels entered Kolahun. The soldiers retreated. And the shelling started, by 1,500 of the government's "Octopus" forces. There were many deaths . . . Rat-a-tat-tat . . . Then the population was moved to Kolahun by the rebels.'

In 2002 Abu's family finally escaped, crossed the border to Guinea and reached the frontier village of Tekolo. 'There were Whites who came to meet us. The refugees decided whether or not they wanted to go to the Kuankan camp.' Abu decided to go to Kuankan, a camp located some 150 kilometres south-east of Boreah. He was registered there and given a food ration card. His family left Liberia separately, but they met up again in Guinea.

They were put down in the Kuankan camp for relocation to Boreah. But only part of his family actually reached this camp. The others were unable to follow, as the bridge between

Kuankan and Kissidougou had succumbed to the weight of a WFP lorry three months previously. Since this was the rainy season, the bridge had not yet been rebuilt and the relocation of refugees was interrupted. The situation of Abu's family is as follows: his four wives and thirteen of his children are in the Boreah camp; he is with four of his children in the Kuankan camp. He was only passing through Boreah when I met him. He had come to spend a few days there and see his family, 'analyse the conditions in which they've been settled'. If all is well, he'll move there, otherwise. And if the war ends in Liberia he wants to return there.

What can we conclude from these trajectories? First of all there is the strong impression left by the tales of atrocities experienced, which are repeated in other stories collected in Guinea and Sierra Leone in the same period. These are literally the survivors. Amputations narrowly avoided but seen at close hand, massacres, the death of loved ones (children, father, mother, spouse), the rape of women, and illnesses that are aggravated by flight. These are the physical and moral injuries. Several people bear very visible traces of these, bodily and psychologically: depression, anxiety, etc.

All are also 'old' refugees. Whatever their age, they have been coming and going for five, ten or nearly fifteen years, as the case may be, in a space defined by war. The dehumanization of war (the death that they approached and narrowly escaped) was followed by a disturbed period of social de-identification, which if certainly not comparable with the first stress, does explain why many of the exiles prefer not to become 'refugees' registered and confined in the camps, despite the advantages that this often provides for them and their families. The resistance of life can then be expressed in the camp by the search for a position by way of various 'integrating' procedures, as ways of restoring some order to daily life (the image of the deliberately ordered life of Ibrahim), and by strategies of accommodation, even the use of the humanitarian apparatus as illustrated by Monsieur Abu's decisions. It is also expressed in repeated attempts to escape the solution of the camps. A double resistance – against war and against the camps – has governed the paths of several exiles between the town, the village, the border and the camps.

This is the case with the sixty or so families transferred from Conakry, the capital of Guinea, to the Boreah camp a few weeks before I met them there in September 2003: a transfer carried out in accord with a decision by the UNHCR and the Guinean government, that only those who agreed to live in the camps would be registered as refugees (and subsequently as applicants for resettlement in a third country).

I conducted a small survey by questionnaire of the sixty-four family heads (thirty men, thirty-four women) transferred in July–August 2003 from Conakry, where they had been registered by the UNHCR, to the Boreah camp. The average size of the families transferred was 5.4 individuals, though ranging widely from just 1 person (thirteen of the sixty-four cases) to more than 10 persons per family group (five cases).[9] Forty of the families were Liberian, and twenty-four Sierra Leonese. Their movements from their initial place of residence in Liberia or Sierra Leone (which they left when the war affected them) to Conakry (the last stage before their collective transfer to the Boreah camp) had been as follows:

- eleven of the sixty-four families had reached Conakry directly.
- eight families had reached Conakry after first stopping in another town.
- thirteen families had reached Conakry after staying in a camp.
- eleven families were in Conakry after staying in two or more camps.
- twenty-one families were in Conakry after staying in several camps and towns.

Finally, if we consider the length of the refugees' final stay in Conakry (where at that time they had neither refugee status nor UNHCR protection) before their transfer to the Boreah camp, a very large majority of them (fifty-eight family heads out of sixty-four) had been settled there for over two years – in the case of nearly a third of them, more than four years, i.e. since before the start of the second war in Liberia in late 1999–2000, indicating an earlier attempt at urban settlement that in part went back to the time of the 'first war' in Liberia or to the end of the war in Sierra Leone.

To sum up, it is clear that these families have lived for several years in the Guinean capital or other towns, often staying for a time in camps. They have worked in Conakry, generally in the so-called 'informal economy', and have therefore attempted a local integration that seemed possible at the sociological level, if not politically. As an 'airlock' for integration, we can note the existence of 'refugee districts' in Conakry (Sierra Leonese around their country's embassy, or Liberians near the fishing port where saleswomen arrive from Liberia). In other words, they have tried to avoid the refugee status that three-quarters of them had already known at one point or another in their trajectory. Until the moment at which making themselves known to the UNHCR meant accepting encampment.

The space for a way of life

If we take into account the stories collected from the refugees that we met not just in the Boreah camp, but also in the other camps in Guinea and Sierra Leone, there are several clear convergences. It is this set of findings that I would now like to present. These concern in particular the region that we have already been speaking of, configured as a network of sites of displacement. In fact, the space that should be considered in order to understand the experience of the refugees is broader than just that of the camps. People have been accustomed to living in a space of war, flight and refuge that has constituted a continuous space–time: a unified geographical zone for fourteen almost uninterrupted years.

There were long periods of life in small towns or villages occupied by armed forces, government and rebel. This meant an experience of daily terror for months or years on end. The 'sound of the war' is an expression heard on many occasions, used by people who do not have very clear notions of the political identity of the fighters who invaded their villages. It denotes the feeling of fear that dominates the tales of the Liberian and Sierra Leonese refugees. Other expressions of the same kind come into their stories: 'the war entered in Monrovia', 'the war met me in Kono', etc. The war is like a subject endowed with a will and a power of its own: it comes, it arrives, it bursts into their life and drives them hastily into the 'bush', into flight and the repeated discovery of humanitarian establishments on the margin of the spaces of war.

There were also long periods of coming and going between villages and the bush, the border zones and the camps, between camps and villages, etc. A particular way of life and a social organization of survival appear in the context of flight. Food is hidden in precarious constructions; forest shelters called 'kitchens' (because this is where in peacetime farmers were accustomed to sleeping and eating when they went to work in the fields) permit the villagers to take refuge as soon as danger threatens. There is then the custom of eating wild roots and fruit (the 'bush yam', the wild potato, palm fruit and nuts), stealing food from other villages, etc. There are also problems of health and death linked indirectly to the war: the many stories of untreated illness among old people, premature births and post-partum complications during stays in the bush suggest a mortality that is additional to that of war itself.

A new way of life is formed in the context of the humanitarian spaces – one that, from the standpoint of the anthropologist, is a complete culture in the broad sense of the term. This bears on changes in the family milieu, as I was able to observe in Zone 12 of the Kuankan camp in Guinée Forestière. The older part of the camp dates from 1995. Added to this is a transit centre at the entrance (some 800 Liberians were waiting there at the time of my visit in October 2003), and some distance away is Zone 12, opened by the French section of Médecins Sans Frontières in 2001 and still under the control of this NGO in 2003.[10]

This zone sheltered some 7,500 refugees in the phase of its heaviest population; by late 2003 there were around 2,500 people there, out of a total of 31,000 in the Kuankan camp as a whole. In material terms, it was an intermediate level between the transit centre (made up of large plastic tents each designed for 50 persons, but actually able to hold up to 100 occupants, with ready-made meals provided) and the relatively stabilized refugee camp (family 'houses', also of plastic sheeting, minimal sanitary facilities, food ration supplied for preparation). In 2003, Zone 12 held Liberian refugees who had been arriving since 2001, some of their number being relatively stabilized (over two years in the zone) while others had just arrived there, after registration and checks in the transit centre at the camp entrance.

A study conducted within the large collective tents of Zone 12 of the Kuankan camp in October 2003 made it possible to establish some precise data on the situation of the groups of refugees who had arrived in the previous weeks and days: a total of 1,454 persons were housed in 25 collective tents, i.e. an average of 58 persons per tent. These broke down into 483 groups of displaced persons, an average of around 3 people per 'family'. The groups were roughly separated within the tents by mats and piles of personal effects.

The people I met in the large tents presented fairly similar characteristics in terms of family structure: cases of family dispersal were common – children who were missing, young women who had arrived by themselves with infants, as well as frequent tales of the violent death of spouses, children or parents. Several months generally passed from the flight from the village – to escape the 'sound of the war' and attacks on the civilian population – through wandering in the bush to settlement in the camps. The recomposition of families gradually responded to the losses and decomposition suffered: widows and other single people, men and women, fairly quickly found new spouses in the camps; residential groups of adolescents were formed on the basis of siblinghood, friendship groups or fellow villagers who met up in the same transit centres; the less vulnerable individuals protected the fragile ones, in the name of village solidarity, neighbourhood in the camps, or to win new local clienteles.

Continuing this study farther east in Guinée Forestière, a few days away is the Lainé camp. This offers a comparable example of what you could call a general ecology of the camps, the premise for a new framework of social life. As in the more recent part of Zone 12 at Kuankan, large tents of plastic sheeting (green here, and stamped 'UNHCR') shelter 50, 80 or 100 persons. These are the most recently arrived refugees, or those still arriving (October 2003) after crossing the points of entry on the border and the transit centres. The forest here has been laid waste: trees cut down to permit the rapid erection of tents. A communal kitchen has been established between four large tents: hearths are built on the ground under a metal roof, where women prepare the American bulgur wheat of the WFP food ration, or other foodstuffs that they have bought after reselling part of their ration: rice, a sauce made from potato or manioc leaves. In the older parts of the Lainé camp (those opened more than a year ago), the collective shelters have given way to individual huts. These were initially made out of the inevitable plastic sheeting – the essential components of the camp 'kit', green or white according to the donor (green for the UNHCR, white or blue for MSF or ACF). They are then transformed by the refugees as best they can, rebuilt in mud-brick or wattle, and covered with plastic sheeting.

Major changes have thus taken place in the course of this apprenticeship to a new life in a habitat and ecological context that are neither completely rural nor completely urban, but close in appearance to poor quarters, small agglomerations, peripheral invasions, townships. The camps can often be seen as 'bare towns',[11] a term that denotes agglomerations that are often dense and heterogeneous, equipped with a certain minimum in the way of collective material infrastructure, where urban sociabilities tend to be rapidly formed, in one or two years, different from anything that those living here would have experienced before in their lives.

Some further information should be mentioned here. This concerns the knowledge that is shared between different camps. In the Lainé camp I met the son of a refugee whom I had known in the Kuankan camp, 300 kilometres west, who had given me the name of his son and of the son's grandmother. The boy and his grandmother had been separated on the flight from Liberia, and the father had known some months earlier that his son 'had to be' in the Lainé camp. This information was confirmed: when I visited Lainé some time later, I was able to locate the boy and his grandmother thanks to a Red Cross employee working in a programme of reuniting families in the various camps and transit centres of the region. However, as this example shows, such intervention can only be effective if the information already exists, however uncertain. In this case, the father in the Kuankan camp had the information that his son 'had to be' in Lainé.

I was able to confirm this spreading of information in other circumstances of dispersal and family rediscovery. There is a great deal of information constantly shared, on the subject of deceased parents, children lost and found, etc. From this point of view, the space of the camps functions as a milieu of mutual knowledge and communication, reinforcing its character as a coherent space or a network of sites. The transit centres located at the entrance to the camps also offer the surprising spectacle of this circulating information, when the older-established refugees come to see the new arrivals descend from the UNHCR lorries in order to identify acquaintances, get news from other places or of missing persons.

Breaking and recomposition of solidarity

Transformations gradually occurred in the distribution of family assistance and humanitarian aid. The stories heard in Kuankan's Zone 12 (which receives the new arrivals), like those of the people I met at the border crossings between Guinea and Liberia, show how the existence of national frontiers becomes more significant for the refugees and their host countries than it was before the war. There was also a further development between the two phases of war in Liberia. In the early 1990s, people arriving in Guinea did so with only little humanitarian aid or recourse to the UNHCR. They would go to the village of their 'family' in a very wide sense – lineage, clan or ethnic group – where they were well received. This was the case with the Kissi (numerous in north-western Liberia and Guinée Forestière) and the Loma from the same region (called 'Toma' in Guinea). But as the war continued and refugees settled for longer periods in Guinea, and due to the political manipulations of the Guinean government, which blamed the refugees for all the country's troubles (1999–2000), and the overspill of the Liberian war into that country,[12] the relationship between the refugees and their hosts began to change. In the second phase of war (1999–2003), ethnic solidarity did not function as well as before, so that resort to the UNHCR and NGOs became more essential, indeed vital, to the Liberians who had crossed the frontier. We can say schematically that the combination of national borders and international humanitarian assistance tended to replace the combination of ethnic borders and assistance from the family as the context of constraints and resources. This also changed the context that displaced persons referred to in their conceptions of their identity and their future.[13]

The radius of matrimonial range also changed with the war and the camps. Thus, in Sierra Leone, not far from Guinée Forestière, the local integration of Liberians in the region and the town of Kailahun was effected partly by way of family relationships or old-established clan ones, even if, as we mentioned above, these relationships have sometimes been 'saturated'. But they persisted whilst being transformed by the context of displacements. In Kailahun as well as in the villages closer to the border, Liberian refugees of both sexes were integrated as spouses of Sierra Leonese. This was the case for persons belonging to the ethnic groups that existed on both sides of the border – the Kissi and Gbandi, in particular – and who were known and accepted during their respective displacements from one side of the border to the other, corresponding to the different phases of the war: war in Liberia and refuge in Sierra Leone, war in Sierra Leone and refuge in Liberia.

There are other forms of integration as well, especially in the crossroads town of Kailahun. Young Liberian women were lodged and helped financially by men here in exchange for their sexual services. This was in the quarter known as 'Kula camp', at the southern entry to the town. Established originally as a refugee camp by the rebel forces of the RUF, but never recognized as such by the UNHCR, Kula camp housed in 2003, over a year after the end of the war in Sierra Leone, both Sierra Leonese 'refugees' from the surrounding rural region who had not been able to recover their lands after the war, and Liberian refugees in a very precarious situation – the UNHCR not recognizing or taking responsibility for them. Other young Liberian women very quickly and easily became the 'wives' of Sierra Leonese soldiers who lived in the SLAF (Sierra Leonese Armed Forces) military camp, and had arrived in Kailahun after the peace agreement made a few months earlier. This camp was located at the exit from the town on the road to Liberia, and its residential part seems completely like a refugee camp.

Living under suspicion:
counting, infiltration and trafficking

At the border crossings, in the transit centres and in the camps, a whole range of journeys can be noted, with an equally wide range of reasons behind them. You also see individuals or family groups practise tactics in order to get into a camp while waiting for the situation in Liberia to improve, to continue an education that has been interrupted several times, to look for parents who have been missing for years, or to benefit from a share of the food ration.

There are also certain kinds of 'trafficking' that contribute to characterizing the space and the culture corresponding to it, one of suspicion and makeshift. This is the case with those practices that the UNHCR terms 'recycling', which consist in moving from the camps to the border zones with a view to re-registering as a new refugee and thus obtaining an additional ration card. This tactic may be supplemented by that of dual residency, living and working not in the camps themselves (where you are then viewed as absent) but in the towns and villages around. The miscounting that arises from such arrangements adds further confusion to misunderstandings over refugee status.

The Lainé camp, which we have already encountered above, thus had 28,000 inhabitants in 2003 according to the UNHCR (this count being based on food ration cards), whereas the 'home visitors' from MSF counted 21,000 at the same time, this number based on counts updated house by house on the occasion of their visits. The difference does not indicate that number of 'false refugees', but rather refugees who accumulated several food rations (a ration is equivalent to less than 1,900 calories per day, and it is rare indeed for this dose to actually be reached). These refugees add to the official status of 'assisted' refugee the unofficial but more real status of active refugee. Deprived of the right to work, such refugees can only do so illegally. In fact, as far as movement in connection with possible work is concerned, or anything similar, refugees are caught up immediately in a network of prohibitions and restrictions that brings any action on their part up against their de facto lack of citizenship, and it is consequently the exercise of a right to life in illegal conditions.

In September 2003, the secretary of the Liberian refugees in Buedu, a small Sierra Leonese town a few kilometres from the border with Liberia, counted the arrivals and departures of refugees: in January 2002 he had recorded 35,500 Liberian refugees in the district of

Buedu (soon after the establishment of this self-settled camp at the entry to the small town, which we already mentioned on p. 39). From that date until September 2003, the UNHCR transferred 10,200 refugees to the Sierra Leonese camps. The others, more than 20,000, were divided between Buedu and the surrounding villages, other villages in the Kailahun district, and the town of Kailahun itself, as we saw above. But the refugees' secretary had no further visitors from the UNHCR to whom he could report his calculations.

According to the latest figures from the UNHCR, in fact (those from the Kailahun post in September 2003), no more than 2,834 refugees were registered in the entire district of Kailahun, of which the Buedu sub-district is only a small part, and no refugees at all were recorded for the town of Kailahun itself. These counts would thus leave some 20,000 persons unregistered and unassisted. It is clear from this case that the UNHCR displays, in the specific regional context, a very firm political desire for the normalization of a country on the part of the 'international community', the national authorities and their local representatives. New 'paramount chiefs' were appointed from Freetown immediately after the war, in 2002–3, so as to 'normalize' the situation rapidly and to prepare elections. The UNHCR follows the political authorities in their tendency to massively understate the numerical presence and the 'problem' of Liberian refugees, though it can at the same time, in a different context, agree to inflate figures or close its eyes to double counting.

The immediate post-war period, from the end of 2003, was marked by many confusions and tensions within the humanitarian spaces – between UN organizations, certain NGOs and the refugees – over the question of the exact counting of refugees, their localization and their rights. Thus, unsuccessful in fixing and counting the number of people displaced, the UNHCR attempted a census of refugees in Guinean camps in 2004 (after having made the same attempt in the capital, Conakry, during the second half of 2003). This count was perceived by the refugees as the preliminary to forced repatriation and a questioning of their status. Facing scuffles and a barrage of stones, the UNHCR official responsible for Guinée Forestière declared in July 2004: 'We have been completely manipulated by the refugees . . . They are rebelling because they are going to lose this possibility of cheating and getting rich.'[14]

The anger of the UNHCR representative at these 'cheating' refugees should be seen in the context of the preparation for a collective repatriation of Liberians at the end of the war. Those who refused repatriation would be considered de facto as illegal immigrants.

110

Finally, there is a double suspicion of refugee populations, marking them with a double stigma: that of being a refugee, and that of being a false refugee. This moral dimension has an arbitrary character which becomes clear if the focus is changed and we compare the context of the African countries discussed here with that of European countries (with their quotas of expulsions and rejections of asylum applications). This a priori blaming of the undesirable is applied case by case, in the midst of the very localized dramas and contexts that successively form the justification for a policy of keeping spaces and persons at a distance – a 'population policy' that uses the language of humanitarianism as a cover.

Returning to Liberia

During the second Liberian war (1999–2003), it is estimated that 900,000 Liberians out of a population of some 3 million fled their place of residence. Out of this total, 340,000 took refuge in bordering countries (chiefly in Guinea, Sierra Leone and Ivory Coast), and some half a million were internally displaced – 314,000 of their number being sheltered in displaced persons' camps located mainly in Bong (in the centre of the country) and around Monrovia.

In 2003, in the refugee camps of the Bô and Kenema regions in Sierra Leone, I met several Liberians who came from Foya in north-western Liberia. Bordering on Sierra Leone to the west and Guinea to the north, Loma county, and particularly the district of Foya found themselves at the heart of the war. The peace agreement of August 2003 that followed the surrender of Taylor and the victory of the LURD, an agreement supported by Guinea and the 'international community', was seen as a promise of peace and stability by many Liberians. They seemed to rejoice in or take reassurance from the visible support of the United States for the process of pacification and disarmament, and they were in a hurry to return to their own country. The refugees in Lofa and especially those in Monrovia had demonstrated in front of the humanitarian compound in Tobanda, one of the regional camps, where the UN High Commissioner for Refugees, Ruud Lubbers, was visiting for a few hours in December 2003. To shouts of 'We wan go', they demanded repatriation while also complaining of the living conditions in the camps. It is hard to separate precisely the respective parts played in their revolt by the desire to leave the camp and by the desire to return home; but the UN High Commissioner responded by heavily emphasizing the second of these, promising a speedy return. Unfortunately, four years later, it is clear to everyone that conditions of life were 'better' in the camps than in the country that the returnees discovered on their arrival.

The repatriation of refugees and the reintegration of internally displaced persons officially began in September 2004. By the beginning of 2007, the UNHCR and other UN agencies claimed that the exercise had been almost completed. All the displaced persons' camps had been officially closed (and no longer received humanitarian aid), but in fact several of them remained partially occupied (the number of occupants being estimated at 30,000 in mid-2006). A further 150,000 refugees were also still in their country of asylum at that time.[15]

A little more than two years after meeting the Liberian refugees in the Sierra Leonese camps, I wanted to see the conditions in which the 'return home' – to Lofa and Monrovia – had been effected, both by refugees coming back from Guinea and Sierra Leone, and by the internally displaced. This study in the Foya district, in January–February 2007, focused on a dozen or so villages, along with the town of Foya itself.

There was certainly an atmosphere of 'reconstruction' in the villages of Foya district. There was no apparent problem among the villagers regarding access to the land. The presence of the UN and NGOs was substantial, but their intervention lagged very much behind the initiatives of the villagers themselves, and was far below their expectations.[16] For example, the supply of zinc roofs for the construction of houses (three packs of twenty sheets per house) from the NGO Peace Winds Japan, acting under contract for the UNHCR, started out at a good pace in 2004–5, but then slowed down considerably. This made the villagers say that the first arrivals had done well, unlike the later ones. The result was that only some of the houses received the corrugated metal sheeting from PWJ. The German technical cooperation agency GTZ supplied some farm tools and seeds to restart rice cultivation. Subsistence agriculture of rice and vegetables is practised by everyone here, but the recovery of commercial crops such as coffee and cocoa has been slow. Another factor of 'reconstruction': all the villages have an established local authority, and the houses of chiefs are being rebuilt.

Let us go back a moment to the recent past, to the war as this was experienced by the inhabitants of Foya county. During the 'second war' of 1999–2003, i.e. the offensive by the LURD, the destruction of villages seems to have been greater in proportion to the distance that the soldiers were from Foya town. Here and in the villages close by houses remained standing, even if damaged; at the same time, inhabitants were requisitioned by the LURD for portage work in Guinea (coffee, cocoa, zinc, loot of various kinds), as well as to provide food for the fighters. All this was more systematic in the town than in the outlying villages, deserted by their inhabitants who had fled en masse, and which were entirely destroyed – according to stories and from the evidence of still-visible ruins.[17] According to the Foya district commissioner, 90 per cent of the population were absent in 2002–3, as against 30 per cent during the first war. At Sombolo, a small village close to Foya town, we were told that the LURD came from Kolahun (the next town to the east) and headed for Foya. The villagers had fled north to Guinea, west across the Sierra Leonese border (Buedu, the villages and camps) or south to Monrovia. The LURD militia came on foot, accompanied by people carrying arms and munitions on their heads. When they heard gunfire, the villagers left as fast as they could.

After leaving Foya district in 2001–2, the refugees and displaced persons began to return on a small scale in 2003, still timidly in 2004, and more massively in 2005 and 2006.[18] Early in 2007, the villages that we visited still had only two-thirds of the population that they had before the war.[19]

It is possible to distinguish three major categories of return. There is the return of those most reluctant about distant flight: villagers who went just to the other side of the Sierra Leonese border, in the frontier zone of Buedu and Kailahun (15 to 40 kilometres from Liberia). These were the first to return, starting in 2004 (there were even a few rare returns in 2003), and they were also the most dynamic and mobilized to resume agricultural activity, the villages' natural leaders. In general, however, they had not been registered as refugees by the UNHCR.

As against this category, there was the return of the most 'vulnerable'. These were elderly people, women and children, as well as families with children, their movements being slower and harder to organize than those of individuals. They first let themselves be taken to the UNHCR camps, either directly or indirectly – in Sierra Leone, for example, after passing Buedu, a small town 15 kilometres from the border, where the UNHCR evacuated a self-settled camp in 2002 and sent the occupants to the camps of Bô–Kenema. On return, they followed what we can call the official refugee itinerary: registered in the camps of Guinea and Sierra Leone, repatriated and registered on arrival at the transit centre of Foya, run by Peace Winds Japan for the UNHCR.[20] (This centre recorded the arrival of nearly 18,000 refugees over the two years 2005 and 2006, 56 per cent of these coming from the camps of Bô–Kenema and Sierra Leone, and 44 per cent from those in Guinea.[21])

Thirdly, we can distinguish the better-off exiles – strong, clever or adventurous, but also those least attached to their villages. These went to Monrovia directly or after a detour in Sierra Leone (this was the case with young people, chiefs and notables), or via the camps for displaced persons in the region of Monrovia. Some of them did not come back; they were hesitant. The general view of the villagers I met in the Foya region was that those refugees and displaced persons who were slowest to return or did not return at all were those from Monrovia. Among them were young people who had completed primary school and aimed to attend secondary school. Many others were missing, and the villagers did not have very precise information about them.

In a general fashion, the atmosphere in Liberia in 2007 was particularly favourable to 'reconstruction' in the rural zone. There was a significant return to the zones of origin: around 60 per cent – even if this means that some 40 per cent of the population displaced by the war are still absent today. The substantial presence of the 'international community' was much noted, but its efficacy is far from meeting the expectations of the villagers engaged in getting local economic and social activity under way again. What exactly is the meaning of this presence? The various UN agencies, the very numerous international NGOs, as well as the regularly renewed presence of 15,000 soldiers of UNMIL (United Nations Mission in Liberia), ostensibly occupy the national territory, urban and rural. This is more a question of controlling the situation than of working to reconstruct the national social fabric, as the official justification of this international commitment proclaims. The most striking effect of their presence is the exclusion from the landscape of the militias on both sides, thus maintaining the image of a reassuring pacification, at least in the short term. The war has left a wide space available for foreign investors, who divide up the zones of rubber, minerals and gold, and for whom the securitization of the country and the control of public order are the indispensable basis and condition of their involvement.

Substantial problems exist in Monrovia, where the economic, social and community precariousness is very great: marginalized quarters like West Point have developed, former camps and squatters either remain or are evacuated without any alternative solution being offered.[22] And yet the state of abandonment of a good part of the capital is ultimately the result of a political choice: to get rid of an excess population, in which the national and international authorities that control the country do not want to invest. Underlying the lack of an urban social policy on the part of these authorities is a conception of 'cleaning up' the city. But this will not be enough to turn refugees and displaced persons, very 'urbanized' in the course of fifteen years of war, into returning farmers. On the other hand, UNMIL regularly stifles attempts at the formation of urban militias, from remnants of the former fighters, susceptible to regrouping whenever the occasion arises – for example, in order to get 'contracts' in Ivory Coast or Guinea. The general view is that the programmed – and regularly delayed – departure of the UN armed forces, and a reduction in American commitment, would have the effect of rapidly breaking the lock that holds the country in an apparent peace and stability, as the paradox of Monrovia illustrates: the city's main avenue is full of flowers, a very large football stadium has just been constructed . . . while the town is turning into an immense camp of displaced persons and squatters.

— 6 —

Surviving, Reviving, Leaving, Remaining: The Long Life of Angolan Refugees in Zambia

The priority given to the 'return' of refugees, whether as a right or as an obligation to send them 'home', is generally presented as the only 'proper' solution to the refugee problem, in both the short and the long term. And yet we have just seen the numerical scale of those 'absent' from the organized return of Liberian refugees and displaced persons to their villages of origin between 2004 and 2007: more than a third of the inhabitants of Foya district had still not returned three years after the start of the repatriation process. Where are the 'missing'? They stayed in Monrovia or in the countries of exile; others, far less numerous, managed to obtain resettlement in a third country (Canada, United States, northern Europe), with the status of refugee; others again ended up in the waiting zones and holding centres that mark the new borders of the European nations. For those who did return to their land of origin, war and the mobile life within the towns and camps generally favoured the settlement of former refugees and displaced persons in large or medium-sized cities; it removed them from the rural world and agricultural activity.

We return to these questions with the Angolan refugees settled at a UNHCR site in Zambia, the Maheba camp. I undertook a study there in January–February 2002 and again in June of that year, i.e. just before and after the signature of a peace agreement in Angola. I was very soon intrigued by the uncertainty and disparity of these refugees' responses to the return promised by the UNHCR in the wake of the April 2002 peace agreement. In fact, my study was set in a context that was dominated, in practical terms, by a demand that the refugees should accept an announced goal (departure of the refugees, closure of the camp), and – more theoretical but just as crucial – by the question of identification in the spaces of exile. A certain conception of identity – in terms of origin on the one hand, and of situation on the other – underlay all the strategies of return, placement and resettlement. These strategies all followed from the experience of years of forced displacement and integration into the humanitarian apparatus. As we shall see in the following pages, the study made it possible to establish a local finding whose general applicability is just as readily verifiable if we keep in mind, for example, the experience of the Palestinian or Sahrawi camps,[1] as well as the Somali camps in Kenya.[2] We can show that a certain social order develops in the camp, an integrative order whose formation depends on the state of war, on humanitarian action and on the relationships formed between the various actors present (refugees of different generations, local population, local and expatriate humanitarian staff), over a long term and in a space that is confined but vibrant.

The peace agreement signed in Luanda in April 2002 between the Angolan government and UNITA,[3] whose historic leader, Jonas Savimbi, had been assassinated two months earlier, put an end to more than twenty-seven years of civil war in Angola, the anti-colonial struggle (from the 1960s to 1975) having been followed by an indirect opposition between the two blocs in the Cold War (1975–88), with the USSR and Cuba supporting the Movimento Popular de Libertação de Angola (MPLA, in power from 1975), while the United States and South Africa were behind UNITA. Finally, from the end of the 1980s, the issues in the conflict became those of territorial control, the development of an international arms traffic and private access to oil and diamond resources.

Increasingly removed from the reasons for the war, the civilian population was its principal victim: half a million Angolans have been killed since 1974; 12 million anti-personnel mines are scattered throughout the country; between 2 and 4 million people (the estimates vary according to sources) were forced into internal displacement, spending years wandering far from their villages, moving on foot into the forest and to temporary campgrounds, leaving these for settlements in rural zones or urban peripheries, before finding themselves again in displaced persons' camps depending on the fluctuations in the civil war. This wandering meant misery for the most destitute of the displaced, and for hundreds of thousands of persons deprived of their means of existence and not receiving any aid; it caused the exile of 450,000 to 500,000 refugees.[4] Those who crossed the border took refuge in the neighbouring countries (Zambia, Congo, Zaire/DRC, Namibia) from where they were sometimes driven *manu*

117

militari, or where they sometimes managed to settle, as was the case in Zambia, in towns and the UNHCR camps opened twenty or thirty years ago. A third of the Angolan population (around 4 million out of a total of 12 million) thus found themselves in a situation of displacement. The most urgent post-war requirements, for the Angolan government, were the demilitarization of some 50,000 UNITA combatants, then the return of internally displaced persons, and finally that of the refugees.

In the Maheba camp of north-western Zambia, 200 kilometres from the Angolan border, 88 per cent of the 58,000 refugees are Angolan, some of them having been at this UNHCR site since it was opened in 1971. Between April and June 2002, i.e. in the three months following the signature of the peace agreement, 3,000 of them left the camp in small groups, or even individually, with some going ahead to assess the situation in Angola before the rest of their family joined them. The general view was that this rhythm of 1,000 departures a month from Maheba was not a massive movement of return to their country of origin; over the months that followed, the effect of the peace agreement declined, and the number leaving fell substantially.

The situation created by the end of the war in 2002 was uncertain. The humanitarian organizations did not yet know whether they should envisage abandoning the camp in order to follow the refugees elsewhere. The UNHCR tried to control the situation by questioning those leaving, and private transporters, but without any real success, and its local officials vaguely mentioned a collective repatriation to be organized in 2003. Finally, the Angolan refugees all distrusted repatriation. On the one hand, they had been burned by the experience of two previous unsuccessful attempts to end the war, and two abortive returns: the peace agreements signed in 1991 and 1994 were broken in the months or years that followed, forcing the *retornados* back to the camps they had left. On the other hand, in the face of the alternative that presented itself, the motivation for leaving or remaining depended on the length of time they had been settled on the site, the quality of this settlement (access to agricultural land, in particular), the family's energy (according to its more or less vulnerable composition and the state of health of its members) and the conditions anticipated in their home district, as reported by rumour. Old people, well settled on the patch of land that the UNHCR had obtained for them, decided right away not to leave, whereas their adult children prepared to return, but after the harvest. Some of the long-standing refugees wished to remain in the camp, whilst others, just as long-standing, liked to conjure up economic plans bound up with a future conditional return. The more recent arrivals were too tired or too distrustful to decide one way or the other, and of course the non-Angolan refugees feared the closure of the camp. In order to understand this uncertainty and the disparity of the refugees' responses to the possibility of return, we have to make a detour and examine questions and descriptions concerning the social organization of the camp and the identification of the refugees with their spaces of exile.

Surviving and reviving at Maheba

How do social contexts of identification arise for those women and men who have survived war, violence and flight? Literally survivors, they settle in a transitory situation while waiting to rediscover a social life, having to care for their bodies and put a dangerous context behind them. Humanitarian intervention cannot be viewed as something simply external, more or less charitable or political. This intervention establishes a power over life (a 'biopower' in the Foucauldian sense) and a space of exception that has to be kept at a distance, in principle, from ordinary social life as well as from war. By establishing this double margin, such intervention at the same time opens a new space of social relationships: relationships established between the victims of war and exodus and the local or international intervention personnel attached to structures of care, health, protection and control. The anthropologist Christian Geffray has shown very well, apropos of RENAMO[5] in Mozambique, how war tends to generate and fix 'social bodies' within which armed factions arise and are legitimated without this corresponding a priori to a precise political project.[6] In the same way, we can observe how the various populations brought into contact in the context of the exile induced by war generate social orders of a new type. Are these just 'bodies', or a 'community', once the emergency has passed? On the ground of humanitarianism, whose action does not attempt to produce a society or found communities but at most to open spaces that are propitious to emergency intervention, a social order of hybrid formation is created; it founds the new locality (in the sense of local identity) of individuals placed collectively in exile here. It is in this new framework, this new social ordering, that inter-ethnic relationships arise, along with cultural apprenticeship, and possibly political conceptions and projects that are specific to such an order.

On the model of all other humanitarian sites, the Maheba camp in Zambia can be viewed like any other human agglomeration that is relatively heterogeneous and massive. It is a localized social micro-cosm: we can interest ourselves in the history of its peopling, in the relations between the different categories of population, their respective localizations on the site, the dominations and relationships of work – in other words, the whole reality of a social order grasped like the order of a village or small town in Africa or elsewhere. This is the spirit in which we shall describe it here.

But there is another and less ordinary dimension that very soon appears, that of the identifications that are formed in the exile situation. When we enquire into the way in which refugees perceive their space of life, we are confronted with several spaces of reference: the concrete and precisely determined one of the camp in which they live; the places that they left, which have become violent and are now distant; and again the more diffuse, 'liquid'[7] and extra-territorial one of the route of exodus. The plurality of contexts of identification is notable in the variety of situations observable: that of the camp as a whole, with the phases in which it was populated deriving from the history of the wars in the region, and that of each person in particular, as shown by the three 'categories' of refugees that I will present here, and which correspond to different waves of arrival.

The humanitarian sites are supposed to be precarious spaces, always provisional. This principle implies that the official end of a war is followed by the departure of the refugees and the closure of the camp. But how does this too predictable closure actually take place? What resistance is put up by those who have remade their lives there? What happens to the space itself, and the improvements made to it, after the departure of the refugees, assuming that they all return 'home'? The reply to these questions depends on the conceptions of locality that the refugees have developed in their exile, as well as on the national and international policies towards these spaces of transit and exception – i.e. the use that these policies want to make of them in the long term – and the conceptions that each party has of the return of refugees to the countries from which they came.

Three generations of refugees

Maheba is not exactly a refugee 'camp'. It is an immense virgin territory that was ceded by the local chiefs to the Zambian government in 1971, and by the government to the UNHCR. A clearing cut into the forest, on a wooded plateau in north-western Maheba, some 35 kilometres long and from 15 to 25 kilometres wide (making a total area of around 800 square kilometres in 2002), between the Maheba River to the west and the Mwatwe River to the east and south. To the north, there is a gateway leading to the only asphalted road in the region, which comes from Solwezi, 75 kilometres away, and continues to Mwinilunga, a distance of about 200 kilometres, close to the Angolan border. This gate is guarded by the Zambian police, but the perimeter of the site has no material limits – these are natural or 'social', i.e. marked simply by the end of inhabited or cultivated zones.

The UNHCR site at Maheba is a settlement of 58,000 refugees in a rural setting. The maximum number recorded was in fact 58,535 in January 2002, and has since declined; the population is made up mainly of Angolans (51,641 at that date, or 88.2 per cent of the total), along with a small number of Congolese (1,649 from the DRC, fomerly Zaire, i.e. 2.8 per cent), Rwandans (3,695 or 6.3 per cent) and Burundi (1,441 or 2.5 per cent), these last two nationalities being chiefly made up of Hutus.

Though these are all refugees and thus live (to different degrees) in a situation of exception, there are major differences among the residents of Maheba. Not all have experienced the same suffering or followed the same itineraries of flight; they do not all depend to the same extent on humanitarian aid; they do not have the same resources and powers within the camp; and they do not all have the same relationship to their country of origin.

A social stratification into three categories of refugees can sum up this diversity, distinguishing between the *settled*, the *recent* and the *new arrivals*. This sociological description largely coincides with the reading of the space, as well as with the chronology of the site:[8] from north to south, from the entrance gate and the 'route 1' of Zone A, opened in 1971, to the farthest 'villages' of the eighth zone to be opened in the camp, Zone H. Some 30 kilometres from the entrance, 'Village no. 17' is the last in the camp, opened in February–March 2002 to receive 900 refugees who had arrived in the preceding weeks. A socio-spatial reading of the camp thus tells us both about the development of warfare over thirty years in this region of Africa – Angola, Congo (DRC), Rwanda, Burundi – and about the formation of the ethnic and national diversity of this specific locality. The context of the observed situation has different scales and temporalities: to account for it, we have to describe not the strictly national or regional framework that surrounds it, but rather the chronological and topographic context of all the different wars that led diverse populations, from different origins and at different times, to converge on a site that is precisely a hybrid one, in a unique local situation. Here we can only sketch the effect of the context on the situation of the refugees in Maheba.

The oldest part of the site, that of the *settled*, starts from the entrance gate of the camp and stretches up the various 'roads' from route 1 to route 46, covering about 500 square kilometres and housing somewhat more than 20,000 refugees. This ensemble includes the original part (known as 'Old Maheba'), which was peopled in the course of the 1970s, and 'New Maheba', a sector developed during the 1980s. The habitat is very dispersed, with large extents of cultivable land: 5 hectares per family in the zones from the 1970s, then 2.5 hectares in those settled in the 1980s. This land is adjacent to the housing and was allocated as soon as the refugees arrived, in order to help them start farming as soon as possible, and become self-sufficient at the end of two years. After their first two years in the camp, their WFP ration was suspended, a principle applied also to the later generations of refugees. In Zone A, the oldest section of the site, the Angolan refugees come from various regional or ethnic groups that took part in the independence struggle against the Portuguese in the 1960s and early 1970s. Among their number, some initially passed through other regions of Zambia, particularly the Mayukwayukwa camp opened in 1966.[9] They were refugees there in the second half of the 1960s, i.e. before the Maheba camp was opened, a site that they are proud to have been the first to till. It was then chiefly Mbundu who arrived from 1976 onward, i.e. in the years that followed the independence of Angola (11 November 1975), very soon marked by the clashes between the MPLA and UNITA. The Mbundu formed the main ethnic group in Angola, around a third of the total population, and their region of origin was the centre of the country, although the war had led them to move to other regions, particularly in the east. The Mbundu, generally viewed as supporters of UNITA (whose leader, Jonas Savimbi, was himself a Mbundu), largely dominated the peopling of the Maheba site from the mid-1970s and the MPLA's taking power in Angola. In the initial phase they filled the remaining parts of Old Maheba (routes 14 to 28, forming Zones B and C). The New Maheba extension was then opened in 1985. It was filled by the early 1990s with the arrival of new Mbundu refugees, as well as Luanda and Luvale, the latter being considered supporters of the MPLA and hailing from regions further east such as Moxico, which were more recently occupied by

UNITA and were the object of regular clashes between the two warring forces.

The Mbundu in the camp claim to be more 'civilized' than the other refugees who arrived before or after them from the eastern regions. They say that they speak better Portuguese, that they have had more education, and that they 'want to dominate them', in the words of a former Mbundu refugee. And yet this does not translate into violent ethnic confrontations on the site. Some refugees also consider that these cleavages, or rather 'frictions' (*atritos*), are not exactly ethnic, but rather derive from the fact that one group are 'UNITA people' and the others 'MPLA people'.[10] For example, some of the 10,000 refugees who arrived as part of the last great wave of September–October 2000 were initially placed at the far end of the camp, in Zone H, opened in 1999 to deal with the influx of new arrivals. As these were Mbundu driven out of the central and eastern regions of Angola by the MPLA conquest, they did not get on well with the Luanda and Luvale who had arrived shortly before them from the eastern and border regions, when UNITA had itself taken control of that region. These groups 'did not let them settle'. The Mbundu therefore asked LWF, the NGO that ran the camp on behalf of the UNHCR, to 'redistribute' them alongside other inhabitants settled higher up on the site at Old Maheba since the 1970s, and belonging to the same ethnic group as them. These recent Mbundu, like those longer settled, were assumed to be supporters of UNITA, whereas the Luvale were seen as close to the MPLA. 'But here', as the Mbundu refugees noted when they related this episode at a collective gathering, 'we are all *refugiados angolanos*'.

In a general fashion, the residents of the older zones are well settled in the camp, and proud of not needing humanitarian assistance. They live off their agricultural products, the sale of a food surplus (chiefly maize, manioc and sweet potato), and a bit of petty trade in the small marketplaces – one in each zone, with between ten and thirty little stalls and some built-up shops. Finally, a far from negligible part receive some income thanks to jobs with the NGOs. This part of the camp population, well established, integrated and seeing itself as only little assisted, comprised in January 2003 something over 20,000 inhabitants, or around 35 per cent of the total population, and occupied about 60 per cent of the total area of the site. On top of this, some of the longer-established refugees 'appropriated' land in the southernmost section of the camp, which was taken back twenty years later when the site was gradually extended to cope with the arrival of other refugees.

Around 30,000 of these arrived in Maheba from the second half of the 1990s to 2001. They were first distributed along a number of 'routes', but as the available space was reduced they were gathered into 'villages'.[11] They form the category that I have called *recent* refugees. These include Angolans from the central and eastern regions (Mbundu, Lunda and Luvale), as in the previous waves, but also Congolese from the DRC, as well as Hutu from Burundi and Rwanda.

A group of some 2,500 Rwandans 'opened' a new zone in the camp in November 1997: Zone C.[12] They arrived from Rwanda, which they fled in July 1994 for Goma, then for southern Kivu in what was then Zaire. Early in 1997 they crossed Lake Tanganyika and entered Zambia, where they were housed for nine months in a transit camp in the north of the country. They were then evacuated to Maheba in November 1997. Other Rwandans arrived rather later. Following their forced evacuation in 1995–6 from the camps of Goma, Bukavu and Uvira, on the border between Congo (DRC) and Rwanda, they spent several years wandering in the DRC. They then managed to enter Angola under the protection of UNITA, after having been repelled by the MPLA and government forces. They lived for a while in the rebel zone: 'UNITA made the strongest ones work', one of the refugees told us, and certain Rwandan Hutus even joined the UNITA armed forces. In 1997, several thousand of them were received in the camps of Angolan 'returnees' opened in the eastern region of Moxico,[13] and placed under the protection of the UNHCR, with the assistance of the Lutheran World Federation and Médecins Sans Frontières. After a year in these camps, the resumption of fighting in the region between UNITA, the government forces and the MPLA provoked their flight, along with that of the Angolan 'returnees'. A group of between 3,000 and 3,500 Rwandan Hutus thus entered Zambia late in 1998, and was placed in the transit centre at Mwinilunga, near the Angolan border, under the control of the Zambian police. They were then transferred to Maheba in the early months of 1999, where a section of them joined the Hutu refugees who had arrived from the east in late 1997, while another part reached a zone already occupied by Congolese refugees. Thousands of Angolans who had arrived at the same time, between the resumption of the war in Angola (in 1998) and 2000–1, also remember the interminable journeys, spending months walking from village to village, feeding on leaves and fruit found in the forest (the *mata*), seeing their families scattered or partly wiped out by attacks on civilians. After a year or more of wandering, they arrived at the Zambian border in small groups. If this difficult exodus is still close for these recently arrived refugees, they are also confronted with problems of settlement in the camp that are all the more preoccupying in that, after the first two years there, they lose their right to the WFP food ration.

The 'villages' in which this category of recent refugees are housed sometimes resemble tiny urban nuclei: along the track are a well and a school,[14] a few shops and a marketplace with twenty or so stalls, but the land they are allowed to cultivate is rarely adjacent to their housing. Most of these refugees have received their allotment of 2.5 hectares, some even taking over additional land alongside without declaring it. This is the case with the Rwandans and Burundi, skilled market gardeners, fishers and traders, who have animated a range of commercial production in the camp, particularly that of fish and rice cultivated in the marshy zones, where they also grow sweet potatoes out of season. Others have not yet officially received their land; some of them 'appropriate' land that is untilled, others cultivate land that the UNHCR grants them for the construction of housing (plots of 50 by 25 metres), or take employment from the *settled*, the 'old refugees' who have long since occupied several plots.

A final category is formed by the generation of *new arrivals*. These find themselves in a situation of extreme dependence on international humanitarian aid, in terms of food, medical and psychological attention, and socially. When they get down from the lorries that have brought them from the border zones where they were initially registered, they are taken to transit centres, in principle for a few days but in fact for several weeks. They are then transferred to empty spaces in the forest, where they form new 'villages', each of these with around 1,000 persons.

The transit centres are lines of tents, more rarely of mud-brick buildings. Medical care is provided on arrival in the health posts and in two clinics, all of these established by MSF in the recent part of the camp where the latest arrivals are located, their needs having a particular urgency in this precarious situation.[15] The WFP food ration is distributed once a month.[16] However, for several months on end, in the years 2001–2, this aid consisted of half rations, i.e. the quantity distributed each month only covered two weeks of minimal nutrition (in maize, oil and salt), which had the effect of worsening the destitution of the new arrivals.

Tired, haggard, hungry or ill, these speak little and remain sitting or lying for most of the time. Their condition is due to their poor state of health as well as the decomposition of families at the moment of arrival – the lack of adults, in particular men of working age. A count made in one of the two transit centres at the end of January 2002 (Transit Centre H) established the presence of 499 persons, including 99 men, 112 women and 288 children under fifteen (58 per cent). Another group of refugees, who arrived in early February 2002 in the camp's other transit centre (Transit Centre 44), was made up of 82 persons divided into 21 families – 6 headed by a man, 15 by a single woman – plus 1 lone adolescent. The under-fifteens made up a total of 61 per cent of this transit group, and adult men 16 per cent.[17]

In the transit centres, the refugees remain grouped in large numbers in immense tents or large empty buildings, or else in smaller tents lined one against the other: these are places of waiting, devoid of intimacy, where they have nothing to do. When they leave these centres they are placed on empty land to be cleared, with a plastic sheet, a couple of covers and a few kitchen utensils. The improvement of this space, the manufacture of huts, the preparation of the ground so that something can be grown – all this minimal settlement takes a number of months.

Access to sites and power over them

The relationship between the settled refugees, the recent refugees and the new arrivals at Maheba does not indicate a 'logic of exclusion', such as Norbert Elias and John Scotson analysed in a suburb of Leicester in late-1950s England: within a group that was very similar ethnically and sociologically, the 'established' inhabitants here stigmatized and discriminated against the 'outsiders', who were marginal simply because of having arrived more recently.[18] On the contrary, the relationship between the three 'classes' of refugee at Maheba shows the existence of a logic of inclusion in domination. And paradoxically, the poor local functioning of the humanitarian system reinforces the functional weight of this logic of inclusion and domination. The establishment of almost 'normal' social relations, i.e. as inegalitarian and as inclusive as they can be in a village or community context, creates the conditions of a locality, in the sense of an identification with place, differentiated as a function of accessibility and of the possibility that various people have of exercising a certain power.

The established at Maheba form a stable population with all-round privilege, who institute relationships of protection and domination with the other two waves of refugees. The powers that they hold over the others concern immediate aid, reception and temporary agricultural work. This power has functions of social integration that are all the more effective and pronounced in that the general administration of the camp, on which the new arrivals are particularly dependent, functions badly. The combination of the power of the established (or that of certain of their number) and the poor functioning of humanitarian aid favours various practices of 'corruption' and misappropriation. Certain people, for example (both locals and refugees), who work for the organization charged with distributing the World Food Programme ration, rapidly unload a few sacks of maize on the road leading to the distribution points. These sacks, piled up in front of one or other of the huts, are then sold retail on the little marketplaces.

The established enjoy more space and more resources; they also have problems of status, and of being the 'second generation': 'All the same, we are refugees', says one of the most long-settled, who has maintained a nostalgia for Angola over more than twenty-five years in his regular meetings with Angolan friends – some of these being Mbundu, like him, others employees of the NGOs, as he is too. Being a refugee, in this case, means being maintained on a UNHCR site as the only legal place to live, except for temporary derogation. In the same way, the right to work exists only in the context of the camp, both for the refugees themselves and, still more so, for their adult children, who require permission to study outside the camp, and do not have the right to work in their host country. In this sense, the established still remain dependent on the humanitarian system, even if they are no longer assisted on a daily basis with food or health care. They find here the context of a certain tranquility, a relatively settled life and a local social status, which is not transferable elsewhere. This explains the lack of enthusiasm that they generally showed in relation to their envisaged return to Angola following the 2002 peace agreement.

The more recent refugees, for their part, perceive very well all the problems that the established ones present to them – the problem of unequal exchange, between the 'solidarity' that they enjoy from those linked to them by origin (the established) and the allegiance paid in return (implying services and agricultural work); a problem bound up with the privileged access of the earlier refugees to cultivable land, an access that makes possible in the medium term not only self-sufficiency, but also an income from the sale of certain products both inside and outside the camp;[19] a problem of competition for access to jobs with the NGOs, the income from which, however modest, makes local investment possible (in agriculture and petty commerce, for example). This is a constant source of complaint on the part of the recent refugees, a source of frustration and potential local conflict, the issues involved in it resembling the customary ones around land or access to employment, but without completely coinciding with these, since nothing – land, housing, capital – is actually legally acquired: everything depends on the context of the war, which justifies the humanitarian framework as a precarious reality with no future, within which these social differences are formed.

The possibility of departure, for the recent Angolan refugees (who have already been in the camp for between two and five years), brings these antagonisms and uncertainties to a head. It is with this category of refugees that the option of return takes concrete form, generally associated, in the explanations that they give of their desire to leave, with the 'bad treatment' that they say they experience in the camp, and which makes that much more understandable their desire to recover the land that they abandoned in their home country not so long ago. This disturbs the non-Angolans, the Hutu in particular, who do not envisage returning to Rwanda or Burundi, and whose agricultural, commercial and organizational dynamism has facilitated their rapid integration in the humanitarian site.

As soon as they arrive at Maheba the newcomers finally learn that their vital minimum, if the UN and humanitarian organizations working there do not take full responsibility for them, is to be negotiated with the established refugees. Whether in the transit centres or on their arrival at the sites where the 'villages' will be established, the distribution of food, covers, cooking pots, spades, soap bars and plastic sheets is conducted very slowly, sometimes after several days of waiting; this gives rise to quarrels with the NGO agents who conduct the distribution, to disputes between refugees, and to endless waiting in line. Everything is delayed and nothing is sufficient. Misappropriation of aid, certain abuses of power on the part of those distributing it, have been the subject of rumour, complaint and observation. To find something to eat, the newly arrived refugees must therefore very speedily ask around them for loans of foodstuffs, or money and seed to begin their own cultivation. They work on tasks for the established refugees, who have already occupied for a long time a part of the space that the new arrivals are supposed to take up. Thus the land envisaged for the site of the last 'village' created by the camp administration in March 2002 ('Village no. 17') was partly taken up, when the new refugees arrived, by older cultivation on the part of people established there for nearly twenty years and living in the New Maheba sector several kilometres away. These people released a section of the land to permit the settlement of the new arrivals (somewhat under 1,000 persons), who then find on other land, also kept and cultivated by the already established, a place of work paid by the task and near at hand. Payment is generally in kind: food, or sweet potato and manioc plants.

If the new arrivals have no other strategy than that of constantly complaining at the 'bad treatment' meted out to them by the NGO in charge of the site, or of hunger and the lack of shelters, and if they note that the solidarity of the other refugees is limited, their desire for return to Angola still depends on institutional guarantees: the organization of return (in lorries) by the UNHCR in agreement with the Angolan government; the pacification of the final zones where warfare has continued; the guarantee of finding agricultural and food resources at their places of return.

Return to Angola?

What was in question in the situation of the Maheba refugees after the announcement of the end of the war in Angola, the possibility of return for the Angolans and the projected closure of the camp was their very conception of locality – understood, as we said, as an identification with a given place. In the political and humanitarian milieus that deal with the refugees, their place of origin is generally viewed as the natural reference of identity and social place for the populations displaced under constraint. It is only in a dominating and unambiguous way that this linear and non-contradictory view of the place from which the refugees come, from which they have been expelled by violence and to which they want to return, can be interpreted as a 'right of return' championed not only as an indisputable political and vital demand, but also as a 'priority of return' – return being presented by the UNHCR as the only long-term solution. The sending 'home' of the populations of the South, as per current European security policies, uses the same identitarian argument of 'return home'. And yet very often the exiles, by the time that international organizations or states project this, have already had the experience of a new emplacement in urban zones or the humanitarian sites where they initially found themselves confined despite themselves, and to which they have had to accommodate themselves over several years. This fact is still more important in the case of the

129

'second generation' of refugees, i.e. those who were born in the camps or who arrived there as children.

The initial violent experience of *dis*-placement leads to reconceiving various aspects of the *em*-placement of refugees. In a first phase, the loss of place of origin calls into question the very evidence of local identification as an original and structuring identification: once this is undone, and is now distant and more objectified, the relationship to the space of 'origin' appears as the result of investments, strategies and 'techniques of production of locality'.[20] However long-established they may be, these symbolic and economic strategies have formed the 'anthropological places' to which people are attached.[21]

In a second phase, exile is the context of individual and collective actions in which other strategies of emplacement can be developed. Since these do not necessarily wipe out the memory of the places lost, a cumulative plurality of local identifications is thus formed. This anchorage to a number of places – and potentially a network of places – confirms the weight of the 'local' (as against the 'global' of the cosmopolitans), while detaching this local from the reference to any rootedness, any unique and definitive origin. For the refugees living at Maheba, it is clear that war and exile have made the conception of place more complex, modifying the conditions in which places are appropriated and bringing about both social and spatial reconfigurations. The formation of a new emplacement for the refugees who arrive in successive waves has depended on the formation of a social order in the space of humanitarian intervention – in other words, of relationships that are formed between the different categories of refugees for access to resources and places. It is on the basis of this kind of dynamic built up over time in this camp, and the changes in identity that have accompanied it, that their responses to the offer of return are conceived.[22]

The camps are the beginnings of agglomerations, sometimes of strings of villages, sometimes of towns, always kept in an incomplete state, but whose depopulation or complete disappearance is disturbing. The end of the camps is always a problem, both practical and political.

Thus at the other end of Zambia, near the border with Mozambique, another refugee site established in a rural milieu, the Ukwimi site opened in 1987, was evacuated in 1994 when the 25,000 or so Mozambican refugees sheltered there were repatriated to their own country under a strong incitement to leave, particularly on the part of the Zambian government and the UNHCR. The government took back the land that had been ceded to it several years before – as at

Maheba – by local chieftains. It put this land at the disposal of colonists and the few refugees who had refused to return to Mozambique after the peace agreement. But these latter found themselves in a more fragile and illegal situation, considered now as foreigners who had to regularize their stay in the country.[23]

At Maheba in 1996, nearly two years after the signature of the second peace agreement in Angola and before the resumption of hostilities in 1998, a Zambian journalist questioned the future of the camp after the war. A 'hot issue' with the Zambian authorities, he revealed, was the possibility that the return of the refugees to their country of origin would lead the host country to discover that there were on the national soil several thousand farmers, part of whose harvest had been sold in the country, as well as a substantial infrastructure (schools, clinics, some official buildings, wells and water reserves, roads and housing).[24] This phenomenon was amplified in 2002, since the camp population had more than doubled since 1996 and the equipment increased correspondingly, as did likewise the product of commercial agriculture.

Beyond each particular case, therefore, there is a general finding: if war generates its own spaces of exception, some of these survive it and give rise to enduring processes of repopulation, or even an urbanization that is precarious, unforeseen and hybrid.

We can imagine a kind of town. This town could be called Maheba, from the name of the river that borders it to the west and that used to give its name to the camp. It could even become, in the terms that Lewis Mwanagombe already used in 1996, 'a large piece of wealth to be appropriated in the middle of nowhere'.[25] We can well understand then how refugees have been not only new tillers, but the inventors of new spaces.

— 7 —

Camp-Towns: Somalia in Kenya

Perhaps it is a rank heresy to assume that all exiles long to return to the country they thought of as 'home'; maybe it is a fallacy to believe that the die of an exile's mind is forever cast around a distant mould, that of a faraway homeland . . . a country frescoed on the murals of a memory, and boasting a set of etches more distinct than any you've ever seen. A long time ago, Somalia would now and then pole-vault into my obsessive recall, with its miragey aridness forming instantaneously into a vapoury realness, and its thorny trees puncturing the air mattresses of my nightly visions. Alas, not so any more, I who have been dispossessed of my dreams![1]

The refugee camps pile together tens of thousands of inhabitants for periods that are generally much longer than the immediate emergency. On every level, humanitarian intervention shows a tendency to become fixed and frozen on the sites of its establishment, even if this process goes together with practices and discourse that only refer to 'emergency'. The hypothesis that I now want to test, from a study of Somalian refugee camps at Dadaab in Kenya, extends the conclusions I drew from Maheba on the subject of locality. Here this means the locality of camp-towns. Humanitarian intervention has transformed the originally empty setting in which the camps were built: these have gradually become the sites of an organization in space, a social life and a system of power that do not exist elsewhere. They impose an 'updating' on the local foundations of identity, and if ethnologists wish to follow as closely as possible the problematic of the refugees that they seek to understand, they must as philosophical pragmatists reach the same conclusion as the exiled Somalian novelist: after all, it is perhaps a mistake to suppose that exiles always desire to return to what was 'their home'.

The question of camp-towns

Camps are paradoxical and hybrid mechanisms; they sometimes form camp-towns. On the one hand, the individuals gathered in these spaces are there explicitly because of their status as victims. This justification of their presence and the existence of the camps transforms them, from the humanitarian point of view, into nameless individuals, in the sense that no identitarian reference is supposed to affect the physical life of the victims being taken in charge (security, health, food): this care is addressed to persons coming from factions, regions or states that may equally well be friends or enemies, allies or adversaries. The recognition of individuals in the practical and ideological humanitarian apparatus thus implies the social and political non-existence of the beneficiaries of aid. This does not mean that the humanitarian actors themselves believe in this non-existence, but it is an essential component of the fiction which they have to accept if they want to give meaning to their presence in the lands of their intervention.[2] Knowing in principle only victims, the camps are spaces that produce an identitarian problematic, in the sense that Michael Pollak has observed in connection with the concentration camp experience: 'identity only becomes a preoccupation, and indirectly an object of analysis, when it can no longer be taken for granted, when the common meaning is no longer given in advance and the actors present no longer manage to agree on the significance of the situation and the roles they are supposed to take'.[3] The ambiguity of action and the paradoxical situation are, in the humanitarian context, elements of a moral constraint that may be more violent the longer it lasts, since it leaves subjects literally without a voice, without recourse to the possibility of open conflict, except to escape from the strait-jacket of the victim identity in which they are caught and trapped, an identity that proves at the end of the day a subtle means of control over individuals. This is an unpredictable and strange situation that they have not been prepared for, and that provokes a questioning of their own identity, already injured by the violence, losses and displacement they have experienced.

On the other hand, this mechanism of minimal survival or preservation of 'bare life' that the camp and its organization represent can also be described in terms identical to those used today to describe towns – heterogeneity, complexity, gathering, concentration. Besides, a particular attention towards everything that arises from almost nothing, for beginnings and the scope of what they proclaim, opens the way to a descriptive and anthropological approach that can be called an urban ethnography of the camps. The point is not to 'compare' the camp with the town as two distinct realities that can be brought together intellectually by a play of analogy, metaphor and superposition of images. In fact, we see repeatedly how, over time, camps create opportunities for encounter, exchange and the reworking of identity for all those who live in them. From this point on, we may ask whether and how the humanitarian mechanism of the camps produces the town.

Can the refugee camp become a town in the sense of a space of urban sociability, or even a political space, a city? And if this is not possible, what prevents it? Is it, or is it not, able to free itself from its initial constraint of enclosure and removal, as the apartheid townships, the African encampments in colonial cities and the various historic forms of ghetto were able to do, even though these were also mutilated forms of urban formation?[4]

I undertook a study in the Dadaab camps of north-eastern Kenya during the months of June–July 2000. I was introduced there by the Belgian section of MSF, responsible for medical assistance in the three camps. I slept in the MSF compound and went to the camps, a few kilometres away, each morning in the NGO's vehicles that drove in a humanitarian convoy escorted by the Kenyan police. For reasons of security I had to leave the camps in the evening, in common with all the Kenyan and humanitarian staff. This did not prevent me, after a number of days, from being free to move around in the camps, and asking a refugee employed by MSF to accompany me, both as a guide and to translate conversations from Soomaali to English as needed.

The Dadaab camps: shelters, 'highway' and video shops

This study enabled me to bring to light three beginnings of a probable form of urban life: the beginnings of a symbolism of spaces, of a social differentiation and of a change in identity. I shall sketch a broad outline of them all, without trying to give a complete description. My aim here is particularly to open up some paths for ethnographic inquiry, in one of these new spaces of life which a few decades ago no one would have imagined could figure among the legitimate terrains of anthropology.[5]

Although as densely populated as the rest of the district of Garissa in which they are located, the three UNHCR sites at Dadaab do not appear on the map of Kenya. The Ifo camp (45,000 inhabitants in 10,000 shelters) was opened in September 1991; the one at Dagahaley (34,000 inhabitants and some 7,000 shelters) in March 1992; and the one at Hagadera (45,000 inhabitants) in June 1992.[6] They are located in a radius of 15 kilometres either side of the village of Dadaab, which is the base of the UN and humanitarian organizations that run the camps. The population is over 90% Somalian in origin, though there are also some southern Sudanese refugees, as well as Ethiopians, Eritreans and Ugandans. The WFP food rations are distributed every two weeks at stores run by the Canadian section of CARE, which is also partly responsible for education,[7] and supports some social and craft activities. The Belgian MSF runs a number of health posts, three bush hospitals and some mobile care teams. Finally, the security of the refugees and humanitarian workers is handled by 250 officers of the Kenyan police, their action coordinated by the UNHCR administration, which also provides their uniforms and vehicles.

The UNHCR has built fences from thorn-bush and barbed wire for the surroundings of the camps and the 'blocs' within, these each being plots of 2 or 3 hectares on which between 100 and 150 shelters are established, with an average of 300 to 600 refugees. The refugees are brought together in blocs on the basis of their place of origin, their ethnic group and possibly their clan of origin, and are generally denoted in broad ethnic (Soomaali) or national (Ethiopian, Sudanese) terms. On their arrival they have all received the same sheet of blue and white plastic from the UNHCR, along with a mattress and some kitchen utensils. They go and find wood around the camp to put together their shelter. Over the years, the habitat has grown denser and more solid: houses of mud-brick alternate with Soomaali huts of branches, all being covered with the same plastic sheeting; material used to transport international aid is recycled – particularly the tin from food boxes and drums, which can be unrolled and used for roofs, doors, windows, tables or chicken coops. The labels 'USA', 'EEC', 'Japan', 'WFP' and 'UNHCR' bedeck the inhabited landscape, along with the respective flags of the donor countries or bodies.

The immediate environment of the shelters is made up of blocs and sections (groups of ten or fifteen contiguous blocs) whose limits have been traced with a measuring tape to permit the passage of control vehicles (police, health and infrastructure). This environment is clearly differentiated according to membership group: the Soomaalis opt for a scattered habitat with family enclosures roughly demarcated by a few low thorn-bushes, and frequently overflowing the marked-out blocs; in the Ethiopian 'quarter' of the Ifo camp, on the other hand, its two contiguous blocs display a high density of habitation, narrow lanes, high fences and the presence of a number of shops – coffee shops, video shops, hair salons, photo studios – summarily erected under cloth sheeting, and the huts are made out of wooden planks, cardboard or metal.

With certain of the inhabitants – particularly those who are minorities within the camps (Ethiopians, Sudanese, 'Soomaali Bantu Refugees' (known as 'SBRs'), Ugandans), the enclosure of their spaces indicates an attitude of fear, rejection, withdrawal and self-defence. Thus at Dagahaley there is a bloc of shelters housing some 500 Sudanese mostly originating from the towns of southern Sudan, more than two-thirds of their number being young men. Rather more than two years after their arrival at the Ifo camp, this group was moved to Dagahaley where they constructed an unusual space, different from that of the Somalian refugees, but also from that of the Sudanese in the two other camps. The habitat was organized in lines of small mud-brick houses, well aligned on either side of a completely straight main road some 50 metres long, at the end of which a mud-brick church had also been built, with a sure sense of perspective. A day nursery, a line of shower and toilet facilities and a little volleyball pitch end up forming what looks like a modern southern Sudanese village, or more certainly a neighbourhood of a miniature town. The whole is surrounded by a fence of thorn-bush and barbed wire, where a dozen men take turns each night, three at a time, at guarding the bloc's perimeter. As in the other blocs, the entrance gate is closed for the whole night at 6 p.m. The night-time enemy here is the immediate neighbour: 'It's the Bantu Soomaalis', the young leaders of the Sudanese quarter explain, 'they want us to pay money for blood'. They mean that at the slightest problem – for example a quarrel between the children of the two groups – these neighbours immediately come and aggressively demand financial compensation. The words 'Equatoria Gate' are inscribed in recycled metal on the gateway, as a reminder of the department of southern Sudan from which the refugees here fled in 1994–5.

Other spaces are more open and can be visited with no problem even by those whose own habitat is apparently confined to their ethnic or clan group (Soomaalis, Ethiopians or southern Sudanese). This is the case with the 'coffee shops' at Ifo, run by Ethiopians, or the 'video shops' in all three camps, run by young people who may be Ethiopian, Sudanese or even Soomaali, in the latter case being the target of moralistic reproach from their Muslim elders. For 10 Kenyan shillings (0.15 euros) you can attend one of the two daily video sessions in a hut made from planks and branches, at which Indian films are shown, and occasionally football matches.

All these activities presuppose certain uses of space, which transform the usual vision people have of refugees. They are accompanied by a tentative form of symbolism of the sites, as witness the fact that some anonymous spaces have been named by the inhabitants. In the Hagadera camp, in particular, the space of the market located at the entry to the camp has become 'the town' in English, and *magalo* in Soomaali; here, the refugees sell part of their food ration and some people from the surrounding region sell other daily needs, along two little sand streets bordered with stalls, also serving coffee or offering video sessions. Similarly, the larger road to the market is known as the 'main street' of the camp. Finally, a broad stretch of sand (50 metres wide, 1.5 kilometres long) which runs from this space and which the refugees take on foot to reach the main group of shelter blocs is known in English as the 'highway'.

Social and ethnic recomposition in the camps

These 'inventions of daily life' – comparable with those that, according to Michel de Certeau, mark the resistance of townspeople in the face of the spread of out-places, resistance to the individualization and anonymity of urban spaces[8] – are supplemented by a second attempt at urban life, relating to social differentiation. The problem of inactivity, however, dominates the life of the camps. As a corollary to the feeling of abandonment this problem affects everybody, but most directly those who had a recognized and more or less formal employment before the exodus, thus principally men and townspeople.[9] Moral suffering, or even psychological disturbance bound up with lack of occupational activity, play an important part in individual daily life: as witness the Somalians who previously worked in commerce, services or administration in Mogadishu and no longer know what to do; the young unemployed Sudanese who spend their days 'pushing time', as they call it; the former Ethiopian government officials who see themselves, after nine years of exile in the camp, as physically and mentally imprisoned – 'homeless and hopeless' as they say – and talk of suicide. In a repetitive way, the refugees express, above all, feelings of impotence and uselessness.

137

There is no official employment market in the camps, and, being viewed as foreigners without work permits, 'those who work outside the camps are illegal', a UNHCR official stresses. More or less recognized or tolerated commercial activities exist, however, and are visible as you pass through the camps: the resale of a part of the food ration and the buying and selling of vegetables or daily needs (brought from Garissa, the district capital) on the market stalls; the raising of goats around the camp; small handicraft activity (basket weaving, sewing, carpentry, metalwork, shoe repairs, building) in and around the huts and cabins; service shops for coffee and tea, hair salons, etc.

If this embryonic economy is to turn, it needs capital, networks and institutions. The Soomaali traders and growers play a major role here. For the members of the Ogaadeen clan of Soomaalis, which is the largest of their groupings, the camp has an ecological and cultural air that is continuous with their own, located just the other side of the Somalian border. They move around the region with ease, and sometimes enjoy support from their host population, rural or urban, in acquiring financial independence (work, loans, etc.).[10] A Kenyan identity card or driving licence, or even a temporary work permit regularly renewed, all obtained by purchasing the complicity of officials responsible for issuing or checking these documents outside the camps, enable them to pursue various business dealings. Eventually, they may be able to settle illegally in the district capital of Garissa or the suburbs of Nairobi, or even make return trips to Somalia. In the same way, some of the refugees living in the camps regularly receive help from sons or brothers circulating in the country and working undeclared – neither as foreigners nor as refugees. There are also those who receive financial help from abroad, sent by relatives who are refugees in third countries (Europe, Canada, USA), or even living in Somalia or elsewhere in Kenya. These financial operations are conducted through local banks and networks of trust in the places from which funds are sent. Two banks of this type exist in Dadaab, near the camps, eleven others in Garissa, and four more in the Soomaali quarter of Nairobi.[11] These funds enable refugees to supplement the WFP ration, but also to embark on various petty business activities in the camp markets.

Commercial and handicraft activities, moreover, are supported by international NGOs, on the grounds of combating the inactivity of the refugees, and above all because they offer an educational or social interest. In fact, this support was conceived in order to give increased social value to certain so-called 'vulnerable' categories: young orphans, the physically handicapped, and women who have been widowed, divorced or raped.

The NGOs also target minority groups who have a lower position in the context of the camp (for example, the Soomaali castes and clans that are considered as inferior or servile). By way of loans of 5,000 Kenyan shillings (about 75 euros) and sometimes more, some 250 groups of four or five persons had developed by June 2000 projects of 'income-generating activities'. In fact, the strictly economic profitability of these is uncertain, and does not seem to be the main motive for the financing bodies. Thus the products of basket-weaving are sold at a derisory price (50 to 100 shillings for a basket, depending on size, or the price of a bus journey from one camp to another); unsold willow baskets pile up in the huts of the women artisans. Only welfare initiatives make it possible to sell a few, wholesale – for example when ambassadors or UN representatives make official visits to the camps. Everything happens as if, from the point of view of both financers and beneficiaries, the point was to keep up an economic appearance in which regular work activity was the tangible proof of social utility.

Finally, the NGOs operating in the three camps employ and pay a total of some 1,500 refugees as 'voluntary community workers' (400 employed by MSF, more than 600 by CARE, the others by UNHCR, WFP, GTZ, etc.). These receive unofficial wages[12] that range from 2,500 to 4,000 shillings per month (38 to 60 euros). This income enables them to supplement the food ration, possibly also to pay others to build more solid and comfortable accommodation than the tents of the UNHCR, and others again to work for them (cooking and housekeeping), to invest in petty business (the sale of vegetables on the market stalls) or help with the operation of the few actually profitable activities ('photo studios' and 'video shops') run by friends – for example, copying onto video cassettes sporting events transmitted live via satellite on the TV sets in the compounds of the humanitarian organizations, in order to replay them the next day in the camp 'video shops'.

These few activities and resources display a social differentiation in the camps, even if this only appears in relief against a common background marked chiefly by destitution and inactivity. Four levels of social hierarchy can be distinguished. At the top is a small minority of Soomaali notables – traders, stock-raisers and the heads of clans with superior status. Their incomes are hard to estimate (around 5,000 Kenyan shillings a month, i.e. 75 euros, maybe more),[13] likewise their number,[14] but the position that they hold also depends on their membership of the superior clans in the Darood clan confederation,[15] from which they draw a legitimate precedence that enables them to occupy representative functions, as elders in the blocs and sections of the camps.

The 'voluntary community workers' are a second social category that are locally dominant. This is an alternative minority, fairly close to the former in terms of income, but smaller numerically (less than 2%) and competing with them in terms of ideology. Their place close to the representatives of the UN and humanitarian organizations gives them prestige and power in the internal camp relationships. As well as this, some of them are or have been bloc 'leaders' in competition with the elders.

The group formed by the petty traders, occasional craft workers and informal employees forms a third category dependent on the two first groups, but also on the aid and support of the NGOs. Thus the wives and daughters of NGO voluntary workers are among the salespeople in the camp markets, but the artisans supported by the humanitarian organizations also include groups that are marginalized in the ethnic relationships within the camps.[16]

A fourth and lowest level of the hierarchy is formed by the beneficiaries of minimal aid (food, health care, water, firewood, shelter), possibly supplemented by occasional assistance from the other categories or from relatives living outside the camps. This destitute group, with no resources of its own, is by far the most numerous.[17]

We can see in this attempt at social classification how the tensions deriving from ethnic membership constantly cut across the social positioning generated within the camps. However, just as the social hierarchy presents an unusual configuration in both its elements and its structure, so a singular ethnic chessboard is established within the camps and makes it possible to relativize this dimension of affiliation, at the same time as it presents itself under the guise of the immediate truth about collective and individual identities. On the contrary, contacts made in the camps, and the conflicts experienced there, suddenly challenge the self-evidence or certainty of identities among the refugees.

From the point of view of changes in identification, it is tempting to contrast towns and camps. This has been done in a very explicit way by Liisa Malkki, who studied in the late 1980s the Hutu refugees from Burundi in Tanzania, comparing the camp occupants (at Mashamo) with those settled in town (at Kigoma). According to this anthropologist, the exiles' attachment to their place of departure was more or less strong in different cases, and the effects of detachment also depended on their place of settlement. In this context, Liisa Malkki held that the camp had become both a spatial reference and a politico-symbolic one: within it, a specific moral and political community was reconstituted among the Burundi refugees, with the memory and myths of origin being retained. In the camp, she noted, Hutu identity was reinforced. On the other hand, those refugees who settled separately in the city produced more 'cosmopolitan' forms of identity, with their ethnic identity losing its mythic and historical reference: this could be more readily manipulated according to the particular context. The cosmopolitanism of the latter was thus counterposed to the ethnic nationalism of the former. They found their place among the actors and conceivers of a 'post-national' cosmopolitan order.[18]

Gaim Kireab, however, drawing on studies of the Eritrean refugees in Sudan, has criticized the idea of a de-territorialization of identities.[19] He particularly argues that, if the self-settled refugees on the urban peripheries seem more cosmopolitan than those in the camps, this is because they are forced to hide behind 'fictitious identities'. Finding themselves without protection, they have the wrong ethnic membership in the wrong place, and they seek therefore to pass as something else. In the Sudan, he continues, some Eritrean refugees, simply with the object of passing unperceived, have changed their name, their language, their way of dress and even their religious allegiance – Christian men and women aiming to pass as Muslim. Some men, while remaining Christian 'in their private world', have even made the pilgrimage to Mecca in order to become 'fictitious *hajjis*'. But all this, he concludes, does not prevent them from being active within Eritrean political circles and, being able to circulate more freely, knowing better than others how to get round the legal prohibitions in Sudan in order to organize political resistance by the scattered refugees. So it is not a matter of loss of identity, but rather a 'strategy of invisibility'.

The experience of the Dadaab camps makes it possible to supplement this discussion in a number of ways. We can approach the description and interpretation of the camps in a different fashion. Speaking very generally, this shows first of all that the camp *creates identity*, both ethnic and otherwise. It is from this point of view an experience of identity that is just as relational and dynamic as that undergone by refugees not under the protection of international organizations, who have self-settled on the urban peripheries. This contention can be qualified in various ways: the patching together of new identities, the strengthening of particularisms, as well as anti-ethnic behaviour and inter-ethnic exchange. I shall deal with these briefly below.

The first qualification concerns the 'patching' of new identities onto existing ones. This can be seen in the fact that nationalities can become ethnicities in the relational sense. If there are, for example, refugees from Ethiopia in the Ifo camp who belong to a dozen different tribes, as well as Eritreans, they are all identified here simply as 'Ethiopians'. Whereas the accounts of warfare and flight are marked by 'tribal' opposition and violence, and reference to the nation was profoundly abused in ethnic conflicts, the term 'Ethiopian', like that of 'Sudanese', refers to what we can call a national locale. These 'ethnonyms' do not eliminate previous group membership, but they do indeed become real and functional terms of identity as long as the camps persist. Thus, in the mechanism of an ethnic 'chessboard' specific to the camps, each affiliation gains its meaning and position in relation to the other 'pieces' around it – competing, hostile or allied.

A second figure of identity in the camps is that of reinforced particularisms. This is shown by the following conflict. Those people known in the Dadaab camps as Bantu Soomaalis are outcasts, i.e. minorities of non-Soomaali origin, immigrant farmers viewed by the 'superior' groups as serfs or slaves. These 'superior' groups include the Darood Ogaadeen, who are numerous in the region and in the camps, and certain of whose representatives display arrogant and dominating attitudes towards the Bantu – sometimes even violence. For centuries, the 'inferior' groups identified themselves by reference to the supposedly noble clans to which they were tied.[20] On the ethnic chessboard of the camps, however, they have been gradually recognized as autonomous and apparently detached from the overall Soomaali identity. Their official designation uses just the initials SBR ('Soomaali Bantu Refugees'), and they address the camp administration as a recognized minority with the right – just like other ethnic or national groups (Soomaalis, Sudanese, Ethiopians, etc.) – to loans for handicraft activity or jobs as volunteers with the NGOs. The camp thus enables them to escape from a low valued intra-ethnic position. Furthermore, this context promotes a search for ancestry that separates them more radically from the Soomaalis and links them with lands in Tanzania and Mozambique, from where they say that they came several centuries ago. The SBR representatives asked the camp administration for collective resettlement in those two countries. This demand was unsuccessful, but a response came from the United States. Under its commitment to the UN to take its due share of refugees, the US administration showed interest in these Africans attached to their land of origin and showing a great ethnic unity, compatible naturally enough with American representations of ethnic identity. In mid-2000, screening[21] procedures were announced to prepare for 10,000 SBRs to be accepted by the United States. Their resettlement was finally accomplished in 2004–5.

But the strategy of reinforcing ethnic particularisms is a potential challenge to the existing ethnic dominations. This ambivalence makes it possible to escape or criticize ethnicity in a third type of identitarian process, which can be seen at the very heart of intra-ethnic relationships. In fact, among the Soomaali groups deemed to be of lower status and made up of a series of minority clans referred to as 'tool people' (*Waable*), the dynamic is not so much an ethnicizing one, as in the previous case, but rather socio-economic. As members of trade castes, a group of craftspeople (blacksmiths, shoemakers, tailors, carpenters) attracted the interest of humanitarian NGOs concerned to maintain a semblance of occupational activity in the life of the camps, and for this purpose to support projects of 'income-generating activities'. This does not proceed completely without violence. Artisans receiving support from the NGOs are reminded of their inferior status and systematically taxed by the elders of the 'superior' Soomaali clans; others see their workshops sacked, if they are not themselves the target of physical aggression by gangs contracted by these elders.

In this case, the camp does not reinforce ethnicity, but on the contrary opposes it, counterposing it to an alternative that relativizes it. The chessboard is no longer strictly ethnic in its operation, but more widely relational. As we have observed above, for example, in describing the levels of social hierarchy within the camps, what distinguishes the two 'superior' classes in the Dadaab camps – the traders and the NGO volunteers – is the different weight that they give to the ethnic legitimacy of their status: imposing and decisive for the Soomaali notables and traders, this is secondary for the NGO workers, and even criticized by them. The ins and outs of the relationship between leaders, elders and NGOs deserve more detailed study. Competition here, whatever its immediate outcome, leads in the direction of an opening up of identity, and thus also a certain cosmopolitanism.

A fourth figure of identity must finally be mentioned – embryonic in this case, but definitely urban in its principles. This tends to undo the pattern of the identitarian boxes on the chessboard and to change the appearance and role of the 'pieces' themselves. What we have here is a set of contact situations sometimes marked by aggressiveness and even serious physical violence, but which represent new exchanges, learning processes and translations (linguistic, cultural), contradicting the ethnic divisions established on arrival. Thus in inter-ethnic encounters inconceivable before the camp, contacts are made in the market, around the wells, at the distribution centre for food aid, at the health post. The Soomaali elders would like to close down the 'video shops' and 'coffee shops' in the camps, but they have not managed to do so, and the young people of their ethnic group visit them often. The Ethiopian refugees, for their part – the great majority of whom are young men who arrived alone – sometimes find wives among the Somalians. These women are then rejected by their own kind: Soomaali gangs may even enter the Ethiopian 'quarter' to take back women from their ethnic group by force, leaving the children to the husband as they see them as illegitimate (since not Soomaali by patrilineal filiation). But these marriages continue, and, here again, the 'matrimonial range' expands considerably.[22]

All these situations experienced in the Dadaab camps enable us to challenge the opposition on which Gaim Kibreab and Liisa Malkki seem to agree, in their respective points of view as presented above. In fact, both make a contrast between closed ethnicizing spaces (in the one case the place of origin, in the other the refugee camp) and open spaces such as towns and their suburbs, where identities are seen as 'fictitious' by the one author and 'cosmopolitan' by the other. The example of Dadaab shows that the camp is a new context and, to a certain point, an innovative one, even if the social and identitarian changes here are experienced in terms of personal suffering and conflict. It generates experiences of hybrid socialization, not just multi-ethnic but also plural, in which clan strategies intersect with ethnic or socio-professional ones, and again with the global programmes of the international humanitarian organizations.

The possible beginnings of urban life

In conclusion, I return to the question of camp-towns which I raised at the start of this chapter. The major interest of the Dadaab camps, in the context of this study, will have been to illustrate a mechanism that has been relatively well 'run in' at the level of 'care, cure and control' – to use the words of a UNHCR official I met precisely at Dadaab. This is why the Dadaab camps are celebrated in the humani-

144

tarian world. Certainly less well known, but just as important for our study, are the complexities of the social life that has been built up over the years within the three camps.

As we said, the management of spaces under the regime of humanitarian government makes these camps a space of pure waiting, devoid of subjects. Opposed to this principle of power are the attempts at 'subjectivization' that are glimpsed in initiatives aiming to create work, and in circulation, meetings and even conflicts. To be human, to reconquer this minimum in the way of identity and being-in-the-world that war and exodus endanger, means therefore for each refugee a redefinition of their place by taking advantage of this ambivalence of life in the camps, between emergency and duration, between the feeling of death, physical or social, and the resumption of life.

The Dadaab example shows that the process of the camp is indeed that of a town in the making: an embryonic economy, since people are willing to work (and many of them ready to remain where they are) rather than resign themselves to their assisted status; a social division adapted to the plurality of constraints and resources (Soomaali clans, the NGOs in the camp, the Somalian diaspora in the world);[23] an occupation of space that, however precarious, gives meaning to a place that was originally deserted and is already no longer so. To speak of urban life in this descriptive context is not metaphorical, and the impression of incompleteness provoked by this analogy that I use to some extent by default ('It all happens as if . . .') reproduces, fairly faithfully I believe, the paradoxical situation experienced in the camps. Everything happens 'as if' it was a town. Everything is potential, and yet nothing develops, as distinct from the townships of apartheid South Africa or the African encampments of the colonial towns, other models with which the refugee camp shares an incomplete and unfinished form of urbanism. The camp, even when stabilized, remains an amputated town, bare by definition.

There is an equivalent tension among the international organizations present in the camps. As always, nothing is simple or homogeneous. Some of them want to promote dialogue, integration, inter-ethnic encounters, cultural learning processes, and go as far as questioning their own justifications for their presence in this broadly socialized context which offers little purchase for the language of emergency.[24] Others, in the same context, seek to avoid, as much as possible, contacts between different clan, ethnic or national groups, which they view as potential conflicts, and to keep control of the overall mechanism. These conflicts, when they arise, are ended by forced repatriation or by moving those involved to other camps. Paid activities remain informal, even if some are tolerated, just as is movement outside the camps, which still requires permission. The town is indeed at the heart of the camp, but it is only ever so in the form of attempts that are permanently foiled.

— 8 —

In the Name of the Refugees: Political Representation and Action in the Camps

At Maheba – the vast UNHCR installation in Zambia, which we described above[1] – one of the two transit centres stands opposite a space called the 'camp for the vulnerable' on the other side of the main road through the site, some 20 kilometres from the entrance gate. The transit centre has twenty tents and two large hangars in which the refugees (mostly Angolan) settle themselves on their arrival, while they wait for emergency care and provisions. The camp opposite is made up of tiny straw huts scattered across the enclosed space, where some 130 individuals deemed 'vulnerable' – old people, the sick, and children without families – remain lying or sitting; there is not enough height for them to stand up. It is neither their age nor their physical condition that makes them absolutely and equally vulnerable, and explains this confinement. Many other people share these characteristics, among the nearly 60,000 refugees present on the UNHCR site, and the vulnerable are still more numerous if we consider all those who fled from the war in Angola. What makes them vulnerable is the loss of their own social resources, the absence of connections, family or local, that could shoulder the burden of their suffering. Their distress may be temporary or lasting, but it exists only because their physical or moral handicap is part of an overall de-socialization: no longer having ties or anything to do, no interlocutors or voices. The 'vulnerability' of humanitarian language is the 'bare life' of philosophical language, from Walter Benjamin to Giorgio Agamben: mere biological existence (*zoê*) without social existence (*bios*), life placed under a 'ban', i.e. a space of exception set apart from the common world but still under control.

No matter how indisputable the evidence of a suffering body, this vulnerability is regularly relativized and 'replayed' on other terrains

147

of the humanitarian stage. Vulnerability becomes a 'resource' on which a voluntary identification is based, as well as the sense of a certain legitimacy among the populations taken charge of in the humanitarian spaces, especially refugees, action on whose part may be directed against the humanitarian and UN organizations themselves. Does this represent a perversion, in the moral sense, of humanitarian action? Or is it rather a slow transformation, more or less hidden, of its meaning? Are we not facing here a reappropriation and re-signifying of humanitarian language by its beneficiaries, when individuals display their refusal to remain locked into the status of absolute victim – identity as the negation of any political recognition – and make the words of identity assigned to them (victim, vulnerable, refugee) words under which they take the initiative? Can their action transform the refugee camps into *public spaces*? Can it, finally, change the very meaning of vulnerability by imposing through negotiation a widening of its criteria? I shall try in the following pages to give these questions greater precision, and open up lines of reflection and study with a view to offering attempted responses. I shall draw here on the studies conducted in the camps that I have already presented, in particular those in Guinea and Sierra Leone.

The denial of citizenship to refugees

The label of 'refugee' denotes the acme of denied citizenship. It is denied, first of all, in the combined police and humanitarian treatment of undesirable populations, transformed into hordes of placeless individuals – frightening or pitiful as the case may be. At different levels, the camp 'events' – those that particularly received media coverage – at Goma, Sangatte, Nauru or Guantánamo have symbolized, in recent years, the existence on the world scale of an ensemble of spaces and regimes of *exception*. The hunt for the undesirables of the world system does indeed seem open, and the period after 9/11 has removed any sense of guilt from those set on their removal. In this order of things, the intervention of the humanitarian NGOs themselves, and that of the UNHCR, has not been exempt from suspicious thoughts towards their 'clients' – suspicions bound up with the place assigned to them today in the world system.

The refugees are also denied citizenship by their political exclusion. This is regularly displayed around questions of social integration and political rights at both local and national levels: only their suffering ultimately justifies their being kept alive by the action of humanitar-

148

ian intervention. Save for rare exceptions, refugees see themselves refused any local political or legal integration: the only alternative offered them can be summed up as either passive submission to humanitarian assistance or the quest for illegal solutions and channels. The passive refugee is the norm; the active refugee is a scandalous hypothesis: at the most, he or she is allowed to seek a right to life illegally.

What is true at the level of social integration is also true at that of political existence. Under the humanitarian regime, human rights and civic duties are dissociated and even become incompatible. Civil rights are in principle tied to membership of a nation-state, but the refugees' states of origin are generally in crisis – and it is precisely the conjuncture here (a society in meltdown, war or internal violence) that leads the civilian population to flee and places them in the net of humanitarian intervention. Through this flight and change of context, the relationship between citizenship and humanity is turned upside down. The experience of refugees literally underlies the question of what universal human rights people effectively have access to if they lose the use of their national citizenship?

The police and humanitarian treatment of refugees thus applies two modes of exclusion from citizenship: exclusion of the placeless on a world scale; exclusion of the right-less – those without the rights of citizenship – on the local and national scale. But we need only shift the representation that we make for ourselves of the refugee and vulnerable populations, from the 'humanitarian stage' where they find themselves confined to the 'democratic stage', to see that some behaviour ceases to be scandalous and misplaced. It is then understandable how forms of politics can emerge in the extremely unlikely space formed by the camps.[2]

Here we shall consider two categories of initiative on the part of refugees in the camps: demands targeting the NGOs and UN agencies; and strategies and conflicts around the winning of representative functions, on the basis of which refugees come to 'speak out'. In both cases, negotiating the status of 'vulnerability' is at the centre of repoliticizing the context.

Camps, vulnerability, politics

In the life of the camps, screenings are constantly made by the UNHCR and NGOs with a view to the distribution of aid, these being experienced by the refugees either as benefits to be gained or exclusions to avoid. It is interesting to note that the categories of vulnerability officially recognized by the UNHCR (fifteen in all)[3] are defined by a broad spectrum distinguishing physical causes from social ones. The vulnerability counted and recognized by the organizations running the camps concerns above all the social conditions bound up with the state of war and exodus. This is what is observed, for example, when we examine the figures for the vulnerable in the Boreah camp, one of the three camps around Kissidougou in the Forest Region of Guinea.[4] The categories of vulnerable population are common to all the UNHCR establishments throughout the world, but they are represented to different extents in each camp. Just taking the Boreah camp (7,500 refugees), there are 1,140 persons viewed as 'vulnerable', i.e. 15 per cent of the total.[5] These break down, in increasing order, into seven categories of vulnerability used here:

Mentally ill	12
Unaccompanied minors	51
Separated children	83
Physically handicapped	92
Single elderly people	104
Single women	115
Single parents	683
Total	1,140

(Data from UNHCR, Boreah camp, October 2003)

Physical handicap represents 8 per cent of the total vulnerable. If we exclude the category of 'mentally ill' (1 per cent), which is highly heterogeneous and fails to take into account the psychological traumas bound up with the experience of war and flight from violence, we see that vulnerability characterized as a social trait affects 1,036 individuals, or 91 per cent of the vulnerable total. It is thus a condition that changes over time: often a consequence of the state of war, it can disappear with the social organization of life in the camp. Thus a widowed woman finds a new spouse who also arrived alone; a lone child is taken in by a family, etc. But a condition described as vulnerable in the camp may also not be a direct effect of the war (physical handicap, single parent, etc.), which only makes responsibility for this person more difficult. Vulnerability is thus a negotiable status, as we shall see from the example of a movement of women refugees.

In the same camp of Liberian and Sierra Leonese refugees at Boreah, women refugees from Sierra Leone demonstrated one day in late

Plate 1 Aerial view of Zone 12 of the refugee camp at Kuankan (Guinea, 2002)
© MSF

Plate 2 A displaced persons' camp in Liberia
© Geneviève Libeau / MSF Liberia

Plate 3 UNHCR refugee camps, displaced persons' camps and transit centres in the Mano River region (2003)

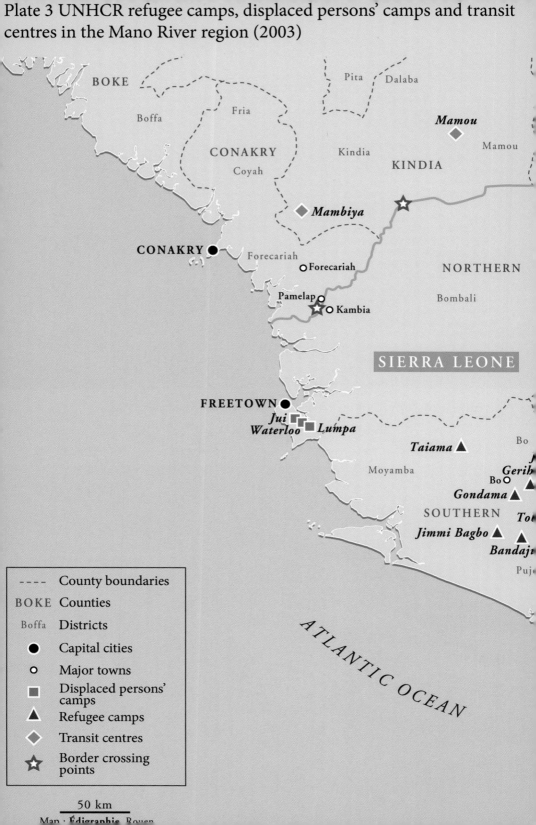

BOKE

Boffa

CONAKRY

Coyah

Fria

Mambiya ◆

Pita   Dalaba

Kindia

KINDIA

Mamou ◆

Mamou

☆

CONAKRY ●

Forecariah

○ Forecariah

Pamelap ○
☆ ○ Kambia

NORTHERN

Bombali

SIERRA LEONE

FREETOWN ●

Jui ■
Waterloo ■ *Lumpa*

Taiama ▲

Bo

Moyamba

Gerih ○
Bo ○   ▲
Gondama ▲

SOUTHERN   *To...*

Jimmi Bagbo ▲   ▲
Bandaj...

Puj...

ATLANTIC OCEAN

---- County boundaries
BOKE Counties
Boffa Districts
● Capital cities
○ Major towns
■ Displaced persons' camps
▲ Refugee camps
◆ Transit centres
☆ Border crossing points

50 km

Map · **Édigraphie** Rouen

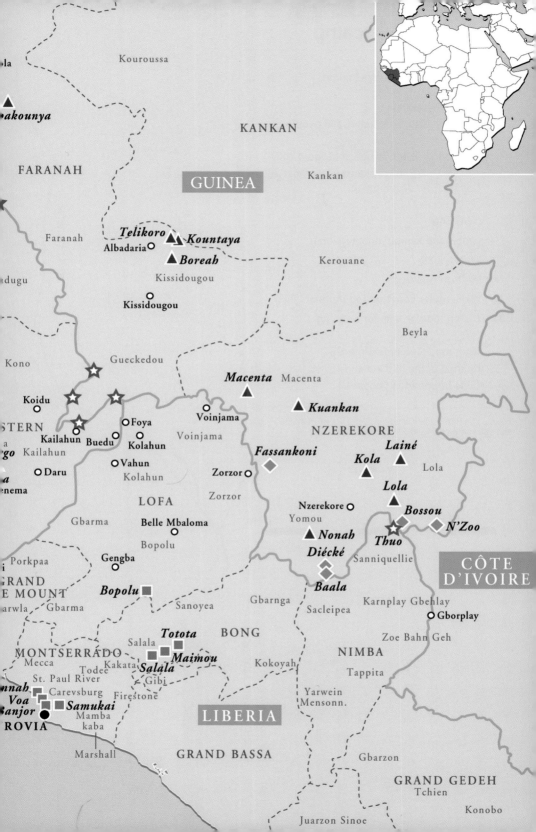

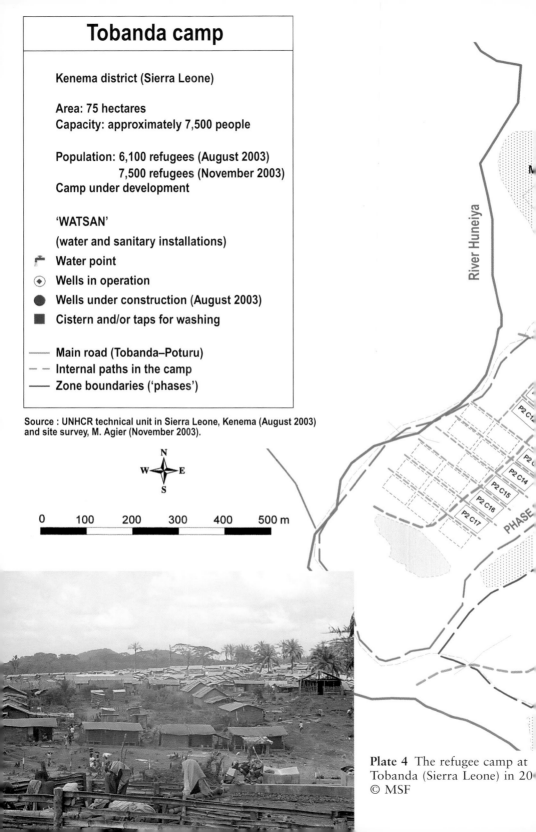

Tobanda camp

Kenema district (Sierra Leone)

Area: 75 hectares
Capacity: approximately 7,500 people

Population: 6,100 refugees (August 2003)
7,500 refugees (November 2003)
Camp under development

'WATSAN'
(water and sanitary installations)

🚰 Water point

⊙ Wells in operation

● Wells under construction (August 2003)

■ Cistern and/or taps for washing

—— Main road (Tobanda–Poturu)
– – Internal paths in the camp
—— Zone boundaries ('phases')

Source : UNHCR technical unit in Sierra Leone, Kenema (August 2003)
and site survey, M. Agier (November 2003).

N
W ⊕ E
S

0   100   200   300   400   500 m

River Huneiya

P2 C1
P2 C
P2 C14
P2 C15
P2 C16
P2 C17
PHASE

Plate 4 The refugee camp at
Tobanda (Sierra Leone) in 20
© MSF

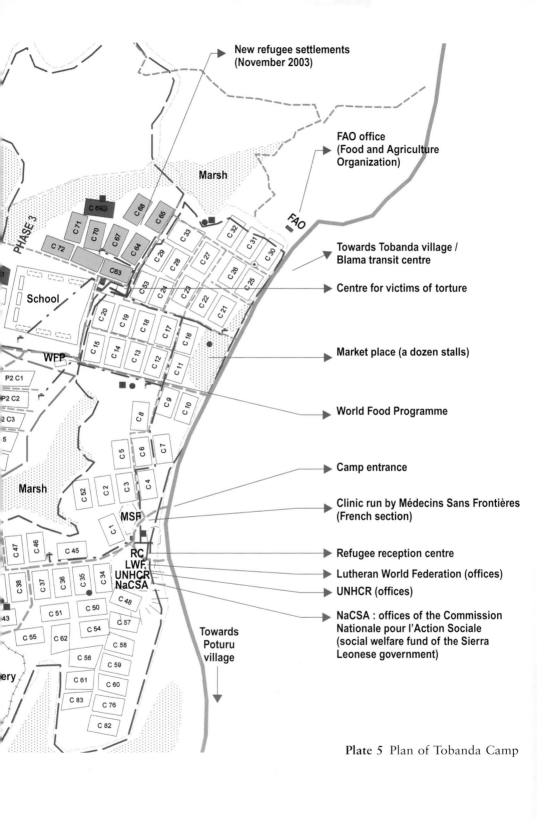

New refugee settlements
(November 2003)

FAO office
(Food and Agriculture
Organization)

Marsh

FAO

Towards Tobanda village /
Blama transit centre

Centre for victims of torture

School

Market place (a dozen stalls)

WFP

World Food Programme

Marsh

Camp entrance

MSF

Clinic run by Médecins Sans Frontières
(French section)

RC
LWF
UNHCR
NaCSA

Refugee reception centre

Lutheran World Federation (offices)

UNHCR (offices)

Towards
Poturu
village

NaCSA : offices of the Commission
Nationale pour l'Action Sociale
(social welfare fund of the Sierra
Leonese government)

PHASE 3

Plate 5 Plan of Tobanda Camp

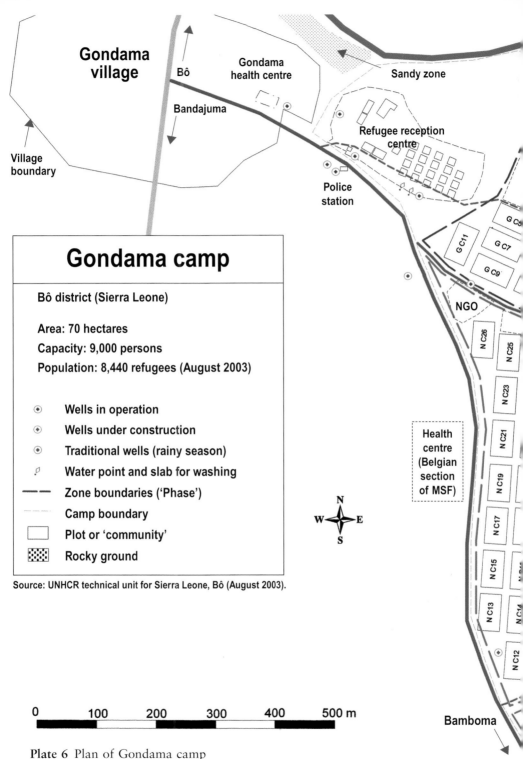

Plate 6 Plan of Gondama camp

Plate 7 New arrivals in the Maheba camp (Zambia, 2000) © Pascal Freneaux, MSF

Plate 8 Plan of Maheba, a UNHCR refugee camp in Zambia (July 2002)

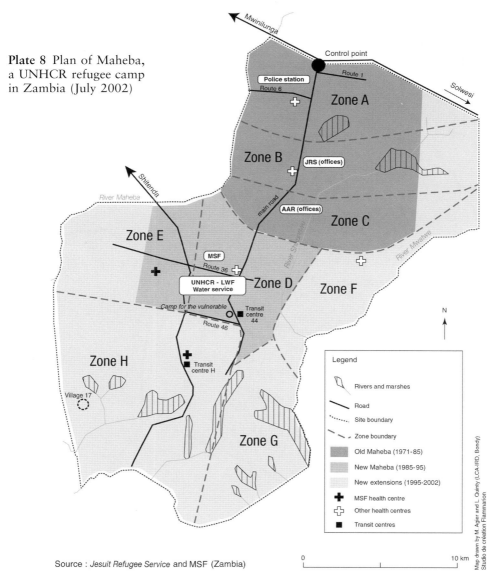

Mwinilunga

Control point

Police station

Route 1

Route 6

Zone A

Solwesi

Zone B

JRS (offices)

AAR (offices)

Zone C

River Maheba

Shitenda

main road

River Mwatwe

Zone E

MSF

Route 36

River Shi...

UNHCR - LWF
Water service

Zone D

Zone F

Camp for the vulnerable

Transit
centre
44

Route 46

N

Zone H

Transit
centre H

Village 17

Zone G

Legend

Rivers and marshes

Road

Site boundary

Zone boundary

Old Maheba (1971-85)

New Maheba (1985-95)

New extensions (1995-2002)

MSF health centre

Other health centres

Transit centres

Map drawn by M. Agier and L. Quinty (LCA-IRD, Bondy)
Studio de création Flammarion

Source : *Jesuit Refugee Service* and MSF (Zambia)

0   10 km

August 2003. Some fifty of them gathered on the main roadway through the camp, and in the late afternoon forcibly detained NGO vehicles that were heading for the exit. It was the rainy season: at this time, violent storms and heavy rain often last the whole night. The walls of the camp housing are mud, the framework is wattle, and the roofs are straw. In this season, the interior soon gets wet: floor, mats, mattresses, clothing. A month earlier, when the rain was strongest, the walls of one house collapsed while a child was asleep inside. Other shelters suffered the same fate in the following days. At the same time, the UNHCR was distributing plastic sheets to newly arrived refugees, who had mostly come from Liberia, leaving the longest-established, who had been in the camp nearly three years, without protection. A group of women – exiled from their country for between five and ten years, and living alone with their children after the disappearance or death of their spouses – then came together to ask the UNHCR for plastic sheets. They explicitly made clear their 'vulnerability': as we saw, the categories 'single woman' and 'single parent' are the most common categories among those that the UNHCR views as vulnerable. They opened a breach through which demands from the refugees could pass in the name of a 'vulnerability' that is ambiguous from the point of view of the UNHCR and the humanitarian organizations: generic for the external legitimization of humanitarian action, excluding for internal management. In fact, in relation to the surrounding population, whether local or global, vulnerability is what characterizes the target population of humanitarianism and legitimizes its existence. This population is far more numerous than just those people suffering a physical fragility. All refugees in the camp are 'vulnerable' from this – external – point of view. Internally, as we have seen, the refugees have to confront a diversity of criteria and classes of vulnerability to justify their demands for rights – among them, in this case, the right to shelter.

Faced with the UNHCR's refusal to meet their demand, the widowed and separated women demonstrated in the rain, along with their children, and stopped some NGO vehicles that happened to be driving along the main road through the camp at that time. Their number increased, and their boldness as well. They chanted: 'We want sheeeting!' The occupants of one car were pulled out of their vehicle 'so they could see what it's like to be under the rain', as the movement's leader later explained. The refugees asked for a written commitment to obtaining plastic sheeting for them. The humanitarian officials protested that this did not fall under their remit, and that they wanted to continue their own assistance work, but the women

151

had a radical reply to this: 'We see you all as NGO workers, just like you see us all as refugees.' Against the idea of compassion doled out case by case, which frustrated any right to make a claim, they proposed a meeting between two different worlds: that of the 'UNs' (generally White representatives of the UN agencies and NGOs) and that of their 'beneficiaries', the refugees.

The women then blocked a Red Cross vehicle and detained its occupants until, after several hours' discussion, they obtained a reply from the departmental prefect as well as the local representative of the Guinean office responsible for refugees (the Bureau de Coordination des Réfugiés), which agreed to receive a delegation from the demonstrators. They obtained their sheeting in the days that followed this meeting between four of them and the prefect.

The leader of the movement had been a refugee for five and a half years, and had lived in the Boreah camp since its opening in early 2001. A seller of clothes in Sierra Leone, she had fled the war with her seven children in 1998: her husband had been seized by the rebel forces, who had also killed her eldest son, aged about twelve. Five years later, she is a trader in the little marketplace of this Guinean camp, selling each day cooked meals of rice with sauce. Her elder daughters help her – twins of sixteen. She was also assisted, both in settling in the camp and in the market, by a man who is the father of her eighth child. She is involved in various occupational training activities organized by NGOs in the camp, and represents 'vulnerable' women even though she herself has more or less risen out of extreme vulnerability. She has managed to reorganize her existence in the Boreah camp, which is the third UNHCR camp she has lived in since 1998. She feels stable there and does not wish to be repatriated to Sierra Leone. A few days before the demonstration of 23 August, she had herself received the plastic sheet for her roof, but she says that she had not installed it out of solidarity with the other women, and suspecting the UNHCR of having given her personal satisfaction so as to disarm her and thus break up the movement of which she was the principal inspirer.

Food tactics and strategies

Boycotting the food ration, or diverting it, are two types of survival action that refugees take in the face of the insufficient quantity, inadequate composition, or simply bad quality of the rations distributed in the camps. Boycotting the distribution is a collective action. The other more widespread action, though seemingly individual, also has substantial effects from the point of view of the resocialization of refugees: this consists in reselling a part of the ration received, so as to be able to purchase, in the camp or outside, foods with the vitamins that are lacking – vegetables, fruit, fish, meat.

Protest actions of this type have occurred in the refugee camps of Dadaad in north-eastern Kenya.[6] In June 2000, there was a boycott in protest at the poor quality of certain products in the food ration, during which a group of refugees informed the BBC World Service so that their action would be known of throughout East Africa.[7] We can also note how a few months earlier a strike lasting several days had been organized by those refugees employed with the NGOs as voluntary workers, with a view to obtaining an increase in their monthly remuneration – unofficial in so far as the refugees have no right under Kenyan law to work or receive a wage.

In Guinea in 2004, while repatriation operations for the Liberians living in the camps were being prepared, the UNHCR census takers were met with a barrage of stones. I have already mentioned this event[8] in connection with the conflicts over the counting and filtering of refugees, but will return to it again here. That day, not only was a dissonant voice expressed on the humanitarian stage, but also there was a violent confrontation between the refugees and the agents of the international organizations, both sides 'negotiating' their respective positions in a space that was certainly common to them both, but highly contradictory.

Let us dwell first of all on the findings and commentary of the IRIN[9] document of July 2004:

NZÉRÉKORÉ, 22 July 2004 (IRIN) – Tens of thousands of Liberians who have registered as refugees in neighbouring Guinea are abusing their status by crossing the border to trade their food rations and prepare their eventual return before returning to their camps for the next handout, aid workers said. Strictly speaking, someone who can enter his or her own country without fear does not need to be protected and should not be getting UN refugee assistance. Aid workers admit that this unofficial flow of food across the border is probably helping to keep thousands of needy people fed in outlying districts of war-ravaged Liberia, where rebel gunmen still control the border. Recent attempts to clamp down on wandering Liberian refugees by counting the population that is actually resident in four official refugee camps in Guinea's south-eastern Forest Region have sparked violence. Cars have been being smashed and UN workers stoned[10] as aid workers try to check their suspicions that the real number of Liberian refugees in the country is well below the official figure of 90,750, on which current aid levels are based. 'We have been completely manipulated by some of the refugees', said Cesar Pastor-Ortega, head of the refugee agency UNHCR in Nzérékoré, the capital of the Forest Region. 'By our own estimates we think that around 80,000 refugees have already made at least a partial return to Liberia, with about 35,000 part-time resident in Voinjama alone', he said.

Pastor-Ortega told IRIN that in early June he was personally attacked by stone-throwing residents of Kouankan refugee camp, less than 100 km from the Liberian border, as a UN team tried to conduct its first head-count in the camp for two years. "That day at Kouankan, I was frightened', he added. 'It was the first time... Before that there were no such security problems.' 'Food is very important for refugees. As soon as they know they won't get food any more things can turn ugly', said one UNHCR security agent at Kounkan as he waited for the head-count there to resume. Another humanitarian worker in Nzérékoré painted a similar picture. 'There are a lot (of refugees) who come and go, though they are ready to fight to keep their food intake or their shelter in Guinea', he said. Refugee cards which entitle the bearer to food packages were on sale to the highest bidder, he added.

Back in the regional capital Nzérékoré, Pastor-Ortega complained that many Liberians only crossed into Guinea in the hope of claiming a refugee card for the benefits which it conferred. Many UN aid workers say the fraud involved in aid distribution to refugees has become so widespread that the situation is no longer tenable. 'All the food has gone to the markets, in Guinea and of course in Liberia', one WFP official in Guinea told IRIN. 'They diverted the aid, but now we have financial problems and cannot continue like this. Too many of them are fraudsters.'

Conducting the census is a fraught business. At Lainé[11] refugee camp, a visiting IRIN correspondent saw tempers boil over as UNHCR workers tried to establish who was a genuine Liberian refugee deserving assistance, and who was making fraudulent claims.

'Get out!' an aid worker yelled at one man. 'You're lying, you think you're very funny? It's impossible! This is the second time I've seen you, only now you don't have the same wife! And these children are not yours! You're cheating me!' Less than one kilometre away, Liberian refugees could be found selling their food packages at the local market.[12]

This scene of conflict, including its forms of verbal or physical violence, displays a disagreement – subjects acting *against* what is dictated by their assigned identity of refugees/victims/vulnerable. This disagreement seems initially to involve a 'misunderstanding' (from the point of view of the humanitarian official), or, more accurately, a conflict of interpretation of humanitarian language; it is by way of this conflict that the protest is expressed. A few comments here will enable us to pinpoint the issues involved in this type of action and the tensions around it, which are by no means uncommon in the refugee camp context.

Refugees are adopted by national or international NGOs and UN agencies in the name of human rights, and these take responsibility for them as pure victims, as if they owed their survival simply to the fact of no longer being present in the world, i.e. being de-socialized and in a state of purely biological life – a life that the representatives of the international community decide to extend rather than let it extinguish. Defined in this way, the condition of refugee breaks the relationship between man and citizen. This is substantially what the philosopher Giorgio Agamben notes when he says that for refugees 'the rights of the citizen are now progressively separated from and used outside the context of citizenship'.[13] In fact, this hypothesis is only effective if it stimulates empirical research – *a contrario* – into situations in which politics emerges in the most improbable spaces, and particularly refugee camps. For we can see on all sides that, even if the space experienced by the refugees is a priori an out-place and a vacuum, on the sociological and political level it is full of relationships.[14] These relationships are created by the humanitarian intervention and the formation of a specific space–time for the refugees – an intervention and space–time diverted from their initial functions, as witness the tensions described in the IRIN document reproduced above.

To act and speak out in their places of exile means for the refugees rejecting the principle of their 'vulnerability' as justifying their treatment as nameless pure victims. From this is born the only revolt that is logically possible, one embodying a politics of resistant life. The boycott actions, just like the siphoning off of food rations, from this point of view occupy the same political stage, the former being more collective (demanding time, stability and organization) whereas the latter is more individual, rapid and spontaneous. Diversion of food is more tactical in nature, the boycotts more strategic. In each case, however, if we want to account for the refugee situation in all its complexity, and particularly the refugees' political existence, it is impossible simply to tie the question of political rights to that of national citizenship. Other spaces emerge, in this age of globalization and the local interventions by the 'international community', and these become sites of a political expression of a new type, which are invented and acted out in and on the limits.

From victim to subject

In parallel with their material construction, refugee camps form themselves into social and political milieus. Very often this process is visible only after the event, when these camps have become over time something like projected towns left in a state of abandonment, or more generally spaces of identification for those people who have lived there for years, even decades – who have been born there, married there, and buried their dead. This transformation is also visible in a beginning of political life, when leaders emerge and become, officially or not, spokespeople for the refugees, even if they do not immediately want to be recognized in this imposed collective identity. It is they who, at the end of the day, champion the position of the 'vulnerable', whatever their own material condition – and even if it is precisely their relatively better condition in comparison to the majority of refugees that enables them to exercise this leadership. This is the moment, that of speaking out 'in the name of the refugees' (all 'vulnerable'), that politics is introduced into the camp, and with it a bit of citizenship. This is illustrated by the strategies of various refugees whom we met with in the Tobanda camp in Sierra Leone.

This camp held 7,500 Liberian refugees in November 2003. Opened six months before, it was the most recent of the eight camps opened since 2001 in the Bô region of south-eastern Liberia, which house a total of 55,000 refugees.[15]

There are conflicts in this camp over the official representation of the refugees to the camp administration.[16] The election of the 'chairman', the refugees' spokesman and representative, was challenged several times during the first six months of the camp's existence. There was first of all an indirect election, with the electors being something over 100 persons: the tent heads of the first 1,500 arrivals. Then there was a direct election, when the camp had reached a population of around 5,000, in which every adult dropped a voting slip in a ballot box – in the course of which, we were told, certain frauds took place. This election was annulled by the camp administration – not, however, because of fraud, but because the 'chairman' who was elected threatened the tranquillity of the camp. According to certain people, he was suspected of seeking to launch 'riots', according to others of stoking up 'tribal quarrels'. The administration deposed him and nominated in his place an 'acting chairman', postponing any new election indefinitely. This acting chairman, a man in his thirties, had little formal education (as distinct from the usual

156

young leaders), no experience of representation, and an often aggressive and biased attitude towards the other refugees. A virulent supporter of Charles Taylor, he had no active support among the refugees, but he seemed to the camp administrators (for whom he occasionally worked) sufficiently collaborative to assist them in the function of control. In fact, under the pressure of the refugee leaders, the 'acting chairman' steadily found himself substituted by other representatives in his function of spokesperson for the refugees. This did not spur the administration to organize new elections.

At least twenty or so refugees exercise various kinds of influence that they try to 'fix' in the social and political system of the camp that is coming into being. This influence is generally based on male functions of relative prestige, or a power already acquired:[17] pastors and preachers of Christian churches (Pentecostal, in particular, whose number in the camp is rapidly growing); NGO staff working in the camp; leaders of the camp's 'communities'.[18] There is a doubling-up of powers – economic, religious, political – and at the end of the day those in a position to speak 'in the name of the refugees' are the least 'vulnerable' among them. This does not mean, however, that what they say is 'untrue'. It is the very principle of representation, of speaking 'in the name of . . .' in a specific scenario of speaking out, that is at work here, and that enables a political subject to be formed. In this enlivening of the internal space of the camp, the humanitarian stage becomes an unforeseen political one. In fact, representation takes place according to an active modality of 'subjectification' – a modality quite distinct from that of representation in the sense of a representativity of the refugees as a category. In this latter modality, the human rights of the beneficiaries of aid are automatically ascribed, by those bodies managing the humanitarian assistance, on the basis of assigned identities, whether these are general ('refugees') or particular (various 'vulnerable categories'). Human rights of this kind disappear as soon as the local humanitarian government is interrupted by decision of the UN and aid agencies. The refugees are then victims twice over: of the war and forced displacement that led them there; and then of their political powerlessness in the face of the power of the humanitarian organizations over their lives.

Here again, then, the distinction between the figures of active (unforeseen) and passive refugees (envisaged even if occasionally criticized) is determining. It is a question of the transformation of the victim into a subject. A single example is enough to explain this, though certainly not enough to give it a thorough response. I transcribed this while making some notes in the field. They show the personal impression that one of these leaders casts around him – particularly on his European interlocutor – while offering some preliminary questions for a political ethnography of the camp.

'All refugees are vulnerable'

Tobanda camp, Bô, Sierra Leone, 18 November 2003

Tom M. is forty-five years old. He was born in Lofa (the region most affected by the war), then moved to Monrovia where he worked first of all in the port. He then began dealing in diamonds, buying them at the Esewé Diamond Camp and selling them in Monrovia. 'The war did not stop me working', he says; 'Even with the rebels there, people carried on working.' He was able to conduct his trade in diamonds by paying off the soldiers and rebels who taxed him on the road.

He left Monrovia in January 2003 to go and collect his mother, who was living in a different region. On his return, he was unable to enter the city because of the war. He made for the Sierra Leonese border, at the crossing point of K. He was threatened there by Taylor's soldiers: they beat him (he points out scars on his body, chest and shoulder, though I have trouble making them out) until he gave them all the money he had on him. But they did not find the diamonds he had hidden in his belt – a fact that he proudly illustrates to the fifteen or so people who surround us during this conversation. He lifts up the belt that he wears round his trousers, and shows on the inside the little pocket that served as a hiding-place.

After crossing the border, he reached the 'way station' at Zimmi, then that of Dauda, the classic trajectory of recent refugees from Monrovia. He arrived here, at the Tobanda camp, in April 2003. He is the 'community leader' of a sector including more than twenty refugee dwellings. 'Here at the Tobanda camp everyone is poor', he says. 'There is no possibility of doing business.' He sold his diamonds to a Lebanese dealer in Bô, the main town in the region, which is why he still has money. He is better established than the average refugee: his wooden hut has two storeys and a lock; there is a verandah in front with a number of chairs, a hammock and a small machine for grinding the American bulgur wheat from the food ration, which belongs to him and which his neighbours use regularly for free.

158

Tom M. makes the interview difficult, because, taking his friends and neighbours as witnesses, he protests – rather than just complaining about – at the conditions of life in the camp. The food is not sufficient; very few people receive the promised covers ('sixty covers were embezzled', he says, 'and sold outside the camp by a [Sierra Leonese] policeman from the camp, who was arrested by a [refugee] volunteer from the security service'); there are not enough toilets, constant problems with the plastic sheeting, etc. He says: 'The Whites and the Sierra Leonese are together against us. We want to leave.' Seeking to question him more on his life story, I tell him that I can well understand his demands but I have no power to answer them, these are questions for the UNHCR people. Then he replies to me, in front of friends and neighbours who are already more numerous than an hour ago and enthusiastically agree: 'You're White, you know the organizations, the UNs, so you should answer them.'

I suddenly feel that things are going to get awkward! I'm not sure of being on firm ground here. But the lesson is an interesting one. On the one hand, I understand and approve of all the protests, demands and claims that have been made, in so far as they are formulated not as complaints but as rights – even if this man sometimes speaks about the 'vulnerable' in order to justify the demand for covers and protests against the embezzlement of aid (the 'old and vulnerable', he says, 'really don't need this'). But then he also says that 'all the refugees are vulnerable', confirming by this his public persona, and publicly setting the tone of an ideological challenge to the principles of the humanitarian organizations, removing the gloss of self-evidence from their compassion towards the victims.

On the other hand, I note that it is the least badly off who are sharpest and most demanding in their contacts: the tone of the 'businessman' Tom M., like that of other 'community' and religious leaders, is generally aggressive when it is a question of the camp administration and the Whites. Their demands are well informed, and they occupy the position of spokesperson. One might imagine that they have lost more than the others in their forced displacement and exile; but, more than anything, they have not lost the awareness of their social value on the labour and consumer markets. There is no trace of the supposed 'tribal quarrels' that the camp administrators accuse them of in order to delegitimize them.

159

At that moment in front of the house of Tom M. – a businessman and refugee leader who is aggressive and rather unsympathetic, increasingly surrounded and approved of by the neighbours from his sector – I really do believe I had the experience of a 'democratic stage' at a humanitarian site! A stage that is precisely political – apparently out of place but completely real all the same, the most immediate conflict to my mind deriving from the fact that I perceived a misunderstanding about my own role, whereas my interlocutors, for their part, did not at all seem to share that point of view.

—— 9 ——

Who Will Speak Out in the Camp?
A Study of Refugees' Testimony

Throughout the present study I have reconstituted the stories of the refugees I met in their camps by way of prolonged interviews with them, learning to place individual and local stories in the national or regional contexts more or less well known to people interested in these regions at war.

These exchanges have taken place at a distance from the violent events to which they testify; indeed, the context of my reflection is a study that is both within and about the humanitarian spaces. The violence that my interlocutors experienced was known to me only through the stories that I requested ('tell me what happened to you, how did you come to be here?'). In this way I found myself faced with people who had survived episodes of war and violence, having fled when the arrival of armed groups was announced, whether these were government, rebel or private forces. They had known moments of fear and wandering, extreme conditions of life with their lot of sickness and injury, and been close to the death of their loved ones. This violence may have been already well in the past (several years, or even decades in the case of the Angolan and Palestinian refugees), or else very recent and present to mind (a few months, even weeks, as was the case with the Liberian refugees).

If these experiences of violence are fairly similar on the whole, I found on the contrary a wide diversity of forms of account: chaotic statements, collective reconstructions from memory of a particular event, long coherent monologues that were repeated several times, a 'book' of testimony written by a group of literary refugees who had interviewed others, refusal or silence, etc. Here I shall present a number of examples of evidence collected in the camps, and broadly compare their form and content. From speech that was

161

almost impossible to a worked-out and collective form of 'writing down',[1] we see an evolution in the form of evidence that I have been trying to understand.

The point, in fact, is not to challenge the actual 'truth' of the facts related, but rather one of a gradual shift in meaning, from evidence defined in the context of humanitarian and police 'screenings', through to the speaking out by which a subject of speech becomes author and is thus released from the assigned identity of victim which is affixed to the memory of suffering.[2] If speech conceived as testimony is still informed by the requirement of constructing 'credible' accounts, normative and controlled, speaking out is the means of bringing subjects into being, i.e. authors detached from an identity essentially associated with suffering. Our attention can then be directed to the testimony itself (testimony as event, if you like), as the construction of a mode of speech that has its own contexts and issues, its own forms and authors.[3] We shall do this by returning to the camps in Guinea, Sierra Leone and Zambia.

Feeling fear, speaking forgiveness, preparing return

'I crossed the Sierra Leone border at Buedu on 12 January', says Mr L., a Liberian refugee who has lived in the Jembé camp in Sierra Leone for two and a half years. Like the majority of his compatriots, he gives the date and the month of his journey, but it takes a little while before he recalls, at my request, the year of this event, and still longer until he gives the name of the rebel or governmental forces that made him flee. He can recall the name of the villages and hamlets that he passed, but not the length of time he was fleeing through the 'bush' – until we manage to make an estimate together: five months in the forest, perhaps six. Nor does he recall the name of the international NGO that took him in on the other side of the border – him and his family.

The memories and forgettings of Mr L. are not an isolated case among refugees hailing from the Lofa region of Liberia. The dates that these Liberian refugees remember are personal anniversaries. They remember when they left their village for the first time – during the 'first war', some of them say rather vaguely – between 1990 and 1996, at the time of the offensive by the forces led by Charles Taylor. They remember the 'second war' (1999–2003), i.e. the rebel attacks against Taylor's forces, which took over the government after the elections of 1997 when there was a brief return of peace. They can state the day on which they crossed the border, the day that they arrived at the 'way station', then reached this or that camp in Sierra Leone. These are events inscribed in their personal history. It is harder to inscribe them in a collective and national history, though it is in this history that these events occurred. Almost all the Liberian refugees that I met experienced the same difficulty in 'settling' on a geo-political commentary. The official discourse of the war – with its precise dates, the advances or defeats of its protagonists identified by their respective acronyms, the occupation or 'pacification' of different regions, the good and the bad – only coincides very approximately with the personal experiences related by the women and men whom I met in the camps of Sierra Leone and Guinea a few months after the signature of a peace agreement in Liberia (August 2003). This might reinforce the idea that it is hard for them to make sense of the events. But is this really the case? Is there not a social meaning that escapes political discourse – or at least is formed outside of this?

In October 2003, in the Kuankan camp in the Forest Region of Guinea,[4] Hassan (my guide, the MSF 'home visitor') and people from the camp, knowing that I wanted to meet people who had had contact with the belligerents, took me to a young girl of fifteen who had come from Liberia. During her flight she was taken charge of by a male refugee from her home village, who has been for the last few months the leader of this new zone in the camp, Zone 12.

She lives in a tiny dark room. During our meeting she often remained silent, speaking only a few words at a time in a low voice. People around her tried to help her express herself. Her story was reconstituted with the help of people who were there: the attack on the village by the LURD forces; everyone fled; her father was killed; then she was captured by an armed band of Taylor's forces; a new attack by the LURD enabled her to escape from her captors; it was during this flight that her mother disappeared; our interviewee was then caught by another group of Taylor's forces; she was compelled to transport weapons, then to 'take up arms' under threat; but she refused, she says, to fight; the soldiers took her, abused her, tortured her (the people around us asked her to show me the traces of this on her body, which she did); she asked pardon from the soldiers; then she was raped by four men; she remained there for a few more days, until an attack by the LURD forces during which everyone ran away, and it was then that my guide, the leader of Zone 12, met up with her and took her with his own family to Guinea and the Kuankan camp.

In a psychological approach this young girl would be perceived as a case of 'trauma', and it is as someone 'traumatized' that she was introduced to me by refugees who were in regular contact with the NGOs: the head of the zone, the occasional workers. But her story can also be interpreted by expanding the perspective to the overall situation of the interview: three other refugees were with her and helped to tell her tale. Bit by bit, a brief history began to emerge, conveyed by the commentaries of other individuals present during the violence of the most recent episodes in the Liberian war (2002–3). The spontaneous reaction to her is a desire to help her: from trying to measure the suffering she experienced and lacking terms to describe the incomparable horror, one also imagines all the rights she could claim if this was given as testimony. This compassion gave rise in me, as in her compatriots, to a desire to help her to express better what had happened to her. That is precisely what is done by the NGOs who have specialized in the formulation and writing of testimonies by people seeking asylum in Europe.

The attempted interpretations that the Liberian refugees make of a war that they experienced at first hand, in their own person, may not tally with the demands for justice and reparations put forward in the sphere of the media and political organizations of the 'international community'. To sum up, it emerges from these interviews that the Liberian refugees are still afraid of their war, that they are trying to forget it, that they want to pardon all the crazy fighters, and above all to restore order in their country.

The field notes that I have transcribed below make no other claim than to share my own discovery: the refugees' active desire to wipe out their sufferings – and the understanding that one gradually comes to from contact with them, which thus makes it possible to explain and relativize, without suppressing, the strong impression of trauma left by the young woman in Kuankan.

Brief notes from a field diary in the Tobanda camp (Sierra Leone)

Tobanda camp, Bô, Sierra Leone, 6 November 2003

In this war, with no clear image of friend and enemy, the people who speak of atrocities identify the authors of these as drunken, drugged, or crazy – very often they speak of them like dangerous and uncontrollable children. These people – victims from the time they were displaced and wounded, or saw at close hand the death of loved ones – are ready to forgive when they use these terms. They are not in the register of 'truth, justice and reconciliation', as in the case of post-apartheid South Africa or the aftermath of the Rwandan genocide. It may also be that, being seen as a war 'without cause' or responsibility (not even on the part of the murderers, though of course their accomplices have still to be judged), this war has merely been interrupted, and not definitively ended. I have the impression that these people in the camp have not emerged from the mental state of the war; they feel it inside them as a fact of social degradation, not externally as a political fact. The way in which the official 'chairman' and his assistant quoted me from Taylor's speech against the 'international community' makes this clear: Taylor wasn't given a chance, the international community abandoned Liberia and Taylor had to draw on his personal funds to help the country, pay teachers, etc.

8 November 2003. Mr R. is the head of the 'small grievances committee' in the camp. Before the war he worked as a court clerk in Liberia. His attitude is certainly that of a judge, but it is perhaps only the most developed formulation of an attitude that one can confirm in the case of the Liberian refugees in general: an attitude in which fear and forgiveness alternate, an attitude more subjective than objective, formed in the proximity of war. Fear is visible when we speak of the possible presence of 'ex-fighters' in the camp (there certainly are some of these; he spotted one and tried to investigate him before he disappeared); forgiveness, since there is no precisely identifiable enemy, ethnic or political, for whom one would demand 'justice' before a reconciliation. The authors of the war – the 'fighters', whether 'rebel' or 'loyalist', and the militiamen assisting them – are often dangerous and uncontrollable people, and so there is a fear that they may reappear. But for the same reasons, one can only pardon them. In the name of what, or what principle, can justice be demanded? The economic and political degradation of an entire country is the cause of the loss of control: this requires no other 'cause' for which everyone would have to explain themselves.

I 'test' the apparent absence of ethnic or political hostility in the camp by reporting to some individuals that the young 'acting chairman' is ardently pro-Taylor, to which Joseph (a refugee from Lofa, who is my guide in the camp throughout this study) replies by explaining nicely that the 'chairman' comes from a region that had been spared and even defended by Charles Taylor's forces, and that he had been very active in the organizations established under his government. This, according to him, is what explains his partisan statements, as distinct from the works of those who suffered under Taylor. This absence of hostility is the mark of forgiveness.

12 November 2003. 'Reverend Moses' is the founder and head of a Pentecostal church established in Tobanda camp for the refugees, though he already had a chapel in Monrovia where he lived with his wife.

Reverend Moses's wife returned from Monrovia a few days ago. She is very enthusiastic. 'Monrovia is back', she tells me. Many people are leaving the camp, say Moses and his wife, like their neighbour opposite whose hut is now closed: he left for Robertsport (in the Cape Mount area). Both believe that the former government (pro-Taylor) forces will be disarmed and the whole army reorganized; all the former rebel groups will be integrated into the army with their own regions to control. They say that the Liberian police are working with the UN military forces: 'The marines are there.' 'With this president [the provisional president installed by the UN and the US administration after the fall of Taylor], things will be different.'

On her return from Monrovia, Moses's wife explains that their house and their church had been pillaged by neighbours. She saw some of these who were wearing her and her husband's clothes. The couple laugh it off: 'They think that we're dead, lost in the bush. It's normal. I told them: "Feel free."' The house itself was not destroyed. They don't contest the existence of the armed groups. In their speech there is a burgeoning enthusiasm to return.

20 November 2003. 'We wan go' has become the slogan circulating in the camp, since the demonstration by some 200 refugees outside the camp administration compound when the UN High Commissioner for Refugees, Ruud Lubbers, made a lightning visit just a week ago. I also heard it at Jembé, another camp. 'We wan go.' They want to return in January or February, like one person whose brother arrived at the Tobanda camp after having been to Foya (in the Lofa region of Liberia) to see how things were going, and while waiting was living at Buedu, a large village in Sierra Leone 15 kilometres from the Liberian border.

What will the refugees keep from their stay at Tobanda? What memories? What ideas? The whole population was more or less implicated in the war. They think rather in terms of forgiveness and social reconstruction. These two terms refer to various kinds of individual involvement that the refugees had in the war. According to the interviews I conducted, there are three different registers to consider: (1) the loyalism of the 'hunters', who responded to the demand of the government forces by offering them their skills; (2) the legitimacy of their defence of the forest against any invader;[5] (3) the recruitment, indoctrination and blindness that affected adolescents or younger children seeking groups and associations in their phase of transition to adult life. These different registers correspond to the differences between 'hunters' and 'fighters', between on the one hand the one-shot hunting rifle (this is how the traditional hunters who defended the territory and responded to the loyalist demand are identified) and, on the other hand, the Kalashnikov (people say 'AK 47', 'AK 48'): a differentiation that is not a condemnation but rather a social and generational distinction. On the basis of these significations (reversible according to the developing war situation), it is hard to see what demands for 'justice' and reparations would mean, since what these attitudes (found also in genocide and apartheid) correspond to in terms of identity is either absent here or largely superficial. It was only belatedly and very partially that all this acquired the air of a 'tribal war'.[6] But, according to the time of their exile and the region from which they came, people still fear a possible resumption of the war. This fear refers not to war in general, but to the horrors that accompanied it (and which they saw).

The way in which the Liberian refugees relate their experience of war is connected with the question of how to live together after the war. The accounts taken down in this camp and others, in Guinea and Sierra Leone, all indicate a strong relationship between the victims and their murderers, the civilian populations and the combatants – soldiers, militia and rebels. Many refugees, especially young men and women, were enrolled by force: the men to work for the armed forces – as 'slaves', some of them say; the women to serve as 'wives' after being captured in the bush and frequently raped; others, finally, to fight for the different groups – either being forced into this in the case of some of the young men captured, who fled as and when they could, or in a more voluntary way like the 'hunters' of the Lofa region in northern Liberia. The relationship of civilians to the war in which they were victims is not generally conceived as a political one. It is rather a social relationship under constraint, in which war became a personal matter, violently drawing in the 'civilian population'.

Between war and return, there are the camps, i.e. a space in which exchanges take place on what happened in the war – but the desire to forget is more spontaneous than the formation and upkeep of a collective memory, which assumes an individualized and painful effort to recall suffering.

In a further camp in the Bô region, Jimmi Bagbo – the 'chairman' elected by the refugees – undertook to consult his fellow citizens from Foya and discuss things with them. (Foya was one of the main places of origin for the refugees in the Sierra Leone camps at that time, i.e. 2003.) He organized meetings both in his own camp and in the others around. He proposed projects of 'social reconstruction'. With him, these projects were associated with attempts at a posteriori explanations aiming to justify pardoning the authors of war crimes. For example, as regards the pillage perpetrated by soldiers, he explains: 'The pillage is because the soldiers weren't paid, or because between Monrovia and Lofa their pay disappeared into the officers' pockets, or because they drank up very quickly what they earned, and afterwards they made the inhabitants pay. They stole their food, their goats, their animals. What is important now really is to re-integrate them.'

Forgiveness does not come by itself. It is associated with, and preceded by, a desire to forget, because authors and victims of violence are close to one another, either in terms of relationship or in their social or regional position. And it is followed and balanced by a desire to control, even strictly 'contain', and a desire for social reconstruction. These are the responses I hear repeated, as if my interlocutors were seeking to overcome the individual fears and the memory of collective panics aroused by several years of a war close at hand.

Keeping silent or speaking out

We can see from this last example how silence about atrocities witnessed or suffered derives from a deliberate attitude, which can be seen as the expression of a desire to forget. This is a strategy associated with the forgiveness of combatants who were most often young (the figure of the 'child soldier' remains emblematic of innocent error), sometimes socially close (same village, region or family) and often viewed as having been not in their right mind due to alcohol, drugs, etc. This attitude is also associated with a desire to return and rapidly reconstruct their ordinary life in the urban and rural zones that were devastated by the war. For the Liberian refugees, silence is not (or not just) individual and traumatic, it is also 'political', in the sense that keeping silent is designed to enable them to 'survive their memory',[7] to revive after a war of which every individual account, if it is effectively expressed, is marked by confusion and ambiguity. This duality is very present in experiences of the Liberian war, and leads to aporias in which silence seems to me a very reasonable outcome, in so far as I presume to judge the reasoning of my hosts: the victim is guilty not so much for having survived, but in a very direct sense for having done everything to survive. The experience of the young girls who were raped and went on to live with the soldiers or militia who violated them, that of the imprisoned villagers who became fighters, are stories of people who are not too clear whether and to what extent, after the war and in the eyes of the Law (the eyes of a state that has regained its sovereignty, or those of the 'international community'), they will be viewed as victims or culprits. Who could say all this fearlessly to a 'special tribunal' or a 'truth and justice commission'?

For the Liberians, therefore, it may be that the past, neither completely forgotten nor completely memorized, takes the form of a 'family secret'. And testimony does not fit well with this policy of silence. To use here an association that Paul Ricoeur suggests,[8] amnesty needs amnesia, at least for a while.

Why then speak out, when there are good reasons to keep silent? Another case, arising from the same war, gives this reflection a further nuance. Marayama was a woman in her forties, likewise Liberian, whom I met towards the end of 2003 in the Jembé camp in Sierra Leone. She had personally experienced several episodes of war and various forms of violence. Stories of successive flights, confrontations with armed groups, the disappearance of two of her children who were taken off by an armed gang, threats to her life and bodily injuries to herself (without mentioning rape) and her husband, fear, the difficult border crossing. She tells her story in a remarkably fluid fashion, at the same time informative and moving. The facts follow on from each other chronologically, details are offered without my

169

needing to ask for them. No one interrupts here. She speaks an English comprehensible to a European, as distinct from the Liberian pidgin that is most frequently heard in the camps.

Some significant elements in Marayama's trajectory help us to understand her attitude. She had previous experience of contact with European NGOs and even worked with these on several occasions during the Liberian war, in Ivory Coast and Guinea, where she lived for a number of years, generally in refugee camps. Her husband, who is in the Jembé camp with her and some of their children, has for many years been a Pentecostal preacher. Marayama takes part in the meetings of the church that he founded in the camp, called Abundant Life in Christ, and like others she speaks in public, when she wants to, of her experience of war, in sessions that are precisely called 'testimony'.[9] She herself compares these sessions with the meetings of an NGO specializing in the organization of encounters and dialogue between the victims of torture, meetings that she has taken part in two or three times in this camp, and that she finds less interesting than those of her church.

To sum up, what differentiates this last case from those previously described? We can say that Marayama's testimony, her elaboration and her force of conviction are the product both of her intellectual – and particularly linguistic – skills, in a family and religious context that has been preserved despite the displacement, and of her experiences of contact with European NGO staff, who were both interlocutors and shapers of her testimony. After fourteen years of war in Liberia, she is well accustomed to the ways of the camps and the humanitarian organizations.

The camp as a space of generalized testimony

In the Boreah camp in the Forest Region of Guinea, my study of the trajectories and living conditions of the refugees gradually turned into a space for speaking out, complaints, demands and, in part, requests for 'resettlement' on the part of the Sierra Leonese and Liberian refugees.[10] In this context, the form of direct study was diverted and given a new signification by certain interlocutors: the mere soliciting of speech from the refugees triggered an event.

From this point on, the notion of the testimony-event should be taken in a literal sense. The uncertainty of the ethnologist's status is patent, in the sense that my study, in the context of the camp, is a trigger for speech: the attempt to produce stories brings speech into being, at this very moment, as a generalized testimony and no longer just a series of singular accounts. During the last few days of my study, I received several written testimonies from refugees whom I did not have time to see. At this point my interpreter-guide and I had to establish our meeting-place in the small MSF office inside the camp clinic, instead of ourselves going round to the huts or tents occupied by the refugees, as we had done at the start of the project. Our office then came to be transformed into a kind of complaints bureau. The thirty or so letters I received from refugees (written either by these individuals themselves, or by others acting as public scribes) offered accounts that were certainly stereotyped, but all perfectly credible: the dates, place names and events mentioned fitted with well-known episodes in the war; the personal details were precise. Finally, the authors of these written testimonies were all well informed as to what they should say in order to be considered for resettlement: the impossibility of returning to their place of origin, and of remaining in the host country, justified their settlement in a third country for reasons of 'protection'.

In reaction to this event, almost a collective public 'demonstration', the attitude of two UNHCR representatives in charge of resettlement who were on a mission in that region at the same point in time is significant – both as a kind of outburst that I was able to verify myself, and beyond this in indicating the importance of testimony in deciding the fate of refugees. The local staff of the UNHCR maintained that they were 'deceived' and 'manipulated' by the refugees, which led to a general suspicion on their part regarding testimony of any kind. At that point in time (late 2003) the two representatives from the UNHCR head office announced that 4,000 resettlement places in a Western country were available for the refugees presently in Guinea, but at the same time made it a condition that the NGOs operating there would act as mediators between refugees and the UNHCR in order to determine for themselves cases of extreme and 'genuine' urgency that justified resettlement. The UNHCR thus decided to stop hearing refugees present their own testimonies, and only take into consideration the files forwarded to them by the NGOs. Certain NGOs operating in the Forest Region at that time, including MSF, refused to play this role of intermediary, on the grounds that it meant a change in the resettlement procedure, which is in principle the responsibility of the UNHCR alone, and guided by the sole criterion of 'protection'.

From victim to author

I was given a final example of refugee testimony in the Maheba camp in north-western Zambia.[11] Around 5,000 Rwandan and Burundi refugees, mainly Hutu, arrived there in 1997–8. In November 1998 some of them formed an 'Association d'Entraide pour l'Autodéveloppement' ('mutual aid association for self-development'). With a reputation as good farmers, particularly in marshland alongside the camp abandoned by the Angolan refugees, they organized themselves, supported one another and made possible a relatively acceptable and peaceable existence in the zone allotted to them, a refuge which they said they did not want to leave.

In 2000, four teachers, two of whom were in charge of an association of this kind, published a text in French which made a kind of synthesis of their own stories and those collected from other Hutu refugees in the camp; this became a 'book' circulating in the camp, under the title *L'Itinéraire le plus long et le plus pénible (Les réfugiés hutu à la recherche de l'asile)*.[12] This mimeographed work is dedicated 'to all the world's refugees'. It sets out to construct the victim identity of the Hutu refugees by detailing the many sufferings – exhaustion, hunger, mistreatment, fear, flight – experienced in three or four years of wandering (between April 1994 and November 1998) on the roads and into the camps of Rwanda, Zaire (now the DRC), Angola and Zambia, ending up with settlement in the Maheba camp. This 'journey' occupies some sixty pages, after ten others devoted in a very elliptical fashion to the 'origins and causes of exile' (pp. 4–14). The whole account aims to demonstrate that 'there has been a twentieth-century exodus [of the Hutu people] similar to that of the people of Moses'.

What is important for our present purpose is the desire here to give a written form to testimony, and the personal commitment of four 'authors' who identify themselves as such, as they explain in a preface: 'The authors, having themselves experienced these tragic moments and seen the hecatomb of these people whose story is narrated, have felt the need to put them down in writing to serve as a historical reference for the benefit of the future generation of this people who are victims of war.'[13] These authors are also the founders of the association and local intellectuals. While investigating in order to collect or complete their own information, and thus to write a collective testimony, they were among the leaders who spoke 'in the name' of the refugees from this zone in the camp.[14] They set out in their text to construct an identity of their 'exodus' as against the 'policy of demonizing Hutu refugees'[15] – a journey of 'five thousand kilometres on foot' undertaken in the midst of misfortune and suffering, and a dynamic integration in the camp: these are the two components of the figure of 'refugee' that arises from this literary work. At the cost of certain ellipses, rubbing out, forgetting – or, on the other hand, certain emphases and emotional commentaries – the label of 'refugee' becomes the common term of identification: it serves to make the Hutu exiles from Maheba identifiable as 'a people of victims of war', part of 'all the world's refugees' to whom the book is dedicated.

The context, issues and shaping of testimony create an event – an act of speech, writing, even theatre[16] – that is distinct from what it refers to. Furthermore, the relationship between the testimony given in the camp and the events experienced in war and exodus may be inverted. For these past events continue to exist in the long run – and in memory – as soon as they take a narrative form, thanks to the words, or more generally the linguistic, intellectual and physical resources, of the author of the testimony: once a common space of speech exists and makes possible the presentation of this testimony as such.

A displacement of context and a gradual detachment from the suffering 'self' bring into being the *space* and the *author* of the testimony as specific realities that form the basis of this work as an independent act. A displacement and detachment in relation to biographical events mean that the testimony can no longer be simply reduced to simple referential speech (relating a past event experienced by the narrator). This independence is expressed even before any aesthetic consideration: the choice of speaking out or keeping silent, for the Liberian refugees, is in fact a dilemma that is not reducible to reference to a past psychological disorder, but relates, from the point of view of the anthropologist, to the normative perspective of return, forgiveness and a desire for social reconstruction. This independence, in the last case that we presented, ends up with a form of 'artistic testimony' in which aesthetic construction is clear and produces its own cultural event, a 'book' in this case, which circulates in the camp as an object. From this point of view, the aesthetic dimension of work on stories already appears, for example, in the speaking groups or dramatic spectacles found in certain of the refugee camps (those of Boreah in Guinea, or Jembé in Sierra Leone, for example) with a pedagogic or psychotherapeutic purpose.

We can deduce from all this that a dual regime of thought, ethical and aesthetic, is always characteristic of the work of testimony. In principle, the desire to speak out is born as a necessity of an ethical order: it is necessary to speak – or learn to speak – one's misfortune in a well-defined community of communication, capable of immediately recognizing and sharing this experience. It is also necessary to be understood and recognized by the agent who will listen, read and judge the acceptability of the testimony. But this communication, if necessary and even urgent, still involves a certain work. Selecting the most striking facts, modifying accounts, anticipating the expectations of an audience. This work of fashioning constitutes a shaping of events, and presupposes a choice of the best 'ways of telling' the facts that happened.

From this point on, testimony can no longer be defined as a strictly referential or utilitarian act.[17] It no longer refers simply to a past experienced elsewhere, but to the present and to everything that is reconstructed there. It is already a further event in itself. Its existence depends on its own conditions: a space for speaking out, an author and his or her skills, a work of creation. In other words, the shaping of testimony demands its own 'stage'. This stage is offered by the space of the camp, once it develops its own social life over a longer time frame than the immediate emergency, and with a relative freedom of movement within the space of confinement. Testimony now becomes a *performance* whose authors no longer address themselves to a specific audience but to a wider public. Aiming at a still wider and anonymous public (one that writing a book or presenting a theatrical piece makes possible), the initial wider public of the refugee performance that speaks unhappiness and has some prospect of detachment from this is the 'dense and heterogeneous agglomeration' surrounding the refugee. At that point in time, the camp becomes for a moment a space that is both shared and public, a place of coming together and speaking out.

Part Three

After the Camps . . .

Three themes have gradually imposed themselves in this study conducted among the refugees and displaced persons: that of the camps as spaces of socialization in extraterritoriality, both out-places and an unprecedented urban experience ('If This is a Town . . .'); that of representations of the world and the individual, which justify and legitimize humanitarian action and encampment ('If This is a World . . .'); that of an exceptional power, its organization and its materiality ('If This is a Government . . .'). In this connection, three theses arose in the field and now need to be developed beyond the level of analysis of the ethnologist – moving from the local to the global, from the particular to the general. Technically speaking it would be more logical to examine these three theses side by side. They amount to three theories of the camps today.[1] All three give the camps a meaning, place them in a certain context, and look beyond them, even envisaging their extension, prospective or utopian. Starting from the camps, beyond the camps, after the camps, let us try to see what is happening.

The first possible theory of the camps extends their urban ethnography as this is gradually constituted with the advance of research: from the networks of camps on the Mano River to the 'camp-towns' of Dadaab, by way of the broad space of identifications that the UNHCR site at Maheba in Zambia has been. From here we come back to the question of the Palestinian camps that was raised at the start as a (paradoxical) model of reflection on the camps. The camps are towns in the process of becoming, and yet . . .

The second theoretical development starting from the camps seeks to embrace as a whole, and give coherence to, the series of values and representations of the world and the individual that constantly 'exercise' the milieus of humanitarianism, or those laying claim to this, providing the words and images that convince people to act, and finally guiding the choice of intervention and the selection of 'beneficiaries', ending up by accepting the possibility of encampment. The world of humanitarianism is that of the victim as an altered form of human, a 'whole' that leaves no place within it for any alternative thought.

The third thesis concerns the emergence of humanitarian government. I do not use the terms 'governance' or 'governmentality' here, as often heard in connection with the world of humanitarianism and its values. The term 'government' was born from observation of everyday life in the camps. I use it here in the concrete and precise sense of the organization of power in and by way of the multi-local humanitarian apparatus. The level for understanding this mechanism

177

is becoming ever more global. This leads us to traverse and analyse the networks of humanitarian organizations which are inventing, right across the world, the premises of a humanitarian government, and at the end of the day to investigate afresh the possibility of humanitarian action as a movement of international solidarity.

— 10 —

'If This is a Town . . .'

Is a camp better than nothing? I return to this question, both practical and existential, which I raised at the start of my investigation. The operational advantage of the camps has been clearly questioned for a good while now, both in medical and nutritional terms, and from the point of view of their financial costs. Wim Van Damme, for example, challenged the operational character of the camps in medical terms, because, among other reasons, confinement is conducive to epidemics.[1] Two doctors from MSF, Erwann Queinnec and Jean Rigal, questioned the composition of the WFP food ration that produces a deterioration of its own, even such 'unexpected nutritional catastrophes' as diseases due to lack of vitamins (scurvy, pellagra, beriberi).[2] These effects are all the more serious in that refugees find themselves for a long period in an enclosed situation, so that the resale and conversion of rations into fruit, vegetables and dairy products proves indispensable in nutritional terms. Finally, Guglielmo Verdirame and Barbara Harrell-Bond, in their book *Rights in Exile*, raised questions about the economic benefit of gathering refugees into camps as opposed to individual integration: the camps cost more, they say, and show a lesser return on investment than would be had from integration and development.[3] The problematic of the camps as we have dealt with it here, i.e. from the point of view of the socio-spatial organization of the controlling and distancing of undesirables, is all the more reinforced.

Camps are always precarious places, but also spaces in which a relatively stable condition of life is formed. Certain camps are located on the periphery of capitals, and their social and economic life is integrated into the urban market, as with the camps for internally displaced persons at Khartoum, Monrovia or Freetown. Others are themselves the foundation of a new urbanism. In order for this to be achieved, their inhabitants have to take possession of these places, or more exactly of these originally 'out-place' spaces, so as to make them into places of life, relationships and identifications. It is this path that we have followed in order to understand the anthropological dynamic of the camps: from the empty margins of present time and space, grasped at the moment of constitution of the camps, through to the centrality of these margins when they are established in the life of individuals and in the urban landscape, as in the case of the Palestinian camps.

Out-places: the camp as heterotopia

Camps of refugees or displaced persons, transit zones and holding centres, more or less informal campgrounds of 'illegals', etc. – it seemed to me useful, in the context of this general reflection, to begin by giving a generic meaning to all these spaces produced by the multiform and global procedures of exclusion, 'outside of all places', where different categories of undesirables, stateless, pariahs, etc., find themselves 'temporarily' (a temporality that becomes lasting). Experienced as a synonym for 'frontier', 'desert', sometimes 'prison', these are *other* spaces, 'heterotopic' to use Michel Foucault's term: 'kinds of place that are outside of all place, even though they can indeed be actually located'.[4]

These out-places are initially constituted as *outsides*, placed on the edges or limits of the normal order of things – a 'normal' order that ultimately remains still today a national one.[5] They are characterized a priori by confinement and a certain 'extraterritoriality'. This is constructed for refugees and displaced persons in the experience of a double exclusion from locality: an exclusion from their place of origin, lost in the wake of violent displacement; and an exclusion from the space of the 'local population' where these camps and other transit zones are established. This extraterritoriality, but also the attempt to supersede it and the evidence of its literally fictional character, lie at the root of the tensions between local population and refugees. Such tensions are a recurrent theme in the problems of camp management. In fact, there is negotiation between the two positions, and relationships are established between the refugees/displaced and the local population: there are, for example, work relationships around the camps, or conflicts over the temporary use of villagers' land.[6] In these relationships, the refugees occupy a subaltern position imposed

180

by the double handicap of not being 'at home' and being almost totally destitute. But locals sometimes pass themselves off as refugees in order to gain access to the camps' infrastructures of humanitarian aid.[7] Marriages between refugees and locals also take place, with new families appearing, and the matrimonial range for both sides increases, as we saw in the space of conflict along the Mano River. Disorder is introduced within the camp by the active aspect of social relationships, emotional or political, that uncloister it without making its borders disappear, and so constantly raise the problem of its openness and closure, its isolation and its permeability.

I now want to return to the idea of extraterritoriality. In order for the camps to be managed according to a principle of assistance and control at a distance from the 'normal' and national order of things – i.e. a principle that separates the rights of man from those of the citizen and thus justifies the idea of a certain 'exceptionality' – an *extra-territorial fiction* has been created, which is also an *extra-national* one. In the early 1980s, Michel Foucault declared that refugees were the first people to be 'imprisoned outside',[8] a phrase that I have used above to describe the refugee camps. But this outside is empty, a pure mirage without its own idea or identity: its real space is occupied by the 'inside' of another state. In other words, those imprisoned outside are individuals 'distanced inside', within another state space that represents the outside of the one that excludes. The extraterritoriality of 'outcasts' as 'residues' or 'human rejects'[9] on the world scale is thus defined in this repeated tension between an inside that is inaccessible from the point of view of national citizen categories (according to the legal fiction of extraterritoriality) and an outside that is experienced in complete uncertainty, as a form of life kept going 'under perfusion', and equally under constraint. It is in this tension or double constraint that the camp makes itself into an artefact, a space of confinement that seems placed in the middle of a void, but is always *on the limit* and on the border. The space of the camp or transit zone as an 'empty world' situated outside all places, and consequently the reified space of the border, is constructed in this context as a liminal space, a controlled between-the-two. And it is states themselves that define these 'no-place' spaces in relief, making them spaces of physical and material life maintained at a minimum, political voids and – originally at least – social voids without temporality. As we have seen above in relation to the continuous creation of limit spaces in frontier zones, it is possible to say first of all, and overall, that the camp defines itself as an *extra-territorial temporary residence.*[10]

These heterotopic emplacements combine the characteristics of heterotopies 'of crisis' and 'of deviation'.[11] Like psychiatric hospitals, prisons or retirement homes, they are designed for individuals going through a temporary situation, which is also assumed to be one of exile, and they can only be a place or moment of 'crisis'.[12] But by fixing them and gathering them collectively, these other spaces turn their occupants into permanent deviants, abnormals who are kept at a distance. It is true that the camps of today are generally not prisons, but they are often experienced as such, even when life within them is not strictly carceral. It is in terms of 'prison' that refugees who had spent over ten years in camps at Dadaab in Kenya spoke to me of their situation – even though, from another point of view, this is also the context of a new urbanism. However, between the Somalian refugees in a Kenyan camp, depressed at 'feeling' themselves in prison, and another Somalian in the CRA holding centre at Vincennes, manifestly 'incarcerated' or 'detained', and mistreated when the national police pay their nightly visits,[13] there is no substantial difference in terms of morale or identity; they share the same fate. The administrative obsession with categorization ('refugees', 'internally displaced', 'illegals', 'detained', 'tolerated', etc., as we have seen above) goes together with this consolidation of ad hoc spaces designed for 'populations' that are in this way deprived of subjectivity and categorized separately. The distancing of the outcasts and their categorization mutually reinforce one another. The use of 'separate' categories of identity, to conceive and manage these expelled or parked individuals, derives from analogous conceptions of bodies and spaces. The conceptions of confined spaces, out-places, and of individuals as *de-socialized bodies* – another name for the absolute victim – form a specific representation of the persons thus defined in 'their' space of life. This representation is focused on the humanitarian model of the victim and on the sanitary (prophylactic) or security (police) model of space conceived as the means for keeping at a distance a specific undesirable population. The managerial representation of large numbers and large spaces, corresponding to policies that have been called, following Foucault, 'biopolitical', brings together the humanitarian figure of the victim and that of the illegal. The illegal, in fact, presents characteristics similar to those of the victim, the embodied body of vulnerability: the loss of political rights, circulation in frontier or extra-territorial spaces, a de facto social marginality. Besides, the transition from the status of victim (the basis for humanitarian action) to that of illegal (the basis for police intervention) is frequent and random for the exiled and displaced; it is a function of the political and moral choices of governments, which lead to variable official interpretations, either national or by the UN, irrespective of social conditions of mobility that may be equivalent in the exile life of people from both groups. The extra-territorial space of the camp thus merges with the body that inhabits it – human at the limit, and outside all norms.

'The Camp' and camps, yesterday and today

The conviction that there exists a contemporary form of camp as a lasting social and political organization can only be confirmed by the major development of refugee camps in the 1980s and 1990s, especially in Asia and Africa, as well as of holding camps for foreigners and asylum seekers on the borders of Europe in the 2000s. The present return of the 'camp solution', as found in the statements and policies of certain European governments towards asylum seekers, extends an old strategy of the distancing of undesirables, and prefigures the possible future uses of the camp form. It is necessary therefore to recognize the continuity of this form of socio-spatial organization, even while noting its new uses and organizational modifications – in short, its present unity and diversity.

What historical depth and what empirical data can a study of the camps today draw on? The model that imposes itself in what I know of present-day camps is not that of the death camp, the Nazi camp, whose existence derived from an exterminating and genocidal logic, and yet it is impossible, strictly speaking, to avoid keeping to the form of the camp as a space of power, or even of exception.

Several facts that were met with in the course of this research and that characterize the out-places of camps and transit zones can provide empirical arguments for the concept of 'bare life' that Agamben used to demonstrate that the camp is the 'model' of biopolitics'.[14] What raises a problem in Agamben's contention is not so much the concept of 'bare life', which synthesizes the multiple forms of absolute power over life (and conversely the power of death) that the institutions and organizations that decide to care for and/or not care for abandoned persons may have at a given time and place: of keeping them alive or letting them die. The problem here is rather the supposed transformation of this power (more precisely this 'biopower') into a model of politics, and the idea that the exact embodiment of this model is the camp form. By way of this abstract and deductive figuration, the camp is ultimately reduced to a mere space

183

of death – a social death before being a physical one – as were the extermination camps to which Agamben finally reduces the figure and meaning of the camp in general – contradicting all studies on the ground in the camps of today.[15]

Camps existed long before and after the period of Nazi exterminations.[16] To forbid, in the name of the exceptionality and 'unutterable' character of the Shoah, the development of a reflection on the commonplaceness of the camp and its multifunctional character, both in the domain of history and in that of the anthropology of contemporary worlds, would mean closing social science research into a whole field of questions and studies of forms of power and political exceptionalism, as well as into the limiting contexts of political action and the potentialities for social and cultural transformation contained in those spaces apart that I have generically called here 'out-places'. Besides, once this research is authorized, certain writings on 'detention', 'concentration' and 'labour' camps from the 1930s and 1940s in Europe can be adduced to support a critical anthropology of the 'camp' form in general. I have in mind, for example, the works on the 'internment' camps under French administration between 1938 and 1946,[17] as well as the writings of Primo Levi and his descriptions of the camp where he worked and survived for a year.

In presenting and commenting on Primo Levi's *Survival in Auschwitz*,[18] Philippe Mesnard noted how the authors had used the word 'Camp' with a capital 'C', seeing this as a desire to construct a generic camp on the basis of their direct knowledge of the camp of Auschwitz-Monowitz.

The capital may well have value as a paradigm for anthropological investigation, without implying any equation of present-day refugee camps with the Nazi concentration camps. The ends and means are profoundly different in each case. On the other hand, the gap is less absolute from the point of view of forms, and the study of past examples makes it possible to emphasize a certain continuity. For the stateless, in fact, the dice were already cast in the first quarter of the twentieth century. 'The Second World War and the deportation camps were not necessary to show that the only concrete substitute for a non-existent home country was the internment camp. In fact, it was from the 1930s the only "country" that the world had to offer the stateless', Hannah Arendt noted.[19] The continuity of the camp form is well illustrated by the permanence of certain sites, and their social and spatial organizations, which have sometimes used the same infrastructures from one period to another, for example in France from the 1930s through to today: there is a long history of camps here, including, without a break, the concentration camps for Gypsies during the First World War, the camps to accommodate Spanish refugees in the late 1930s, the internment camps for Jewish refugees before their deportation to Nazi Germany, the centres for surveyed residence of collaborators in the post-war 'purge', the centres for assigned residence for Algerian independence activists, the reception centres for Harki families, and the reception centres or waiting zones for asylum seekers since the 1990s.[20] Analysing the continuity of the form and principal functions of camps in France since the 1930s, Olivier Clochard, Yvan Gastaut and Ralph Schor have shown the close relationship existing between a restrictive immigration policy, a xenophobic climate and the development of camps in France seventy years ago.[21]

In the same way, the parallel that I mentioned earlier on, between refugee camps, and prisons may be shocking in terms of their respective purposes. Yet it does have an empirical foundation: in the Australian desert at Woomera, detention camps for Afghan refugees awaiting a response to their asylum applications were recognized as military-humanitarian spaces enclosed by the full panoply of deadly barriers.[22] Following the closure of the Woomera camp, in the wake of atrocities committed there being publicized, the Australian government looked for other solutions to keep refugees away, the latest of these at this point being the construction of a detention centre on Christmas Island in December 2005. We should also bear in mind and understand the repeated statements of refugees who, describing the humanitarian establishments in which they find themselves, speak of prison without this requiring that their camp should be surrounded by walls and barbed wire. Confinement itself, and more generally isolation in spaces that are hard of access, are 'sufficient' to produce the effect of imprisonment.[23]

Nevertheless, the unified representation of the generic camp, however well founded this may be as an institution of biopower, still comes up against not only the multiplicity of actual forms, but also, and above all, the rapid appearance of disorder within the camp space. This disorder is of two kinds. On the one hand, it results from the very wide margin of manoeuvre that the extraterritoriality of the camps gives to 'government employees' in these spaces of exception. As we have seen above,[24] the de facto situation within certain present-day camps is not a moral and social order governed and regulated by the humanistic principles conveyed in messages from the UN and NGOs, but rather a situation of actual imprisonment 'where the scum are in charge',[25] which produces a similarity with camps from another time. Abuses of power, sexual and otherwise, organized diversion of the food ration, and the establishment of illegal work networks are regular features of everyday life in the camps for refugees and internally displaced people in Africa, and they involve government employees in these camps, who themselves wield fragments of power over the lives of the refugees.

On the other hand, and not necessarily conflicting with what we have already said, a further type of disorder can arise from the emergence of various kinds of resistance to imprisonment, whether in the form of everyday survival (petty arrangements with the staff, trafficking in refugee cards, corruption of police, etc.) or that of political action. These two kinds of disorder are shown both in writings on the European camps of the 1930s and 1940s, and in the descriptions of present-day refugee camps.

Even when they are established in the midst of deserted territory, in the savannah or the bush (between Kenya and Somalia, for example, or in the Forest Region of Guinea), the camps gradually transform themselves. From spaces of transit and waiting, some of them organize themselves into 'towns' despite not being endowed with an urban project inasmuch as everything is designed not to last. An organization of space and a certain social life develop despite a general situation of great legal precariousness, swinging in various cases between lack of rights under national law and the pure virtuality of international law, between a very general (and distant) humanitarian law and a power over life exercised by those who are locally closest to the beneficiaries of humanitarian aid and control its resources.

In the same context, certain relationships are established with young men and women who have come from their pleasant countries of Europe, the United States or Australia to spend a few months in the 'heart of darkness' and take part in the great movement of international humanitarian aid, whether in the UNHCR refugee camps or the voluntary associations that help the 'illegals' in their forest encampments. A telescoping of cultures takes place in a time that is suspended for all involved (the expatriates are there from six to twelve months, the refugees waiting indefinitely), and a space that is initially artificial but does not remain so. Without actually realizing it, both sides find themselves in the world of the humanitarian apparatus, whose long history converges here with the equally long history of camps and removals. They transform this into a contemporary social world in which the relationships between space, culture and politics take a new form.

186

Camps, ghettos and towns

Observation of the camps makes it possible to describe a certain tension. There is of course a mechanism of power, categorization, filing, control and imprisonment, in a local framework of government. The camp is then at the same time both metaphor for and concrete realization of the separate treatment of these 'residues' with no voice or place in the world. And yet, at the same time as they are somewhat consolidated in material terms, the camps transform themselves in a few months, or a couple of years at the most, into relatively stable social milieus, worlds of relationships that display various kinds of injustice, violence and frustration, as well as coping, encounters and certain forms of speaking out.

We then see how the mechanism of minimal survival or preservation of 'bare life' that the camp and its organization represent can be described as a 'relatively large, dense and permanent settlement of socially heterogeneous individuals', in the sociological definition – certainly a very minimal one – that Louis Wirth gave of the town in the 1930s.[26] This heterogeneity is what produces the 'extraordinary complexity' of the town, as Bernard Lepetit explains in connection with the history of European towns: 'the very being of the town', he stresses, is a heterogeneous ensemble of identitarian resources, whose confrontation defines 'the citizens' space of action' and determines 'the transformative capacities of the urban'.[27] As a unique and complex place by virtue of the singular and heterogeneous combination of its population and spaces, the town also produces effects of 'convergence', to follow the studies of the sociologist Isaac Joseph on public places and spaces.[28] The philosopher Marcel Hénaff, for his part, conceives the town as a 'technical mechanism' and a 'social machine': 'The town is thus empirically the continuous concentration of a large number of individuals in a built space on a restricted terrain.'[29] Again an elementary form, therefore, which may also characterize the many more stabilized camps. 'This already constitutes a totally new technical and social phenomenon' in relation to the rural mode of existence, Hénaff continues: in technical terms, the town is constructed out of its own resources (materials, knowledge, labour); in social terms, it presupposes the systematic organization of a 'division and complementarity of tasks'[30] among all those who are concentrated there, while personal ties (particularly those of kinship) tend to give way to broad functional categories in determining the bases of social organization. We have seen above how hierarchies

187

are gradually formed between generations of population (on the Maheba site)[31] or between classes defined socio-economically or by prestige (at Dadaab).[32] What forms can these towns have, being neither medieval nor industrial, but still desired and in the process of birth?

The various analyses that we have just mentioned very rapidly describe the town in terms of heterogeneity, complexity, convergence, concentration and apparatus. They foster a constructivist approach to the town, neither essentialist nor normative, which is particularly helpful in grasping camps as extra-territorial spaces outside of norms. This approach seeks to describe the town (each town is both singular and a 'summary of the world'[33]) in its process, its movement and its internal transformation, rather than in the hardened outward form of a double *nature morte* – dead both in the sense that the town would simply be a countryside without its movements, and in the sense that what makes up the materiality that I see here and now is, to take up a famous Marxian concept, 'dead labour', i.e. past and finished construction that is now self-evident, already there, and from which the creative movement has disappeared.

As we emphasized above, for those undertaking research today in the camps that persist and prolong the precariousness induced by a policy of emergency, the model is not the death camp. On the contrary, it is a model of beginnings, with uncertain and hybrid forms. The background model for research on present-day camps is that of the Palestinian camp. In Lebanon, Syria, Jordan and the Palestinian Territories of the West Bank and Gaza, dozens of camps have already existed for more than fifty years, housing a million and a half Palestinian refugees, and where Sudanese and Iraqi exiles have more recently also come to seek asylum. No more than any other camps were these designed to last. Over time, however, they have gradually become places of a local identification and the hard kernel of a Palestinian political identity. Keeping people in the political and legal out-place of the camp fosters the justification of return as the only solution for recognition. But for a long time already the camp inhabitants have reorganized their existence within these spaces. A gap is steadily growing between 'the Camp' with a capital 'C' (its definition in legal and political terms as a space of exception and a place of waiting) and the various Palestinian camps, which are urban and social realities in movement.[34] The camps are transforming themselves, and for a number of years they have experienced an urbanization that is fairly close – in terms of social organization, economic practices and material aspect – to what we know about urban peripheries elsewhere in the world. The distinction between town dwellers and refugees hangs only by a thread.

What has happened to the camps created several decades ago? They are no longer completely camps, but kinds of ghettos or portions of towns: their empty world has been transformed and internally filled; the initial bare space has been populated; social, cultural and political relationships have developed within a space that is delimited if not totally closed. This has taken place in the same way that, in the general history of urban ghettos, the development of an 'other' life within a relative imprisonment has favoured identitarian politics, whatever their foundation (ethnic, racial, national, religious, etc.). In the camp, *place* is formed, and the camp itself is the context in which an identitarian strategy is born, rather than the converse as is often believed. What seems to be debatable in interpretations of the transformation of the camp into an 'ethnic sanctuary', for example, is the idea that basically 'neutral' humanitarian spaces have been invaded by identitarian forces, or even ethnic armies that pre-existed them. It is true that national or ethnic groups may have pre-existed the camp, but in this space they transform themselves, confront one another, even mingle; it is here that they can give rise to ethno-political forces of various different kinds. Besides, the territorial and social consolidation of the camps has several consequences for their inhabitants, beyond the most visible political translations. In other words, when the idea of 'anthropological place'[35] is introduced into the originally empty world of the out-place, the urban form that goes with it is that of the ghetto. We can then ask if a ghetto is not better than a camp, in the sense that this particular ghetto is the camp that has developed a social and cultural life in the very space of its confinement.

To conceive the town as an unending process, and investigate its repeated beginning, thus leads us logically to reconsidering the camps from the point of view of the invention of the town. There is the question of the town to be made, and that of the transformation of precarious spaces into made territories – today still largely unforeseeable in terms of their materiality, economy or future sociabilities – where a local identity is founded. Such an identity, if it is to be transmissible from one generation to the next, can still be displaceable. And the very idea of foundation – the foundation of a town, a village or a house – contradicts any belief in a kind of autochthonous local identity that has arisen 'naturally' from the earth. In a study of myths of autochthony, both ancient and contemporary, Marcel Detienne notes that founding a city means creating a link in and to a place, creating a rootedness without this root having had to pre-exist: a mixture of ecology, smells, markings for neighbours, rituals of foundation or installation – 'Nothing is more trivial for a living being than digging its hole, its immediate territory. The rest follows.'[36] The 'rest' here is everything that will follow technically and administratively from the necessary anthropological foundation of spaces as places of identification. And yet, in order for the camps to found new spaces, durable and liveable, they will first of all have to free themselves from the hold of a representation that confines them to the margins and non-existence.

'If This is a World . . .'

Well, you know, I'm no longer very sure where I am here . . .
I don't know if I'm in heaven or still on earth.[1]

If our research in the camps has led us to reconceive the beginnings
of towns, it has also provided material for new questions in the
debates around humanitarianism. I am well aware that the foundation of the following reflections – on the one hand ethnographic
research in the camps, on the other hand the most fundamental questions of anthropology – presses us into terrain that is little explored
by the specialists in humanitarian aid. But it may at least contribute
to 'deconstructing' analytically this world and its beliefs.

The world of humanitarian aid does not form a rigid and mechanical system, it is flexible and diffuse from the standpoint of its modes
of concrete organization; and yet its specific values give it a style and
language that is always recognizable. Besides, the humanitarian world
is also *the world according to the humanitarian*, i.e. the world (physical and social, political and cultural) as the humanitarian represents
it. This representation implies defining its 'beneficiaries' as well as
taking responsibility for them, these beneficiaries being those with
the right and obligation to enter this world and thus legitimizing its
existence. To put this in terms familiar to anthropologists, I want in
the following pages to investigate fundamentally the formation of a
'representation of the world and the person' within this contemporary social world of humanitarianism.

Fictions of lineage, humanitarian fiction and representation of the person

The philosopher Jacques Rancière has termed the moment that corresponds to the temporality and places of our reflections the 'nihilist

age' of politics.[2] This non-politics is first of all the moment at which there is an identity between the totality (represented in our day by the state, but also and increasingly by the institutions of the 'international community') and the sum of its parts – the moment at which consensus, the submission of the weak or the 'tolerance' of the dominant, as the case may be, annihilates, stifles or dismisses the dissensus that a 'disagreement' expresses. Whatever the particular mode, there is no longer a 'supernumerary part' whose vote falsifies the count and thus the agreement. In the absence of a mediation between the whole and the sum of the parts, each part of the whole is conceived in a state of immediacy within the whole, sharing the same fate and integrating the same logos. This is a consensual system in which the whole is whole and there is no remaining residue. This identity, or generalized transparency, takes the name of humanity. The double with which this humanity is associated is not the expression of an alterity (no 'other' is recognized in this closed and total system) but rather the expression of an identity with two faces: the double is the same, but as wounded, suffering and dying. It has become the 'absolute victim' that is nothing other than absolute humanity when it is suffering. This figure of the unique and dual human (absolute humanity versus absolute victim) dominates the thought of the present: the representation of a world viewed by consensus as a totality, lacking a representation of the different, founds our present as the age of humanitarianism, a world of nameless victims, without a separate identity (or it is only the common identity, when it is damaged and wounded, that creates the victim 'irrespective of sex, religion, ethnicity, political camp, etc.'). A world in which each person plays their role – even 'overplays' it, as is said of actors in the theatre when they lay it on too thick – thus without a representation of the *différend*. This reference to the absolute victim determines the meaning given to the space of the camp that is created and managed according to the specific rules of humanitarian government.

There is a certain analogy here that will not escape the attention of the anthropologist. It brings together two contexts that presuppose with equal insistence a unified representation of the person: the context of lineage (or the domestic context) and the humanitarian world. Anthropology has long been interested in different theories of the person, a notion whose meaning ranges from that of mask – tragic or ritual in the Latin *persona* – to that of a social or sacred status.[3] In this context, the identity or transparency between the part that I observe (ethnographic observation) and the whole that I never see, but which is generally given the names of 'society' or 'culture', is

192

called 'individuation'. I would like here to relate these two ideas briefly, the immediacy and singleness of the human on the one hand, and the notion of person that anthropology has constructed on the other. There is first of all a methodological point that is also a question of the representation of the individual in the world: in the holistic tradition of anthropology, the 'privileged informant' of the ethnologist is one who has no other *raison d'être* than that of telling and embodying the whole of the society or culture which the ethnologist seeks to present – bearing an external regard on it and addressing an audience that is likewise external – as the fiction of a coherent totality, overlooking its conflicts, breaches and heterogeneous forms. In the same way, there exists a humanitarian image of the human, ideally the suffering woman and child, i.e. a representation that compels consent by showing a doubly bare life: on the one hand, pure life in the essential biological mother–child relationship, and on the other hand, life stripped bare in the degradation that suffering embodies. These unified representations of the person, one in terms of lineage and the other humanitarian, are regularly displayed as images in the form of lectures, films and 'exotic' books – even cultural tourism, the anticipated exoticism of war and humanitarianism now coming to compete with ethnic exoticism, especially in certain African countries.[4]

· But a political questioning is also possible on the basis of this analogy of individuation between the world of lineage and the world of humanitarianism. It is because the individual is caught in the constraints of power and meaning given to the society (which includes individuals and in which all their existence is summed up), because he or she is born and remains inescapably within the terrorizing net formed by the power of chiefs and the interpretation of sorcerers, that we can speak, as Marc Augé does, of 'lineage totalitarianism',[5] within which there is no place for the rebel, and the sole response to which has historically been that of flight: in Africa in the years of decolonization from 1950 to 1970, leaving for the cities and urban peripheries was synonymous with emancipation (literally, the search for an 'air of freedom') before being for many the discovery of places of abandonment.

The idea that individuation in the context of lineage should be conceived right through to its totalitarian culmination evidently raises the question of the impossibility of politics within the lineage, the clan, the domestic community. In what way is there this incompatibility between the domestic community and the political community? It certainly does not lie in the natural order of things. The philosopher

Geneviève Freysse has shown the great heuristic interest of a comparison between the 'two governments', that of the city and that of the family. Her research enabled her to describe relations of power within domestic relationships and to compare these with power in the city: 'In each structure, family and city, there is thus a government, an instance, that organizes and directs a society: a place of power.'[6] The comparison between these two places of power helps us to demonstrate an absence, that of politics, within the domestic community. Politics (understood as action and speaking out in a precise context of subjectification) is not power. Politics is both close to and distinct from the exercise of power, which is the everyday prerogative of government. As if she was echoing this question, Hannah Arendt placed the possibility of politics in the only free space that exists, according to her: in a (non-)place – neither abroad, 'where it was impossible to be free because one was no longer a citizen', nor 'in the private domestic home, where it was impossible to be free because of the lack of equal others'. It is only the meeting of such equals that constitutes the space of freedom and the possibility of the *res publica*.[7] This intermediate space in which politics is possible is that of the *agora*, a utopia that we derive from Greek political thought and that still designates the ideal of a space of politics as one of freedom of speech and action among equals. In the end, the exercise of politics within the domestic community is impossible because a community of equals cannot be realized there: relations between sexes and generations are unequal and based on the illusion of 'natural' hierarchies.

'The heart of darkness': a world with no outside

Beyond the domestic context which is the foundation of these considerations, the impossibility of politics extends to a society that is completely one based on lineage; this is the repressive and depoliticizing model of 'lineage totalitarianism' described by Augé. This impossibility of politics is then based on the illusion of totality, which presupposes the absence of an outside, and, beyond this, on the essential emptiness of any 'thought from outside'.[8] Membership of the totality, consensus, subjection itself, are constructed on the belief that there is no alternative, no life outside that which is lived and experienced. This total (totalitarian) conception of the social world betrays a double absence – one as the invisible elsewhere of all visible places, the other as the silent elsewhere of all discourse – both emptinesses are constitutive of the external frontiers of this closed world, or more precisely this single world at the heart of the desert: 'The outside cannot offer itself as a positive presence – as something inwardly illuminated by the certainty of its own existence – but only as an absence that pulls as far away from itself as possible, receding into the sign it makes to draw one toward it (as though it were possible to reach it).'[9] In other words, a point of salvation outside of this world. The very concrete translation, in the life of each inhabitant, of contexts governed by this totalitarian thinking, is the impossibility of an alternative definition of the individual-in-the-world. It is this lack that I shall retain here, inasmuch as it signifies the totalitarian hold of the lineage or the domestic community. It corresponds to the absence of alternative that is produced by the 'whole' of humanitarianism. A simple shift of focus and a change of scale will demonstrate this.

The humanitarian world is based on the double fiction of an identitarian humanity and an equivalence between universalism and globalization. On the one hand, there is a regime of universalistic thinking: it is the unique human being and his or her extreme embodiment in the problem raised by the nameless and unmediated victim, who is thus not an 'other' recognized in their own speech, but the same being when mistreated, when their human qualities are diminished, incomplete or unachieved. Assessment of these deteriorations creates different degrees within the same identity, according to categories which initially seem natural, while opening the way immediately to principles of social and normative classification: child, disabled, inept, incapable, illiterate, retarded, underdeveloped, etc. The different categories of 'vulnerable' now only have to find their place in this human classification.

On the other hand, a globalized apparatus: a set of organizations, networks, agents and financial resources distributed in various countries and crossing the world as heralds of a universal cause, the sole and exclusive declared *raison d'être* for humanitarian intervention. The fiction is realized here and there, for a given time, in what the anthropologist Mariella Pandolfi calls a 'movable sovereignty' applied by organizations and agents – individuals who moreover are often 'committed', trained in the disciplines of human rights, social and political science, the health professions and humanitarian logistics.[10] An organizational globalism thus replicates the universal message of equality in the form of a humanity whose opposite is not inequality (and, still less, challenged inequality) but rather the suffering of silent victims: these victims that the humanitarian world designates as its beneficiaries, or, to speak in terms of economic strategy, as its target.

The counterpart of the anthropological individuation of the person in the lineage – in which the submission of 'juniors' or the 'circulation of women' are classic figures of ethnological village studies – is thus the subjection of the absolute victim, for whom the humanitarian camp is the paradigmatic place of survival and confinement. As Jacques Rancière spells out: 'The eligible party pure and simple is then none other than the wordless victim, the ultimate figure of the one excluded from the logos, armed only with a voice expressing a monotonous moan, the moan of naked suffering, which saturation has made inaudible.'[11]

In both of these cases, the two social orders of lineage and humanitarianism, the village and the camp, no residue is envisaged, no possible outside is described. At best this exists as an absence, the place of a desire and the direction of a flight. And in both cases, the permanent dualism contained in any identification with a social order – both resource and constraint – conditions the possibility of a subjection without evident violence: thus the figure of the *person* is the sign of a social recognition of the individual in proximity (family, neighbourhood), before capsizing into the extreme oppression of the domestic or 'communitarian' collective; while the humanitarian *victim* finds vital help in the refugee camp before observing that his or her voice has no meaning: undesirable as well as vulnerable, they can be forced to remain or to leave from one day to the next, and see 'their' camp disappear, according to the unfathomable goodwill of the international organizations that opened it.

In this swing towards the limit of the power over life that it institutes to excess, the humanitarian world is a totalitarianism that has power of life (to let live or survive) and death (to let die) over the individual that it views as absolute victim, just as the lineage world exercises its totalitarianism over the persons to whom it absolutely dictates their identity, their inheritance and their duties.

To sum up – humanitarianism as a social world and regime of thought resorts to a totalitarian fiction constructed in two stages: on the one hand, the fiction of the singleness of the human without a representation of inequality; on the other hand, the fiction of the transparency between this ideological universalism and the organizational globalism. It can be painful to experience 'for real' the fiction that is realized here. The unwanted return 'home' of refugees (an *additional displacement*), or the human and economic problems raised by the closure of a camp after ten or fifteen years, are experienced as a further violence on top of those that the beneficiaries of humanitarianism have already known. At each step in their trajec-

196

tory, the refugees and displaced persons discover, side by side, the staff and white vehicles – four-wheel-drives and lorries, buses and tanks – of the UN agencies, the blue helmets and humanitarian organizations whose functions, however distinct they may be in technical terms, merge in their experience as the expression of a single international force that is totally sovereign.

The imagined victim

As a sign and condition of this fiction and all-powerfulness of humanitarianism, we have the strange presence-cum-absence of its beneficiaries. Omnipresent symbolically but absent intellectually, this separate world – the inevitably ambiguous world of 'victims' – is indeed exhibited sometimes in striking forms: the evening news fleetingly shows images of despair, and the poster of a humanitarian organization focuses close-up on the supplicant eyes and skeletal body of a naked Black child. But there is no place in the conceptions of the social world that our own world produces. What can be said of these beneficiaries, except to sympathize with them or condemn them? A form of intellectual relegation accompanies the distancing of 'victim' populations and other undesirables, who only appear in general in the revealed form of the 'unthinkable', 'intolerable' and 'unutterable': extreme figures of speech – sometimes 'scandalous',[12] sometimes terrible[13] – which provoke a shock effect and thus confirm, by an emotional presentation, the exceptional character of their unexpected incursion into our images of the world.

This way of seeing justifies and even makes commonplace the exceptional treatment accorded to these 'victims'. The exception is intellectually associated with everything that is impossible to conceive, i.e. an unthought 'residue' of reflection on the world, left on the margin or in shadow by the representation of social systems, like an indefinably blank page that thought abandons to the void and the Nietzschean 'desert'. Emotion (fear, compassion, hatred) then occupies the place of reflection, and spreads over the blank page. And the gesture linked with emotion (that of the well-wisher who gives or the volunteer who travels off) is directly bound up with the image of suffering that is a 'revealed' image of absolute form: with no before or after, no context. Emotion, well-wishing, suffering, absolute revelation: these movements of the self towards the world make up the most powerful wellsprings of the humanitarian effort. The moral gesture that conceives itself as an immediate response to the revelation of extreme suffering may even be assumed by its author to be spontaneous, rebellious, unreflective. It then grants itself the right to be dominating as well as donating. The heroic saviour figures have a fearsome reverse side in those of the all-powerful who seeks to 'control the situation' and the master-thinker who dictates to the beneficiaries their 'proper' responses. This moral gesture may seek to be reparatory, but it constructs victims who keep the appearance of absolute victims, without name or voice; such victims must know how to conform to their victim image, to receive money without 'wasting' or 'misappropriating' it, without using this support for other purposes than those conceived by the world of donors (individuals, organizations or donor countries) – in other words, without disorder. They must know how to receive while keeping their place. The same moral demand bears on those organizations responsible for transmitting charitable gifts abroad, towards a generalized suffering that is maintained, by the rich and do(mi)nating world, in the modality of the spectacle and of virtuality that are expressions of distancing.[14] Organizations that show public signs of moral ambiguity are then violently attacked, without the underlying ambiguity of contemporary humanitarian intervention itself being challenged, even though this lies at the origin of its possible cruelty in extreme situations. We thus heard in France, at the time of the Arche de Zoé affair in autumn 2007, that it was the incompetence or immorality of certain individuals that lay at the root of the scandal of the children who were rescued/kidnapped in Chad. Did people really take into account the fact that, if such behaviour was possible, it was because there exists today an exceptionalist view of Africa that is firmly anchored in the society and political milieus of the Western world? The imagery of an infantile and irresponsible continent, whose political and legal institutions are therefore contemptible, ultimately leading to contempt for people themselves in the name of the humanitarian representation of nameless victims.

— 12 —

'If This is a Government . . .'

It seems it's not a matter of opening political ministries anymore there. Instead the State of Emergency sets up its administration.[1]

The long and now converging histories of humanitarianism and camps are not only a history of the treatment of refugees, whether this is inscribed under the discursive regime of 'protection' (referring to the image of 'victim') or that of 'control' (referring to the image of the 'guilty'). What we have is a modality of social organization deployed on a global scale and treating a separate part of the planet's population according to a specific regime.

From camps to the formation of humanitarian government

To say what humanitarianism is or should be has in recent years become a popular political and journalistic exercise, with unanimous approval for its aims but combined with frequent denunciation of mistakes and abuses that stain an undertaking which is still defined and defended in essentially moral terms, despite the importance it has acquired in other domains – political, economic, professional and media. The consensual adjective 'humanitarian', attached to what was in origin simply a temporary act of relief, well shows how this activity has established itself in our social environment and is promised a long future. The substantial number of books, periodicals, seminars, conferences and lectures with 'humanitarianism' as their theme also indicates the wealth and diversity of the opinions expressed there. Without being a single organization or a homogeneous institution in social, spatial and strategic terms, the world of humanitarianism well and truly exists today at the level of representations and globalized actions.

In my visits to refugee camps I have discovered the concrete reality and micropolitical legibility of the humanitarian world, which are hidden when people simply speak of humanitarianism 'in general'. In actual fact, despite its globalism, this world only ever exists in local forms, though none of the spaces of this apparatus falls outside the great network of humanitarianism.

The function that the humanitarian apparatus performs today on the world scale may be described as the *left hand of the Empire*.[2] It acquires its meaning at the global and multi-local level in so far as it closely follows and attenuates the devastation of military intervention – a police operation that acts simultaneously at different points on the globe. There is a hand that strikes and a hand that heals. We have seen this in a crude fashion in the military interventions led by the US army in Afghanistan in 2001 and Iraq in 2003: the aerial distribution of supplies and medicines accompanied the dropping of bombs; assessments of the number of survivors and potential orphans to feed were published in advance; the precise localization and cartography of future camps for a predicted total of 'displaced populations', as well as the erection of tents and the delivery of thousands of shelters, all anticipated the programmed effects of military operations.

On the one hand, a global 'police' exercises control, and if necessary intervenes militarily in the extreme crises that regularly shatter certain parts of the world seen as wretched and 'vulnerable', or in so-called 'low-intensity operations'. On the other hand, since this represents a normal and constant activity in planetary life, the hand that heals requires a whole permanent apparatus – an organization, budgets, staff – whose extent has considerably expanded in recent decades and which has integrated the discourse of rescue and emergency into a permanent and powerful system. On the one hand is a consensual world order with an 'imperial' form in the sense that any political adversary is denied and the world conceived simply as divided between a single order (the world, the whole or the 'Empire') and an outside represented by 'rogue' individuals, organizations or states.[3] On the other hand are relief actions based on a single representation of humanity, and practised only on the figure of the absolute victim, which is also the *raison d'être* of the humanitarian world. This world is thus caught in the iron net of an unwanted and yet determining relationship (if only to indicate sites of intervention), with multiple ramifications for global policing.[4] Its task well reveals the conception of 'endless emergency' that we mentioned in our introduction.

This conception gives the humanitarian apparatus unprecedented functions, the whole thing taking the form of what I have called humanitarian government, both global and multi-local – or rather, global because it is multi-local. It is as a minimum a descriptive concept: each camp is governed by a series of organizations that locally exercise sovereign power. It becomes a theoretical concept in the sense that it can be literally abstracted from any specific terrain in order to conceive the totality (invisible as such) of the global humanitarian apparatus.

In a way that is very palpable in the case of refugees and displaced persons in the countries of the South,[5] humanitarian government is the entity that constructs, manages and controls camps, everywhere that these are needed, in order to keep there populations who are viewed, simultaneously or alternatively, as vulnerable and undesirable, victims and dangerous. This demands the development of virgin territory, with access roads; the installation of tents and huts; piping, wells and drainage; facilities for transporting materials, foodstuffs and people; bush clinics and schools, etc. Corresponding to this infrastructure is a division of tasks and a coordination between workers (foreign and local) from different NGOs and UN agencies that are all 'branches' of a government operating locally, by delegation, under the control of the head of the camp. Food, health, roads, transport, youth, shelters, security, literacy programmes, environment – each has their 'ministerial portfolio' in the organization of the camp's life.

But if refugee camps are today the most developed example of the new form of government, this is spreading across a range of situations marked by the same triptych of extraterritoriality, relegation and exception. These three characteristics have to be fine-tuned and qualified in the study of each particular case, but they identify a common 'space' on the world scale in which the humanitarian apparatus is logically deployed, without obstacle, with its own specific modes of intervention, legitimization and government. A flexible and multi-local apparatus, with material and human deployment 'on demand' and spaces for camps: it is in the intertwining of these different 'places' that the humanitarian government takes shape. This series of organizations, networks, agents and financial resources, distributed in a number of countries, is deployed with flexibility, establishing its own exceptional spaces for a given time.

This is how 'humanitarian situations' are created, in the sense that humanitarianism occupies the whole space of life, including the political space: situations in which the victim and the guilty, the true refugee and the false refugee, the vulnerable and the undesirable occupy the whole representation of the person, and sound the end of the citizen who may say what he or she wants without condition. Everything is set for a governmental humanitarianism to play its part in the 'government of the world'.[6] We could then generalize Paul Virilio's comment apropos of the creation in Ukraine, twenty years after Chernobyl, of a 'ministry for emergency situations': 'It seems it's not a matter of opening political ministries anymore there. Instead the State of Emergency sets up its administration.'[7] And the convergence of all the world's miseries (or catastrophes), whether 'natural', epidemics, social or political, in the same regime of thinking and government (distinct, emergency and exceptional) inaugurates the age of humanitarian government.

It is already possible now to trace the outlines of this on a global scale. Humanitarianism is deployed according to the principle not of a rigid system or structure, but rather of an apparatus with the form of a network of networks, in which different groups, small lobbies, experts, and more or less charismatic leaders, intersect, ally with or confront one another, with all these communications and a substantial part of their personnel in constant movement around the globe. Its reticular forms lead towards multiple and diverse spaces, dispersed across the planet with greater or lesser density in different continents – Africa, the Middle East and Asia being today the regions of heaviest 'investment' by the humanitarian intervention apparatus.

Far from simply involving non-governmental organizations acting in the humanitarian field, this includes all participants – public and private, governmental, inter-governmental and UN – that use the term 'humanitarianism' as a mode of recognition, distinction or legitimization of their action on the ground. The collaboration, willy-nilly, between all these entities in the same parcel of global space is further evidence that the apparatus as a whole acts as much for control as for relief.

Humanitarian government does not have an actual organized global coordination, even though this is indeed imaginable, and even to some extent already imagined. Let us examine this point a bit more closely.

The UN High Commission for Refugees plays a leading role in both political and economic aspects. It 'subcontracts' its operation through agreements with various NGOs to work with refugees under its responsibility: more than 500 NGOs in the year 2000, and 575 in 2007 (424 of these being national and 151 international). Attention should be drawn to the key role of this special institution, inasmuch as it is today the great UN coordinator of this specific government, even if it does not entirely control the situation, being most frequently caught in a vice between the local and national authorities in the countries of intervention, the pressure of the Western governments that finance it, and the NGOs that work with it.

The creation within the UN in 1992 of the Office for the Coordination of Humanitarian Affairs (OCHA) represented an attempt to coordinate humanitarian action in the different branches of this apparatus. Conflicts of competence have sometimes appeared between the UNHCR and the OCHA in the last two decades, particularly in African contexts, as was the case around the management of internally displaced persons. Finally, responsibility for handling the internally displaced in camps was given in 2006 to the UNHCR. In the same sense, but at the European level, European Commission Humanitarian Aid (ECHO), also established in 1992, occupies a key place in the financing and therefore steering of intervention by European NGOs, in particular the far-flung nebula of small NGOs without independent financing.

The apparatus also includes those large NGOs with international range. Some of these developed from local or national organizations that appeared in the first half of the twentieth century, others were born in the 1970s. But for all these organizations, the 1980s and 1990s were decisive for intervention on a planetary scale. This was particularly the case with CARE (United States),[8] the International Rescue Committee (United States, 1942), OXFAM International (1995),[9] Save the Children,[10] MSF (France, 1971) and ACF (France, 1979).[11] A dozen or so international NGOs mobilize 90 per cent of the total funds of humanitarian NGOs, and a small number of these have budgets larger than that of the UNHCR itself.[12] All these organizations seek to coordinate the intervention on the ground of their different national sectors, and more rarely to define common campaigns or positions at the international level.

Finally, a Global Humanitarian Platform was established in 2006 to bring together and coordinate the three components of humanitarian intervention: the NGOs, the Red Cross and Red Crescent movement, and the UN along with the international organizations associated with it (International Organization for Migration, World

Bank, etc.). The aim was to bring fluidity and harmony into the relationships between these different actors, and to better integrate the small national NGOs into the 'platform'.[13] In the same year, the UN established its so-called 'cluster' strategy to organize coordination and division of tasks between the different UN agencies active on the same territory.[14]

The present situation of the camps, and the development of waiting zones on the borders or zones of 'internal asylum' in the countries of the South, are just a few aspects of a wider political process that is giving humanitarian action an increasing place in the world in general, and not only in the camps of the UNHCR. Certain spaces, but also certain categories of population and especially certain events, give ever broader range to an 'indirect administration' by the NGO system.[15] Humanitarian organizations and UN agencies intervene on the terrain of all catastrophes – 'crisis', war or chaos – to make the drama of the populations that they reach more bearable. These organizations are not only morally comforting, but spread a culture of emergency – for example, there is a very active market in 'kit', and competition between the major NGOs in the medical, nutritional and logistic fields. On top of this, with the help of habit and media publicity, they lead people to take increasingly for granted 'states of emergency' – even, finally, the actual idea of a 'state of exception'.

Humanitarian exceptionalism or permanent catastrophe

The terrains of humanitarian government extend, renew themselves and form a system that is technically and ideologically homogeneous. The reproduction on a world scale of the domain of humanitarian exceptionalism needs the model, now emerging, of permanent catastrophe. Thus, in the face of a political inaction that is responsible for social and economic 'catastrophes', and a political chaos that is favourable to the development of war and violence of all kinds, in the face of the lack of foresight and the absence of political ecology that make natural disasters that much more deadly for those who are already the most deprived, a politics and economics of emergency and catastrophe (more precisely, of 'post-catastrophe') are developed and structured on a global scale. All this becomes the common and standardized response to the dramas of all kinds that succeed in affecting, moving or disturbing the populations of the rich countries: tidal waves or terrible hurricanes, the spread of global viruses, intense and large-scale warfare, the massive displacement of haggard African populations are all unforgetful reminders of the existence of a 'darkness' from which everyone seeks protection.

Paul Virilio noted that the same battalion of the US army (the Florida National Guard) that specializes in dealing with the consequences of natural catastrophes (various kinds of pillage and crime in the wake of earthquakes or fires on American territory) undertook its first mission outside the United States in Iraq in 2003, two months after the official ending of hostilities, to try to restore order in Baghdad.[16] A further battalion of the same National Guard then appeared on American soil to repress the acts of pillage committed in New Orleans in August–September 2005 after the passage of Hurricane Katrina. So-called 'natural' catastrophes, or social catastrophes such as American 'preventive war' or 'war against terrorism'; the temporary or permanent exile of millions of people driven away by violence, war, famine or the social and economic chaos in which certain regions of Africa, Central and South America are trapped: in all such cases, similar technical and organizational apparatuses are mobilized in response, with military forces and humanitarian organizations intervening side by side. Their 'emergency' modes of operation leave little room for critical reflection or challenge, and politics upsets them.

One piece of evidence of the growing importance of the 'market' in emergency and catastrophe currently being consolidated in world politics is the attraction it now exerts on private business, which is starting to compete with NGOs and UN agencies on their own ground. Too lucrative to be left to the 'charitable souls of the UN', as the Canadian journalist Naomi Klein puts it, catastrophe economics is passing increasingly systematically under the control of the World Bank.[17] NGO interventions represent an attractive economic opportunity, all the more so in that 'post-catastrophe' or 'post-conflict' rescue and reconstruction leave little choice for the 'beneficiaries': 'With the local population struggling to find shelter and food, political organizing against privatization can seem like an unimaginable luxury.'[18] The same thing was noted in New Orleans after its devastation by Hurricane Katrina: the public authorities were so slow in intervening that the media, researchers and organizations did not hesitate to denounce a veritable abandonment of the city's Black population by the state, but reconstruction would rapidly become the soil of a 'laboratory of neoliberalism', according to the sociologist Mike Davis.[19] This experimental conception is also telling about a fact of first importance in characterizing the whole set of terrains of market humanitarianism: the mere announcement of a 'catastrophe', whether natural or political, offers the extraordinary advantage of making a clean slate of the existing situation, in a further moment of exceptionalism.

The silent collapse of international solidarity

If the history of humanitarianism has been characterized by a long and slow process of development, justification and institutionaliza- tion, the acceleration of this history in the last four decades has made the humanitarian tale one of the great stories of globalization, in the sense that its action is among those that have constituted the world as indeed one world. Like others, the global humanitarian story is still only in its beginnings. We can decipher its three most striking steps, noting from the start how this story – which we can call the contemporary humanitarian movement – developed on the basis of a succession of crises.

First phase: the 'French doctors' of the MSF were part of the politi- cal activism of the 1970s (humanitarianism, ecology, alternative urban cultures, ethno-politics), bearers of the generalized critique of the First World's system of production and consumption, its moral and political values.

Second phase, second situation: the turn from the 1980s to the 1990s corresponded to the political and military reorganization of the world after the fall of the Berlin wall; this was the heyday of highly publicized humanitarian operations, carrying the eye and the hand of the First World far afield; the age in which NGOs were internationalized and professionalized, with convergence between them and the UN agencies.

Third phase: the context of the 'war on terror' unleashed after 11 September 2001, which strangely resembles science fiction, but permits the effective global application of an imperial police, with humanitarianism as its 'left hand'; the humanitarian government that is coming into being today is an efficient and globalized apparatus, made up of experts and expatriates who have to carry out the man- agement of chaos, the control and confinement of the 'catastrophic' effects of the division of the world into zones of prosperity and the supernumerary.

The gradually constructed convergence between the history of refugee camps and that of humanitarianism finds expression in the number, diversity and reproduction of the camp form, with humani- tarian activists being the managers – principal or secondary, as the case may be – of almost all the forms of camp confinement in the world today. If it is fully realized, the fragmentation of the world of which humanitarian government is one of the means will probably avoid direct conflicts or make it possible to repel these, orient them and 'contain' them. But by tightly closing off the protected world from the excluded world, it will signal the disappearance of the very question of international solidarity – a difficult moment for a humanitarian movement which many people saw as a new, concrete and effective form of international solidarity, going out into the field to meet the distant 'others'.

My argument is not aimed at denigrating the commitment, skill and sincere devotion of the thousands of volunteers with humanitarian organizations who set off to these distant and difficult parts. Personal commitment in this type of action is a bold attitude, in which each humanitarian 'missionary' seeks to overcome or break the comfortable belief of the sceptics in the rich countries for whom the world today is simply a spectacle leaving no handle for action or change. Reacting to this pessimism, the 'volunteers' of humanitarianism sought – and still seek – to go and take a closer look. Impelled by very varied motivations, these individuals have decided to devote part of their time, their professional and personal career, to this commitment.[20] This experience sometimes leads them to personal questioning and virulent critique of humanitarian action and its 'system'. Some of them have thus transformed their experience a posteriori into a 'terrain' that they inscribe in a reflective approach towards anthropological, sociological or political research. At that point, their critique of the humanitarian world, their disillusion and sometimes their rancour, are very evident.

Thus the cynical belief that humanitarian commitment is necessarily naïve and poorly informed about its own effects and issues does not withstand the test of facts. Criticism, and above all self-criticism, generally arise from an unease that is felt on the ground. This unease was most clearly apparent at the time of the first steps of contemporary humanitarianism, just as it often is with a volunteer's 'first mission'. These two temporalities – the historical one of the first moment of the contemporary humanitarian movement, and the individual one of the first mission in the trajectories of volunteers – are remarkably brought together in the book that the journalist Anne Vallaeys has devoted to the NGO Médecins Sans Frontières,[21] and also presented very well in the film based on this book.[22] MSF nurses and doctors describe their first experiences, and recall with concern their surprise in the face of the very real power over life and death that they wielded: the lives of those people among whom they worked were very directly dependent on the time that they chose to devote to one person rather than another, on selections made when people arrive at a camp as a function of the age or weight of those seeking aid. Gathering refugees into camps, and the selection of the beneficiaries of emergency aid (well known under the name of 'screening'), both illustrate from the 1970s onward, at the level of each humanitarian intervention, the capacity for domination that the Western world enjoys, as paradoxically demonstrated by the action of the 'French doctors' that was sometimes 'rebellious'. It is in the petty detail of the everyday procedures of humanitarian action on the ground that we see most clearly at work its power of life and death, the domination that it exercises at every turn. This observation and the criticisms to which it has given rise (ideological critique, but also personal questioning) fuel discussion, dispute and revolt, which are also part of the humanitarian world with its diversity of trajectories, ideologies and beliefs.

The crises of the humanitarian movement

It is not my intention here, therefore, to repeat for the umpteenth time the arguments and moral chiding about 'wrong' good intentions, the self-interest or 'bad' commitment of the humanitarian world. Besides, if one had to get involved in this kind of moralism and argument, the first requirement would be to take account of the volume and wealth of internal criticisms that constantly nourish the debates, forums, conferences, periodicals and books characteristic of individual NGOs and groups of these.[23]

And yet, despite the many virtues of commitment to humanitarian action, the fact remains that the economics, culture and politics associated with the humanitarian apparatus inscribe a whole part of the contemporary reality of the world in the intersecting registers of exceptionalism, catastrophe management and the keeping out of undesirables. This reality goes very far beyond the good will and the particular operational projects of the organizations involved in it. The formation of a humanitarian government at the global level is the issue at stake today in the history of the humanitarian movement. It is in this context that its crisis is evident.

One of the most powerful contemporary international NGOs, Médecins Sans Frontières, which was awarded the Nobel Peace Prize in 1999, is seeking to redefine the sense and 'perimeter' of its action.

Other French and international NGOs have for some time been undergoing 'crises' whose terms are basically very much the same. On the national as on the international level, everyone agrees that there is a 'crisis of growth'. The vertiginous increase in funds, even a certain 'bureaucratization', are pressing the organization's members to try to do more than just deal with emergencies, perhaps do something other than this (social action or development, i.e. with a longer-term perspective), or else to give medical emergency so broad a definition that an NGO of medical 'relief' risks losing its credibility. But the crisis is also a social one, when the customary turnover of humanitarian 'volunteers' becomes a problem in relation to the need for training and allocation of human resources, for well-identified and recognized skills, and for adequate reward in terms of salaries. Finally, if, for some people, working for the MSF has simply become something 'good on the CV' in a logic of professional competition, this is also because the humanitarian movement is experiencing a moral crisis. Having become a recommendable professional experience, the social and moral specificity of humanitarian work has been obscured. In recent years, volunteers have frequently been in situations of danger, and there have sometimes been 'senseless' accidental deaths, whether because they are Westerners whose vehicles or dollars are envied, or because they are members of the 'international family' working alongside the military forces of the UN or a national army from the Western world, i.e. from where the expatriate humanitarian workers also come. In this context, the 'fundamentals' of the organization – financial and political independence, relief actions, taking 'evidence' on the ground, criticism of the humanitarian 'system' – are no longer as stable or sufficient as they were; dissent is expressed, in an internal dilemma that the majority of international NGOs are experiencing today.

Is humanitarianism being impelled towards a market logic in order to occupy (with skill, experience, effectiveness, etc.) a particular space – 'its' space, as defined by the perimeter of humanitarian government – precisely one to which private companies have also directed themselves? In this emerging logic of markets and expertise, the NGOs are not really assured of being competitive in the face of private companies. At the same time, they are not assured of keeping the social anchorage that was their specific strength, as the motivations of voluntary and solidaristic commitment have suddenly lost their bearings.

This tension – both a crisis of growth and a crisis of identity – is profound and general. It is drawing the humanitarian movement in two possible directions, towards two purposes and two alternative conversions: on the one hand, the privatization of humanitarianism; on the other, state humanitarianism. Drawing on the case of OXFAM among others, Marc Abélès stresses the social proximity of the officials of the major NGOs with the world of business (its staff, its management methods, its financing), as well as the 'qualitative mutation' of NGOs that is expressed in internal tensions whose terms largely echo what we have ourselves explained: 'Does the operation of the NGOs have to evolve in the direction of a rationalization after the model of the most profitable private companies? Do they have to embody above all an ideal of activism and solidarity in the lineage of the movement from which they arose?'[24]

The crisis of humanitarianism in the wake of 11 September 2001 has also been analysed in a special issue of the periodical *Cultures et Conflits*, edited by Wolf-Dieter Eberwein.[25] This focuses on the (de)construction of the 'humanitarian order' (a term that denotes on the one hand a set of norms, and on the other an organizational system), converging therefore, though from different starting points, with the perimeter and content of humanitarian government that we have described in this chapter and the preceding one. In addition, the analyses in this periodical show the extent to which humanitarianism is already an image and a language with uses that today go far beyond the actual humanitarian organizations properly so-called. These can be found as forms of legitimization or professional practices in the contexts of diplomacy and government policy.[26] We find this same presence – displaced and reconstituted – of humanitarian language and practice within the armed forces, as analysed by the sociologist Sami Makki in relation to so-called 'civil-military operations'.[27]

The crisis that the humanitarian movement has been experiencing since the first years of the new decade is thus at the same time economic, social and moral. A profound transformation is under way. On its outcome will depend the possibility of an internal critique of the global humanitarian apparatus.

Conclusion

By way of conclusion, I will sum up the overall picture I have been able to draw from this study undertaken in refugee camps between 2000 and 2007, chiefly in Africa, along with some final comments. The result is clear: the legal categories of 'refugee' are everywhere steadily giving way to a diversity of 'rejected'. And yet these are the same individuals – or could easily be so. They become stateless and illegal, lacking resources of any kind. On the cursor of biopolitics, they are moving away from 'keeping alive' and towards 'letting die'. In a general fashion, the protection of the stateless (when this is still mentioned) is no more than a euphemistic justification for controlling the undesirables. Other groups are placed right from the start under the policing mode of control, with humanitarian assistance some-times as an add-on (Libya, Australia, camps for foreigners in Europe, etc.).

Despite the praiseworthy efforts and words of certain commission-ers and high officials of UN agencies, it is perfectly clear today that the Geneva convention of 1951 defining the rights of asylum and refugees no longer actually governs the policies of asylum and hos-pitality practised by those Western governments that drafted and voted for it at the time of the Cold War. In the UN agencies, the international organizations, and the majority of Western countries today, direct control of population movements prevails over the pro-tection of the stateless. The UNHCR scarcely now proposes anything more than a humanitarian supplement to this control, even if under-taking – by its mandate, renewed in 2006 – the management of refugee camps and 'emergency shelters'. This no longer has much to do with the universalistic and, in principle, supranational mission that the UN entrusted it with in the wake of the Second World War.

In a fractal fashion, by way of the externalization of frontiers, the rejection of undesirables has repercussions on the most distant and destitute countries. Even if demographically massive, the economic share of those the world over with 'no share' becomes residual in this excluding conception of globalization centred on the 'zones of prosperity'.[1] A form of political, economic and social chaos has been permanently established in the supernumerary parts of the planet, those that largely comprise what has successively been known as the Third World, the developing countries, and the countries of the South.

This permanent chaos has led states and UN agencies to reconceive the treatment and control of the humanitarian consequences of a collateral 'catastrophe' bound up with the project of maintaining order on a planet that is ever more fragmented, and divided into protected and excluded. If this order has managed to impose itself as the unchallengeable form of a globalization that favours those social and national minorities that benefit from it, its collateral and permanent catastrophe will seem just as inevitable as a 'natural' catastrophe – depoliticized and thus manageable in the same terms and by the same apparatus as we have already seen at work in the camps. What can we learn from this experience?

First of all, these are the camps of today and tomorrow, 21st-century camps. What spaces are we talking about? And what are they leading to? They are being transformed and 'miniaturized' along the lines of present-day processes of social control; they are becoming more flexible, and more bound up than ever with an economy and culture that are both standardized and ephemeral: camps for the internally displaced, controlled border spaces and the recuperation of self-organized refugees (possibly via the intervention of certain humanitarian organizations) all provide the future airlocks of control and release for flows of undesirable populations.

Humanitarianism and politics

It is again from the camps that we can see the emergence of tactics, strategies and mobilizations that jam the apparatus and disturb its programmed order, as we have seen in examining various forms of territorialization, protest and speaking out within these places. Humanitarian fiction may ascribe the right to life to a generic human being recognized in the universal and absolute victim, but to all appearance this right is conferred according to membership of certain

212

assigned categories. Thus the refugee, the internally displaced, the woman in the waiting zone, the child without papers receive their survival kit in their capacity of belonging to such a category. Within the camps, the category of 'refugee' is itself broken down into distinct categories of vulnerability, which end up establishing a hierarchy of misfortune. This exercise in division, which is precisely the application of biopower, is also a breach on the basis of which it is possible to express refusal.

This question is often brought up in debates within or about humanitarianism: the question of 'de-politicization' in and by humanitarian action, and still more so in and by the situation of 'exception' that particularly characterizes terrains of military and humanitarian action, and leaves neither time nor space for Hannah Arendt's 'democratic conversation'.[2] But what kind of emergency are we speaking of when humanitarian intervention is set fast in a local space for years or even decades? And what kind of policy and politics does this display? An event at which I was present in the Tobanda camp in Sierra Leone[3] will allow me to draw a conclusion about the potential and effects of politics in the humanitarian context.

In November 2003, during one of the weekly meetings of representatives of the national and international NGOs, national and UN public bodies active in this camp, I found myself alongside the local coordinator of Médecins Sans Frontières. Being then in the process of conducting various studies at Tobanda, I informed her of the fact that those in charge of the camp had dismissed a refugee who had been mandated by some of his fellows to represent them and replaced him by another younger man who had no charisma for the population, but was known to be particularly 'docile' towards the administration. The MSF coordinator presented these facts to the fifteen or so participants at the meeting and asked the head of the camp to explain himself. The response she received made it perfectly clear: 'The camp doesn't need democracy to operate', he said in a tone both rather mocking and annoyed, thereby putting an end to any discussion. This was in a way the speech of a head of government, who directly read the situation politically and laid down the law.

This little event provided me with a key for understanding, which I have used and developed in the present book: there is a specific order and organization of power in the camps, and more generally in the places of humanitarian intervention, which the concept of 'humanitarian government' is designed to express as closely as possible. This power defines its own space as one of exception, a frontier, an out-place in the sense that individuals are treated and managed as nameless victims devoid of identity – as stateless, in fact, in the sense that they no longer have any framework in which to exercise their citizenship.

But behind this first observation, a second immediately follows. To speak of free representation and free speech for the refugees in the government of the Tobanda camp was apparently the most out-of-place question one could raise in this situation, and yet at the same time the most fundamental one – not (or not only) because two expatriates shared a disagreement that particular day, but because this disagreement was expressed and forced the administrator to respond. A few weeks later, in fact, when the UN High Commissioner for Refugees – Ruud Lubbers at that time – made a brief visit to Tobanda, the 'representative' of the refugees appointed by the camp administration as acting chairman was absent . . . due to illness. In his place there appeared one of the most visible public figures among the residents, a preacher, who sat at the meeting table and was able to present some of the protests and demands of the refugees, from a list he had made on several sheets in a school exercise book.

The same double situation was equally visible within the camp: humanitarian government and refugee politics. Other facts of the same order have been observed on other sites. Some of these bear on the exercise of a power of life over various categories of beneficiaries, others on forms of protest, diversion and dispute on the part of these same beneficiaries when they do not perfectly play the role that the apparatus assigns them.

How, finally, can we define this relationship between politics and humanitarianism? It does not seem adequate to me to say that politics is always more or less hidden 'behind' or 'at the heart of' interventions of control, aid or care, so that their ultimate meaning is a political one. The political question I indicate here is something other; it refers to a pragmatic and situational approach – political in the sense of policy, i.e. the actions, conflicts, mobilizations and speech that constantly found and refound the existence of the subject in a particular situation (subject of speech or subject of political action).

This action and speech that form a subject in such a situation are, however, absent from the institutional recognition of the beneficiaries of humanitarianism: whether 'refugees', 'disaster victims' or 'tolerated', or their negative alter egos 'illegals', 'terrorists', 'stateless', etc. – all these are external identitarian categories ascribed according to 'technical' criteria of assistance or control, i.e. policing or humanitarian criteria that have no need of the voice of the beneficiaries to confirm them. At a minimum, a camp 'doesn't need democracy to operate', as we just heard. It is in this sense that we can say that military and police interventions on the one hand, and humanitarian ones on the other, by their nature act *against* politics by producing exceptionality and presenting figures of victims and guilty, vulnerable and undesirable – all incompatible with those of the subject and the citizen. The whole question is knowing in which conditions a tension will appear in contexts that exclude, by definition, politics as action or act of speech. It is to answer this question that I have studied here politics in the space of the camps, by examining the tension between power and politics, subjection and subjectivation, humanitarian government and refugee politics.

It is in the gaps in the system, the failures of humanitarian work, that we can see what could be called the 'raw material' of injustice, contradicting the proclaimed fiction of equal treatment for all suffering humanity – unequal distribution of covers, food ration disastrous in quantity or quality, insult and physical violence against 'crowds' requesting aid, forced repatriation, the prohibition on building huts from rigid material, the hunt for 'profiteers'. But for such injustice to exist, it must be possible to speak it. The political question that is then raised on the ground relates to an enigma that is shared by all the voiceless: how to move from complaint to cry, how to start speaking out? In the space of the camp, in order to be understood this speech must find a place within the language of humanitarianism, this being the only convention of speech that is locally audible. In this context, politics therefore takes paths previously unexplored.

Thinking at the limit

The only genuine *event* in the life of the camps is the speech and political action of the refugees themselves, which for a moment changes this into a public space. Their very existence expresses a refusal of the identity assigned to them in this temporary extra-territorial residence. Over time, these moments multiply, relationships are consolidated and reproduced, spaces materially transformed. Soon they are no longer completely camps. They could well disappear and give way to a squat, a quarter, a ghetto or a town, and at the same time to a local experience of politics. They would then rediscover the double meaning of the city, both urban and political, whatever their material aspect, their management of space and the state of their infrastructure.

215

Are we able to conceive both politics and towns developing tomorrow from these uncertain, precarious and hybrid places?

Ultimately there is no prospectus, no utopia brought back from this long exploration in the camps and the world of humanitarianism, simply a conviction of the urgent necessity (a real emergency) of changing the focus of our gaze on the world. It is ultimately from its margins that we have to conceive politics, alterity and urbanism. Borders, *ban-lieux*,[4] town-camps, refuge-towns: camps can lead on to towns, and the history of wars and population movements has already offered several examples of this. This transformation will signal the end of the camps and the beginning of resilient towns: in Africa, in the Middle East, in Asia, and even on the borders of Europe.

By way of this break with a present that has so far been interminable, today's camps will then finally become an object of history: both the work of a time now past and the worthy objects of a remembrance and reflection to be projected onto our living memories in order to help us to reconceive spaces, Others and politics.

Notes

Acknowledgements

1 Centre de Réflexion sur l'Action et les Savoirs Humanitaires (CRASH).
2 'Corps des victimes, espaces du sujet – réfugiés, sinistrés et clandestins: de l'expérience au témoignage', supported by the joint initiative 'Terrains, Techniques, Théories' of the Ministère de la Recherche and the Agence Nationale de la Recherche (2004–8).

Introduction From Vulnerable to Undesirable

1 *The Humanitarian Impact of the West Bank Barrier on Palestinian Communities*, United Nations – Office for the Coordination of Humanitarian Affairs (OCHA), Jerusalem, Update 7, June 2007, p. 8.
2 The first date here marks the closure of the Sangatte camp in France (by Nicolas Sarkozy, then minister of the interior) and the strengthening of European inter-governmental strategies to tighten border control. The second marks the establishment of FRONTEX (European Agency for the Management of Operational Cooperation at the External Borders of the Member States of the European Union), which is particularly active in the Mediterranean.
3 On the theme of camps in Europe today, see two recent collective publications: Jérôme Valluy (ed.), 'L'Europe des camps. La mise à l'écart des étrangers', *Cultures et Conflits*, 57, 2005, and Olivier Le Cour Grandmaison, Gilles Lhuilier and Jérôme Valluy (eds.), *Le Retour des camps? Sangatte, Lampedusa, Guantánamo . . .*, Paris: Autrement, 2006. On camps in French history, see Denis Peschanski, *La France des camps: l'internement, 1938–1946*, Paris: Gallimard, 2002, and, among a number of case studies, Emmanuel Filhol, *Un camp de concentration*

français: les Tsiganes alsaciens-lorrains à Crest, 1915–1919, Grenoble: Presses universitaires de Grenoble, 2004; Émile Temime and Geneviève Dreyfus-Armand, *Les Camps sur la plage: un exil espagnol*, Paris: Autrement, 1995; Émile Temime (with Nathalie Deguigné), *Le Camp du Grand Arénas: Marseille, 1944–1966*, Paris: Autrement, 2001. A general study of the twentieth-century camps in France has been made by Marx Bernadot (*Camps d'étrangers*, Paris: Éditions du Croquant, 2008, and 'Le pays aux mille et un camps. Approche sociohistorique des espaces d'internement en France au XXe siècle', *Les Cahiers du Cériem*, Université de Rennes-II, 2003).

4 Peschanski, *La France des camps*, p. 17.

5 See ch. 2.

6 I deliberately use the term 'hangar' (also the title of Jacqueline Salmon's photographic exhibition 'Sangatte 2001 – Le hangar') to refer both to the multiplicity and commonplaceness of the material and social forms taken by the camps, and, in relation to this multiple reality, to the need for a theoretical and political application of the 'generic' concept of *camp*. I shall return to this question below.

7 UNHCR estimate, limited to the recognized categories of refugees and internally displaced persons.

8 A critical presentation of numbers and categories of displaced persons is given in the first chapter.

9 A defence of the discovery of meaning from attention to detail is developed by Albert Piette, *Ethnographie de l'action: l'observation des détails*, Paris: Métalié, 1996.

10 See ch. 3.

11 I shall return to this in ch. 12.

12 In order to account for this experience, I have integrated at different points in the text notes and documents taken directly from the field.

1 Refugees, Displaced, Rejected: The Itinerary of the Stateless

1 See Rony Brauman, *L'Action humanitaire*, Paris: Flammarion, 2000, p. 49.

2 Under the Geneva Convention of 1951, the status of refugee is to be attributed to an individual, who, 'owing to a well-founded fear of being persecuted for reasons of race, religion, nationality, membership of a particular social group or political opinion, is outside the country of his nationality and is unable or, owing to such fear, is unwilling to avail himself of the protection of that country'. As we shall see below, this status of 'conventional' refugee is today attributed only to a very small share of asylum seekers (less than 10 per cent in the present decade, and as low as 1 per cent in certain countries).

3 See Michel Agier and Jérôme Valluy, 'Le UNHCR dans la logique des camps', in Le Cour Grandmaison, Lhuilier and Valluy (eds.), *Le Retour des camps?* pp. 153–63.

4 An in-depth historical analysis of these questions has been undertaken by Gérard Noiriel, *Réfugiés et sans-papiers: la République face au droit d'asile, XIXe–XXe siècle*, Paris: Hachette, 1999 (1st edition 1991).

5 Jean-Christophe Rufin, *L'Aventure humanitaire*, Paris: Gallimard, 1994, p. 26.

6 Ibid.

7 The UNHCR officially envisages three 'solutions' to the 'problem' of refugees: (1) repatriation, (2) integration in the host country, (3) resettlement in a third country (i.e. neither the country of origin nor the place of reception). I shall return to this question below, and particularly to the UNHCR's preference in Africa for a fourth 'solution': 'encampment' (see ch. 2).

8 Founder of the Centre for the Study of Refugees at Oxford University, Harrell-Bond was at this time head of a programme for legal assistance to refugees (AMERA – Africa and Middle East Refugee Assistance), and taught at the American University in Cairo. Her account of the events on Mustapha Mahmoud Square is contained in an interview with Fabienne Le Houérou, 'Le drame de la place Mustapha-Mahmoud au Caire raconté par Barbara Harrell-Bond', TERRA editions, April 2006: http://terra.rezo.net/article553.html. See also the page that *Le Monde* devoted to this subject on 8 January 2006.

9 Le Houérou and Harrell-Bond, 'Le drame de la place Mustapha-Mahmoud'.

10 Letter from the UNHCR representative to the Egyptian government, 22 December 2005.

11 An assembly that sometimes had the appearance of a large demonstration, as, according to Harrell-Bond in the interview cited, there were at some points as many as 4,000 individuals gathered in the square.

12 Letter from the representative of the UNHCR to the Egyptian government, 27 October 2005. As I have indicated above, Barbara Harrell-Bond, for her part, insists that two-thirds of the demonstrators held UNHCR cards.

13 H. Arendt, *The Origins of Totalitarianism*, New York: Harcourt, Brace Jovanovich, 1968, p. 287.

14 I have developed this description of the refugees' community of existence in Agier, *On the Margins of the World*, Cambridge: Polity, 2008.

15 Federica Sossi, 'Une tragédie en trois actes', *Vacarme*, 39, spring 2007, p. 56.

16 Marie-Claire Caloz-Tschopp, *Les Sans-État dans la philosophie d'Hannah Arendt*, Lausanne: Payot, 2000, p. 24.

17 Ibid., p. 115.

18 This superfluity, as the disappearance of citizens and their space (the *polis* or common world), is what makes possible the totalitarian regime,

just as the desert is the potential site of a destructive sandstorm: 'Totalitarianism strives not towards despotic rule over men, but toward a system in which men are superfluous' (Arendt, *The Origins of Totalitarianism*, p. 457), cited and commented on by Caloz-Tschopp in *Les Sans-État*, p. 111).

19 See ch. 2.
20 See the recent publications of the UNHCR (UNHCR annual reports 1997, 2000), and *Protecting Refugees: The Role of the UNHCR*, Geneva: UNHCR, 2007.
21 The Palestinian refugees have been 'managed' since 1948 by a special organ of the UN, the United Nations Relief and Works Agency for Palestinian Refugees (UNRWA).
22 Internally displaced persons, in the UN definition, are a category of designated persons who have left their place of origin because of internal violence or war, but have remained within the frontiers of their country. After lengthy discussions among the UN agencies, it was finally the UNHCR that was given responsibility for them in 2006.
23 Information from the Migreurop network, www.migreurop.org (29 October 2007).
24 See 'La crise des déplacements persiste malgré une diminution de la violence et des retours limités' (http://iom.int/jahia/jsp/index.jsp, 24 January 2008).
25 See Coordination Française pour le Droit d'Asile, 'Quelles solutions pour une protection internationale des exilés et réfugiés d'Irak?', Paris, December 2007.
26 See Daphné Bouteiller-Paquet, 'Quelle protection subsidiaire dans l'Union européenne?' *Hommes et Migrations*, 1238, 2002, pp. 75–87.
27 *Translator's note:* prisoners are described as *détenus* in French, and the inmates of the new holding centres as *retenus* – 'retained' rather than 'detained'.
28 On the new European immigration policy, see the synthesis of data and analyses presented by Serge Weber in *Nouvelle Europe, nouvelles migrations: frontières, intégration, mondialisation*, Paris: Éditions du Félin, 2007.
29 Jérôme Valluy, 'La nouvelle Europe politique des camps: genèse d'une source élitaire de phobie et de repression des étrangers', *Cultures et Conflits*, 57, spring 2005, p. 22; also, by the same author, 'La fiction juridique de l'asile', *Plein Droit* (GISTI review), 63, December 2004.
30 Office Français de Protection des Réfugiés et Apatrides.
31 Studies of this have been made not only in France but also in the UK, Switzerland, Denmark and Canada.
32 Valluy, 'La nouvelle Europe', p. 23.
33 Ibid., p. 20.
34 Ibid., p. 23.
35 In France in 2007, the OFPRA, the government organism in charge of asylum applications, was passed from the tutelage of the ministry of

foreign affairs to the ministry of 'immigration, integration, national identity and co-development'. At the international level, the idea of a convergence or even fusion between the UNHCR and the IOM, even if still introduced only in the projections of study groups charged with conceiving a new 'international architecture' on the question of international mobility, is a move in the same direction.

36 Accounts of this particular episode were collected at Bamako, the capital of Mali, by the organization Fortress Europe and the Association des Refoulés d'Afrique Centrale au Mali (ARACEM). See Osservatorio sulle Vittime dell'Immigrazione, *Effeti collaterali: rapporto sulle condizioni dei migranti di transito in Algeria*, Fortress Europe / ARACEM, Rome, October 2007. According to Fortress Europe, at least 1,579 migrants died in the Sahara desert between 1996 and 2007. Though probably an underestimate, as emphasized by the author of a review of the international press on which this report was based, this number also includes 'the victims of collective deportations practised by the governments of Tripoli, Algiers and Rabat, well used by now to abandoning groups of hundreds of migrants in frontier zones in the middle of the desert' (http://fortresseurope.blogspot.com/2006/01/revue-de-presse.html, site accessed 21 January 2008).

37 See ch. 5.

38 Official note of the UNHCR representative in Guinea, Conakry, 7 July 2003. We shall return (ch. 2) to the obligation made on the African exiles to move into a camp if they wished to be recognized as 'refugees'.

39 A certificate as a displaced person, giving right to minimal assistance in the form of food, medical care and housing for six months.

40 See Mike Davis, *City of Quartz*, London: Verso, 1990.

41 *Le Monde*, 4 September 2001.

42 See Philippe Rivière, 'L'asile aux antipodes', *Le Monde Diplomatique, Manières de Voir*, 62, 2002.

43 Eleni Varikas, *Les Rebuts du monde. Figures du Paria*, Paris: Stock, 2007, p. 181.

44 A procedure without prior individual checking, but taking into account the displaced group: added by the UN in 1967 to the initial individual criteria of the definition of 'refugee' under the Geneva Convention of 1951.

45 We shall return to this below in the inventory of camps (ch. 2).

46 *Translator's note:* these 'communities of peace' established in Colombia are discussed by Agier in *On the Margins of the World*.

47 See Stellio Rolland, 'De l'individuel au collectif. Des strategies de survie des déplacés colombiens aux regroupements communautaires', *Asylon(s)*, online magazine of the TERRA network, 2, November 2007, http://terra.rezo.net/rubrique124.html.

48 On this whole series of questions, I refer to various recent publications: the dossiers 'L'Europe des camps: la mise à l'écart des étrangers', *Cultures et Conflits*, and 'Migrations en Europe: les frontières de la liberté',

Multitudes, 19, 2005; also Le Cour Grandmaison, Lhuilier and Valluy (eds.), *Le Retour des camps*.

49 This is also shown by the establishment in 2005 of FRONTEX, the European agency for control of European borders. Endowed with substantial financial, logistical and human resources, FRONTEX has already begun operations in the Mediterranean and envisages other interventions on the eastern borders of Europe – those with the western Balkans – as well as the major international airports (*Le Monde*, 5 September 2006). It embodies the European consensus in consolidating a European 'wall' with variable geometry: the territory of Europe is thus creating itself by producing violence at its margins.

50 Liberians United for Reconciliation and Democracy.

51 www.unhcr.org/pages/49c3646c4d6.html.

52 Varikas, *Les Rebuts du monde*.

53 This was done by the Spanish government in 2005, giving the legal status of immigrant a posteriori to nearly 600,000 'illegals', and by the Italian government in 2006 when it regularized 520,000 irregular immigrants. Serge Weber (*Nouvelle Europe, nouvelles migrations*, pp. 93–6) shows convincingly the sociological pertinence of a posteriori regularizations as a public policy validating situations that are already well 'integrated', as distinct from the arbitrary and unrealistic confusion of a priori 'quotas' ('selective immigration') associated with applications being dealt with at a distance.

54 Noiriel, *Réfugiés et sans-papiers*.

55 Ibid., p. 234 (my emphasis).

56 A history that in Europe, indeed, is very largely colonial and postcolonial.

57 Recall, for example, the great migrations of the second half of the nineteenth and beginning of the twentieth centuries, which took tens of thousands of Italians, Spanish, Germans and Poles to Latin America.

2 Encampment Today: An Attempted Inventory

1 See Z. Bauman, *Liquid Modernity*, Cambridge: Polity, 2002.

2 See UNHCR, *Statistical Yearbook*, 2002 (www.UNHCR.ch).

3 Luc Cambrezy, *Réfugiés et exilés: crise des sociétés, crise des territoires*, Paris: Éditions des Archives contemporaines, 2001, p. 72.

4 There is not a word of explanation about camps, nor any figures given, in the annual 25-page luxury brochure presenting the UNHCR's activities for 2006–7; though the middle of the booklet has a double-page colour photo giving an aerial view of a Sudanese refugee camp in Chad, accompanied by the caption: 'The Djabal camp, which arose in the thirsty desert lands of eastern Chad' (*Protecting Refugees: The Role of the UNHCR*, p. 11). In the same vein, in an internet game with educa-

tional purpose that the UNHCR created to make known the fate of refugees, we can observe a complete absence of camps, detention centres, administrative expulsions, and likewise of Africans (see 'Envers et contre tout', www.UNHCR.fr/cgi-bin/texis/vtx/news/opendoc.htm? tbl=news&id=4731b5064).

5 Amnesty International, *Displaced in Darfur: A Generation of Anger*, 22 January 2008.

6 We shall go into more detail on the Liberian conflict and the forced displacements it has led to in ch. 5.

7 Members of the Kissi and Gbandi ethnic groups are found on both sides of the border.

8 Smaïn Laacher, *Le Peuple des clandestins*, Paris: Calmann-Lévy, 2007, in particular pp. 92–147.

9 Ibid., p. 92.

10 Ibid., p. 116.

11 The doyen of the forest camp had arrived ten years previously, in 1997 (ibid., p. 122).

12 Ibid., p. 128.

13 Ibid., p. 129.

14 This was the case with the West Point quarter, whose demographic increase from 2005 was due to the arrival of former internally displaced persons from the camps around Monrovia, former Liberian refugees returned by the UNHCR from Guinea and Sierra Leone, and Sierra Leonese refugees unwilling to return to their country after the peace agreement of 2002 and the closing of their refugee camps.

15 This squat was evacuated early in 2008.

16 This transmitting station belonged to the Voice of America and gave its name to the camp: VOA Camp. This was the oldest displaced persons' camp in the region. Opened in 1992, it had 26,000 occupants in its first year – refugees from Sierra Leone and displaced persons from Liberia itself – and grew by 1998 into the largest camp in the Monrovia district, with 36,000 occupants. By that date, other camps had been opened around VOA Camp to avoid overpopulating it, and it was officially closed by the UNHCR in 2005. The UN agencies and NGOs that operated it gradually left the camp at the request of the Liberian government and the UNHCR. From that time on, a local association founded by Liberians formerly employed with Action Contre la Faim and Médecins Sans Frontières took over the regular distribution of food aid supplied by the World Food Programme, as well as the health information programmes of UNICEF.

17 The Revolutionary United Front was a Sierra Leone rebel movement supported by the forces of Charles Taylor who had been at war in Liberia since late 1989. The RUF launched an insurrection against the government forces in 1991, permanently establishing itself in the east of the country and especially at Kailahun. The war in Sierra Leone, extremely brutal on both sides, was officially ended early in 2002. See Fabrice

Weissman, 'Sierra Leone: la paix à tout prix', in F. Weissman (ed.), *À l'ombre des guerres justes: l'ordre international cannibale et l'action humanitaire*, Paris: Flammarion-MSF, 2003, pp. 53–73.

18 This was done on 5 December 2003, and involved 1,161 entries made over the previous six months (June–November 2003) at the Internal Patients Department of this MSF clinic, as inscribed in the register and noting the residence, origin and mobility (returnee/refugee/resident) of the patient. The MSF clinic in Kailahun was an emergency hospital set up in 2001 in a building made from earth walls with a roof of plastified cloth; it remains the only institution in the town offering medical care.

19 I have developed these ideas in Michel Agier, 'Le ban-lieu du monde. Marges, solitudes et communautés de l'instant', in Christine Macel and Valérie Guillaume (eds.), *Airs de Paris*, Paris: Éditions du Centre Pompidou, 2007, pp. 180–4. On the intermediate spaces between rural and urban, see Mike Davis, *Planet of Slums*, London: Verso, 2006. On the paradoxical conception of the *ban-lieu*, see also Giorgio Agamben, *Homo Sacer: Sovereign Power and Bare Life*, Stanford: Stanford University Press, 1998.

20 Smaïn Laacher, in *Le Peuple des clandestins*, has shown differing degrees of organization and hierarchy re-invented in the various 'jungles' and 'ghettos' formed by the illegals in a situation of survival and danger. Sandrine Revet, for her part, has retrieved from accounts of a natural catastrophe the formation of a 'community of survival' at the moment of the disaster, before any outside intervention of aid or humanitarian support. At moments such as this there is an exceptional transparency between individual and group; the community exists in the situation, it does not refer to any sense of common identity or essence (S. Revet, *Anthropologie d'une catastrophe: les coulées de boue de 1999 au Venezuela*, Paris: Presses de la Sorbonne nouvelle, 2007, p. 129).

21 We find the same in those urban contexts that are the theatre of action of non-identitarian collectives, momentary communities, ephemeral political moments. See Michel Agier, 'Politiques urbaines sans auteur. Une anthropologie des situations' (interview with C. Petcou and A. Querrien), *Multitudes*, 31, 2008, pp. 51–60, and the entire special issue in which this appears: 'Une micropolitique de la ville: l'agir urbain', *Multitudes*, 31, 2008, pp. 11–121.

22 See below, ch. 4.

23 Claire Rodier and Emmanuel Blanchard, 'Des camps pour étrangers', *Plein droit*, 58, December 2003 (special issue 'L'Europe des camps').

24 European Parliament, *The Conditions for Third-Country Nationals (Detention Camps, Open Centres as well as Transit Centres and Transit Zones), with a particular focus on provisions and facilities for persons with special needs in the 25 EU member states*, December 2007, p. 15.

25 In France, more particularly at the Charles-de-Gaulle airport, reception centres for 'detainees', known also as Zapis (created by the Quilès law of 1992 and redefined by the Sarkozy law of 2003), were initially estab-

lished in waiting rooms, parts of hotels or police stations. Zapi 3, opened in 2001, was 'the first waiting zone specifically conceived and built to accommodate unadmitted foreigners. The centre is located in the freight zone of the airport, next to the offices of the Servair company. Combining the functions of a reception centre and an administrative centre, Zapi 3 is a rectangular building of 3,500 sq. m. on two storeys in corrugated iron and concrete – white, yellow and orange – surrounded by two fences (respectively 2.5 metres and 4 metres high) and cameras: some fifteen surveillance cameras are placed around the building, centralized in a control hall managed by the border police, who are responsible for the site's administration' (Chowra Makaremi, 'Vies "en instance": le temps et l'espace du maintien en zone d'attente. Le cas de la "Zapi 3" de Roissy-Charles-de-Gaulle', *Asylon(s)*, online magazine of the TERRA network, 2, November 2007, http://terra.rezo.net/article664.html).

26 European Parliament, *The Conditions for Third-Country Nationals*, p. 15.
27 Sophie Baylac, 'Pologne – Partie II. Le contexte et l'enquête de terrain', annex to Parlement européen, *Conditions des ressortissants de pays tiers retenus dans des centres (camps de détention, centres ouverts, ainsi que des zones de transit) au sein des 25 États membres de l'Union européenne*, December 2007, 'Rapports pays', p. 3.
28 Ibid., p. 5.
29 Ibid., p. 7.
30 The Assocation Nationale d'Assistance aux Frontières pour les Étrangers combines twenty-two member organizations and, since 1989, has intervened at waiting zones at the borders to ensure respect for the national and international rights of foreigners detained there.
31 Makaremi, 'Vies "en instance"'. See also Claire Rodier, 'Zone d'attente de Roissy: à la frontière de l'État de droit', *Hommes et Migrations*, 1238, July–August 2002.
32 Federica Sossi, 'Entre l'espace et le temps des nouvelles frontières', *Lignes*, 26, 2008, p. 50.
33 See above, p. 29, n. 44.
34 In Denmark, for example, 'according to the most recent report by the Danish Refugee Council, the percentage of suicide attempts has tripled since 2001, from 0.6 per cent of the population residing in centres in 2001 to 1.7 per cent in 2006. This observation is related to the duration of residence in the centres and the resulting deterioration in these persons' psychological state' (European Parliament, *The Conditions for Third-Country Nationals*, p. 200).
35 See ch. 4 below, pp. 81ff.
36 Alain Brossat mentions 'the proliferation of a furtive state of exception', in relation to the camps being developed in Europe as airlocks (prior to expulsion) for all kinds of undesirable foreigners. He emphasizes therefore the malleable and precarious character of these installations ('L'espace-camp et l'exception furtive', *Lignes*, 26, 2008, pp. 5–22).

37 See Jean-Pierre Godding (ed.), *Réfugiés rwandais au Zaïre*, Paris: L'Harmattan, 1997. A series of case studies on the political causes and effects of the production of migrants, refugees and displaced persons in the Great Lakes region, on the categorizations and assembly policies in the camps and those of forced repatriation, is presented in the book edited by André Guichaoua, *Exilés, réfugiés, déplacés en Afrique centrale et orientale*, Paris: Karthala, 2004.

38 See ch. 7.

39 In 1990 there were 140 rural or 'semi-urban' UNHCR installations housing around 1 million refugees in Africa, chiefly in Sudan and Tanzania. Véronique Lassailly-Jacob, 'Des réfugiés mozambicains sur les terres des Zambiens. Le cas du site agricole d'Ukwimi, 1987–1994', in Luc Cambrezy and Véronique Lassailly-Jacob (eds.), *Populations réfugiées: de l'exil au retour*, Paris: IRD éditions, 2001, pp. 260–99.

40 Officially, it corresponded to the objective of one of the three solutions to the refugee problem: settlement where they were.

41 Lassailly-Jacob, 'Des réfugiés mozambicains', p. 273.

42 See ch. 6.

43 See Marion Fresia, 'Aide humanitaire et production de services publics en Afrique de l'Ouest: le cas de la gestion des populations mauritaniennes réfugiées au Sénégal', *Le Bulletin de l'APAD*, nos. 23–4, 2002, and 'Des "réfugiés-migrants": les parcours de l'exil des réfugiés mauritaniens au Sénégal', *Asylon(s)*, 2, November 2007 (http://terra.rezo.net/article675. html).

44 M. Rahmi, E. Rabant, L. Cambrezy and M. Mohamed-Abdi, *Environment, Cartography, Demography and Geographical Information System in the Refugee Camps, Dadaab, Kakuma – Kenya*, vol. III, *Demography, Data Processing and Cartography*, n.p.: UNHCR/IRD, 1999, p. 29.

45 See chs. 8 and 9, on the political representation and action of refugees on the one hand, and the question of testimony and speaking out on the other.

46 Cécile Dubernet, 'Du terrain au droit, du droit sur le terrain? Origines et trajectories du label "déplacé interne" ', *Asylon(s)*, 2, November 2007, http://terra.rezo.net/article670.html.

47 Established in 1992.

48 Nearly 20 per cent of this camp's 21,000 residents (Office for the Coordination of Humanitarian Affairs / UNHCR, *IDP Return Survey of Official Camps*, Preliminary Report, HIC-Liberia, May 2004).

49 See Sabri Cigerli, *Les Réfugiés kurdes d'Irak en Turquie*, Paris: L'Harmattan, 1998.

50 Guglielmo Verdirame and Barbara Harrell-Bond, *Rights in Exile: Janus-faced Humanitarianism*, New York and Oxford: Berghahn, 2005.

51 It is in this way that one can read the 'map of camps' regularly updated by the Migreuropa network (www.migreurop.org/IMG/pdf/L_Europe_des_camps).

3 An Ethnologist in the Refugee Camps

1 Marc Augé, *Le Temps en ruines*, Paris: Galilée, 2003, p. 15.
2 Migrations of Black people from the Pacific coast to Cali, and their cultural and political effects, were the subject of the first collective research programme undertaken at the Universidad del Valle (Univalle) in Cali from 1997 to 2000, in the context of a cooperation between the IRD, the Colombian research body Colciencias and the Centro de Investigación y Documentación Socio-económica (CIDSE) of Univalle. Two works arising from the results of this research should be particularly mentioned on account of the richness of their vision: Odile Hoffmann, *Communautés noires dans le Pacifique colombien: innovations et dynamiques ethniques*, Paris: IRD/Karthala, 2004; and Carlos Efren Agudelo, *Politique et populations noires en Colombie*, Paris: L'Harmattan, 2004.
3 The results of these studies can be partly found in Agier, *On the Margins of the World*. See also Agiers, 'Perte de lieux, dénuement et urbanisation: les *desplazados* de Colombie', *Autrepart*, 14, 2000, pp. 91–105, and 'Violences et déplacements forcés en Colombie: apprendre à vivre avec la guerre', in Gilles Bataillon, Hamit Bozarslan and Denis Merklen (eds.), *Situations limites et expériences de l'incertain*, Paris: Karthala, 2008.
4 More precisely, those of MSF's Centre de Réflexion sur l'Action et les Savoirs Humanitaires (CRASH).
5 These exhibitions are put on regularly for the purpose of raising funds and recruiting volunteers.
6 Several epistemological debates in anthropology have shown the importance of personal relationship and dialogue as foundations of the knowledge produced: dialogism, recognition of heteroglossia, translation as performance, etc., have been common themes of a reflexive anthropology that has played a major role in renewing the work of ethnologists. See, among other important contributions to this debate, Clifford Geertz, *Works and Lives: The Anthropologist as Author*, Stanford: Stanford University Press, 1988; James Clifford and George Marcus (eds.), *Writing Culture: The Poetics and Politics of Ethnography*, Berkeley: University of California Press, 1986; Johann Fabian, *Time and the Other: How Anthropology Makes its Objects*, New York: Columbia University Press, 1983. It should be noted, however, that all this burgeoning reflection remains anchored in the 'classical' anthropological field, and maintains the image of an autonomy of the ethnographic situation in relation to its context, which generally is still either drowned in an artistic vagueness or referred to the more or less adjacent disciplines of sociology, economics or political science. What we maintain here, on the contrary, is that, if the face-to-face relationship is indeed the heart of the anthropologist's production of knowledge, this is on condition that the study never abandons understanding the immanence of the context in the lived situation.

(See Alban Bensa, 'De la micro-histoire vers une anthropologie critique', in Jacques Revel (ed.), *Jeux d'échelles: la micro-analyse à l'expérience*, Paris: Gallimard-Seuil, 1996, pp. 37–70; Jean Bazin, 'Interpréter ou décrire: notes critiques sur la connaissance anthropologique', in J. Revel and N. Wachtel (eds.), *Une École pour les sciences sociales*, Paris: Cerf/ EHESS, 1966, pp. 401–20; Marc Augé, *An Anthropology for Contemporaneous Worlds*, Stanford: Stanford University Press, 1999.) This diffuse and even irregular presence of determinations of context is very concrete: still more so when health, social or security policies keep groups apart, categorize and stigmatize them. It is this that makes the controlled fields of the refugee camps particularly 'sensitive'. A series of reflections and case studies in sensitive fields (camps, squats, reception centres for asylum seekers, etc.) can be found in the book edited by Florence Bouillon, Marion Fresia and Virginie Tallio, *Terrains sensibles: expériences actuelles de l'anthropologie*, Dossiers africains, Paris: EHESS, 2005. More generally, the methodological and epistemological implications of the new terrains of anthropology are described and commented on in the collective volume edited by Olivier Leservoisier and Laurent Vidal, *L'Anthropologie face à ses objets: nouveaux contextes ethnographiques*, Paris: Éditions des Archives contemporaines, 2008.

7 See ch. 11.

4 The Interminable Insomnia of Exile: The Camp as an Ordinary Exceptionalism

1 See, in particular, Fabian, *Time and the Other*; and Augé, *An Anthropology for Contemporaneous Worlds*.

2 'Exile is a kind of long insomnia', wrote Victor Hugo (*Pierres*, 62, cited by Roland Barthes, *Fragments d'un discours amoureux*, Paris: Seuil, 1977, p. 123).

3 Elias Sanbar, *Figures du Palestinien: identité des origines, identité de devenir*, Paris: Gallimard, 2004, p. 246.

4 Éric Hazan, *Notes sur l'occupation: Naplouse, Kalkilyia, Hébron*, Paris: La Fabrique, 2006, p. 53.

5 Some sixty camps were established in the 1950s and 1960s in Lebanon, Syria, Jordan and the Palestinian Territories. The latter today host thirty-two refugee camps, twenty-three on the West Bank and nine in Gaza, with a population of over 600,000; around a quarter of the Palestinian population of the Territories live in a refugee camp. See Hélène Seren (ed.), *L'Urbanisation des camps des réfugiés dans la bande de Gaza et en Cisjordanie*, research report, GEMDEV, Programme de Recherche Urbaine pour le Développement (PRUD), Palestinian Diaspora and Refugee Centre (SHAML), project 93, n.d. [2004?], n.p. [Paris?].

6 See her descriptions and analyses of the Palestinian camp of Shu'faat, located within the Jerusalem city limits (Sylvaine Bulle, 'Domestiquer son environnement. Une approche pragmatiste d'un territoire confiné: le camp de réfugiés de Shu'faat à Jérusalem', *Asylon(s)*, s, 2008, http:/terra. zero.net/article672.html).

7 Young people imprisoned or killed by the Israeli army for committing or allegedly intending to commit bombings.

8 The key is a symbol of the native land and the expectation of return on the part of the families in the Palestinian camps. Thus in May 2006 Éric Hazan met a Hamas member who sat on the committee of the Balata camp at Nablus: 'Were you born here?', he asked. 'Yes, but it's not my native land. My native land is Jaffa. Before he died, my father gave me the key to his house there' (Hazan, *Notes sur l'occupation*, p. 20).

9 The same duality is brought out by the studies and impassioned commentaries of Muriel Rozelier on the town of Nablus (*Naplouse Palestine. Chroniques du ghetto*, Paris: Presses de la Renaissance, 2007). On the one hand, you have a leader who declares: 'The right of return is sacred, it is inalienable. Each one of us, as a refugee, has the right of return inscribed in his genes' (p. 188); or again another leader exclaims: 'Destroying the camp means abandoning the right of return. Here in Nablus we are temporary guests' (p. 190). On the other hand, the author noted a social division in Nablus between 'the top people – townsfolk' and 'the lower plebs – the refugees' (p. 199). A very real urban social segregation, which brings about a 'ghettoization' and spurs the refugees to leave the camps if they want to rise socially, or to transform them by developing an informal economy. Commenting on her visit to the Balata camp in June 2006, Muriel Rozelier again writes: 'Before entering a camp, I imagined I don't know what haunted place. An emptiness of misery, perhaps, or mud and desperation. Since then I have learned to see, behind the urban wasteland, a mushrooming of life that is far more intense. The camp is a village life in a world of mad urbanism' (p. 191). I shall return below to the urban character of the camps, from the point of view both of their actual organization (ch. 7) and of their potentialities (ch. 10).

10 These historical developments of the Palestinian cause are related in an extraordinary fashion in Elias Khoury's novel *La Porte du soleil* (Arles: Actes Sud, 2002) and the film of it with the same name by the director Yousry Nasrallah. On the sense of political commitment of the Palestinian youth as transformed between the first and second Intifada, passing from the dominant figure of the fighter (*fedayin*) to that of the martyr (*shahid*) who is both hero and victim, see Pénélope Larzillière, *Être jeune en Palestine*, Paris: Balland, 2004.

11 The contradictory construction of this humanitarian cause in Palestine and Israel is discussed by Didier Fassin, 'La cause des victimes', *Les Temps Modernes*, 627, 2004, pp. 73–91.

229

12 The following passage is based on studies currently in progress in the Sahrawi camps by the anthropologist Alice Corbet and the geographer Julien Dedenis.

13 Sahrawi Arab Democratic Republic.

14 Alice Corbet, 'Les campements de réfugiés sahraouis en Algérie: de l'idéel au réel', *Bulletin de l'Association des Géographes Français*, 1, 2006 ('Territoires d'exil: les camps de réfugiés', ed. Véronique Lassailly-Jacob), p. 15.

15 Ibid., p. 14.

16 The space of the camps on Algerian soil, and the resources provided by international organizations, have in fact been placed under the control of the Sahrawi state (the SADR).

17 Julien Dedenis, 'La territorialité de l'espace des camps des réfugiés sahraouis en Algérie', *Bulletin de l'Association des Géographes Français*, 1, 2006 ('Territoires d'exil: les camps de réfugiés', ed. Véronique Lassailly-Jacob), p. 27.

18 Ibid., p. 33.

19 I am echoing here a contribution by Alain Brossat to a debate organized by the TERRA network, 'Camps/prisons, rétention/détention', Paris, 28 February 2006. Brossat explains that this political risk – 'the refugee camp makes people Palestinians' – as well as other associated factors (the static heaviness of the camp, for example), mean that the camps, when they intervene in the present policies of control, are no longer an end in themselves (a pure distancing whose final model would be the disappearance of such distancings), but a more or less well-improvised 'airlock' in strategies of expulsion and rejection, and more generally strategies for controlling flows. See also, by the same author, 'L'espace-camp et l'exception furtive'.

20 On the contemporary idea of a present with no future, and the controversial rise of presentism in the last quarter of a century, see François Hartog, *Régimes d'historicité: présentisme et expériences du temps*, Paris: Seuil, 2004, pp. 113–62. Marc Augé has shown how the meaning of anthropological sites is formed when space is the crucible of a memory, an identity, relationships that vanish in the development of out-places (Marc Augé, *Non-places: Introduction to an Anthropology of Supermodernity*, London: Verso, 1995). As for ruins, they are the concentrated material of a 'pure time', now absent from the fragments of our violent contemporary world, which no longer has time to produce ruins (Augé, *Le Temps en ruines*).

21 See again, on the subject of these 'faults in the present', Hartog, *Régimes d'historicité*, p. 127.

22 'The UNs': the term commonly used for staff of the UN agencies, and, more widely, organizations and individuals representing the 'international community'.

23 The status of individuals in the camps where the fieldwork for this study was carried out is that of prima facie refugee unless otherwise indicated.

The result of this is that the individual attribution of an UNHCR refugee card is not automatically associated with this status, that refugees use their card from the World Food Programme as an identity card, and that their refugee status is not recognized outside the camps. We shall return to this question below (ch. 5).

24 'Big men' is the name by which the minors who testified to the Save the Children inquiry denote their 'sexual exploiters'. These analyses have been developed in Michel Agier and Françoise Bouchet-Saulnier, 'Espaces humanitaires, espaces d'exception', in Weissman (ed.), À l'ombre des guerre justes, pp. 303–18.

25 A detailed analysis of the different generations of refugees and the power relations within this UNHCR establishment is given in ch. 6.

26 ECHO is the European Commission Humanitarian Aid department, UNDP the United Nations Development Programme.

27 Verdirame and Harrell-Bond, *Rights in Exile*.

28 Ibid., p. 333.

29 Ibid.

30 Ibid.

31 Ibid., p. 271.

32 Ibid., p. 332.

33 I shall continue this analysis of exceptional situations in Part Three of this book. Here I have deliberately confined myself to presenting actual facts and commenting on them closely.

5 Experiences of Wandering, Borders and Camps: Liberia, Sierra Leone, Guinea

1 Formed in the early part of 2000 and soon supported by the Guinean authorities, as well as by certain British military advisers, the Liberian diaspora in the United States, and the 'international community' more generally, LURD sought from 2001 to 2003 to overthrow Charles Taylor at all costs (see in particular Jean-Hervé Jezequel, 'Libéria: un chaos orchestré', in Weissman (ed.), À l'ombre des guerres justes, pp. 171–90).

2 On the war in Liberia, see Stephen Ellis, *The Mask of Anarchy: The Destruction of Liberia and the Religious Dimension of an African Civil War*, London: Hurst, 1999, and the above-mentioned synthesis by Jean-Hervé Jezequel, 'Libéria: un chaos orchestré'. On the Sierra Leone conflict, see Weissman, À l'ombre des guerres justes, pp. 53–73, and Paul Richards, *Fighting for the Rain Forest: War, Youth and Resources in Sierra Leone*, Oxford: Currey, 1996, in which the author gives a detailed analysis of the armed mobilization of young people by the RUF in the early 1990s.

3 The relationship (both continuity and breaks) between the 'colonial situation' and the post-colonial present is discussed in a collective work devoted to such developments in the second half of the twentieth century, and their interpretation: Marie-Claude Smouts (ed.), *La Situation post-coloniale: les* 'postcolonial studies' *dans le débat français*, with a preface by Georges Balandier, Paris: Presses de Sciences Po, 2007.

4 On the different registers (intellectual, political, social) of the relationships that led to a reciprocal desire and need for the other among both Africans and French, in the colonial period and since independence, see Jean-Pierre Dozon, *Frères et sujets: la France et l'Afrique en perspective*, Paris: Flammarion, 2003.

5 I shall return to the question of testimonies and speaking out in ch. 9.

6 An armed force formed by the union of the RUF rebels with the soldiers of the Sierra Leonese government army.

7 United Liberation Movement of Liberia for Democracy.

8 The camps of Waterloo and Jui are close to Freetown.

9 If young men who arrived by themselves made up thirteen 1-person 'households', I also noted the presence of thirty-four widowed women family heads. They had with them children and parents, possibly also brothers and other members of their deceased husband's family. The average size of their household when it was moved was 6.35 persons, little different from that of the seventeen households headed by a man (apart from the single men living alone), whose average size was 7.11.

10 This raised some particular problems. In fact, the establishment of this zone (even in terms of occasional assistance) could correctly be equated with the building of a camp by MSF. Tensions arose within the NGO on the question of the maintenance of this zone for a period of years and the stabilization to which it contributed. An exceptional initiative and a controversial one within MSF, the establishment and management of this section also made it necessary to deal with the UNHCR and place itself under its authority, whether it wanted to or not (see the photo of the Kuankan camp on the first page of the picture section).

11 See Michel Agier, 'La ville nue: des marges de l'urbain aux terrains de l'humanitaire', *Annales de la Recherche Urbaine*, 93, 2003, pp. 57–66.

12 The formation of the ULIMO and LURD rebel groups, which fought and eventually overthrew the government of Charles Taylor in Liberia, took place largely in Guinea and with the active participation of the Guinean authorities.

13 In the same way, the appearance of distinctions of status between indigenous Guineans and Sierre Leonese refugees gave rise, according to Douglas Henry, to 'strategies' and 'manipulations of identity', as well as a 'border citizenship' (Douglas Henry, 'Réfugiés sierra-léonais et aide humanitaire en Guinée', *Politique Africaine*, 85, 2002, pp. 56–63).

14 IRIN document, 'Refugees criss-cross a fluid and volatile border', 29 July 2004. I shall return to the political significance of this event in ch. 8.

232

15 An overall balance-sheet and an analysis of refugee returns have been supplied in a study by Action Contre la Faim; see Thomas Laporte Weywada, *Liberia – Halfway through the Return Process*, ACF, Monrovia, June 2006.

16 Some ten or so international organizations, UN and humanitarian, were present in Foya.

17 It would also be possible to count the deaths for each village. The villagers have precise and well-identified figures for both the first war (1990–6) and the second (1999–2003).

18 The disarmament of the LURD took place in 2004.

19 This estimate partly coincides with information from the Foya district commissioner: for the district as a whole there were, according to him, 80,000 people before the war as against 60,000 now, i.e. three-quarters; for the town of Foya itself, there were 22,000 before the war as against 15,000 or 16,000 today, i.e. around 70 per cent. We should note that in 2000, MSF counted the population with a view to a vaccination campaign, making a total at that time of 122,800 for the district as a whole, which would give the present situation a recovery rate of 50 per cent or 60 per cent of the population before the war.

20 At the PWJ centres they received a food ration for two months (renewable for a further two months), some household utensils, covering, soap, etc.

21 For the 2005–6 period, PWJ registered in the Foya transit centre 17,750 repatriations in 59 convoys (33 from Sierra Leone with 9,954 persons, 26 from Guinea with 7,796); these returnees included 55 per cent women, 13 per cent vulnerable and 20.5 per cent children under five.

22 I have described above the living conditions in the former displaced persons' camps and squats of Monrovia (see ch. 2, pp. 43ff.)

6 Surviving, Reviving, Leaving, Remaining: The Long of Angolan Refugees in Zambia

1 See ch. 4.

2 See ch. 7.

3 União Nacional para a Independência Total de Angola.

4 The situation in Angola and the chances of peace in the country at the point when the peace agreement was signed have been analysed by Christine Messiant ('Fin de la guerre, enfin, en Angola. Vers quelle paix?' *Politique Africaine*, 86, 2002, pp. 183–95).

5 Resistencia Nacional Mocambicana, a guerrilla movement active from 1977 to the early 1980s.

6 Christian Geffray, *La Cause des armes au Mozambique: anthropologie d'une guerre civile*, Paris: Karthala, 1990.

7 Bauman, *Liquid Modernity*.

8 See the detailed map of Maheba in the central picture section.

9 Somewhat fewer than 20,000 refugees still lived there in 2002.

10 This is confirmed by a few incidents (related by Julia Powles) in the camp in the early 1990s between UNITA and MPLA supporters, when the Angolan elections were held in September 1992, as well as by the existence, mentioned by the same author, of 'a high level of political consciousness among the refugees', which we have equally noted, but more among the older and more established refugees (J. Powles, 'Tales of fish . . . a field report: Angolan refugees in Zambia, September 1992 to July 1993', eighteen-page unpublished manuscript, 1993).

11 The new extensions of the camp from 1995 are known as 'villages'.

12 This zone now numbers 3,500 residents.

13 Returns that followed the second Lusaka peace agreement of 1994.

14 The Jesuit Refugee Service has a programme of literacy and pre-primary teaching on the site as a whole, conducted in twenty-five schools and accommodating over 2,000 pupils. The Zambian authorities, for their part, run four establishments of primary education and one middle school in the older part of the camp, for which fees are charged. The refugee families settled there sometimes have the resources to pay these fees, and the JRS also has a programme of bursaries to enable some refugee children to get access to middle school.

15 Clinics run by the Zambian authorities also operate in the older parts of the site.

16 As we have said, the refugees receive this ration for two years after their arrival, after which they are supposed to live off their own crops if they have actually been given a plot of agricultural land. There were 25,000 beneficiaries of food aid in May 2002, i.e. 43 per cent of the total number of refugees in Maheba.

17 Elsewhere, a 'camp for the vulnerable' houses 130 elderly people, handicapped, and children without families.

18 See Norbert Elias and John Scotson, *The Established and the Outsiders: A Sociological Enquiry into Community Problems*, London: Frank Cass, 1965.

19 Zambian traders come to the camp entry to seek agricultural products (chiefly maize, manioc and sweet potato), which they buy very cheaply from the refugee farmers (unofficial purchases, untaxed and outside the market, though perfectly open), and then sell in the towns of the Copperbelt and the capital, Lusaka, at the local market price. In this context, the technical skill of the Rwandans and Burundis in market gardening enables them to occupy cultivable land left untilled by the Angolan refugees and thus to integrate themselves without difficulty into this commercial agriculture.

20 Arjun Appadurai, *Modernity at Large: Cultural Dimensions of Globalization*, Minneapolis: University of Minnesota Press, 1996, p. 182.

21 Augé, *Non-places*. On the subject of the relationship between displacement and emplacement, see Liisa Malkki, 'Refugees and exile: from "Refuge Studies" to the National Order of Things', *Annual Review of Anthropology*, 24, 1995, pp. 495–523.

22 Thus the organization of a collective repatriation by the UNHCR (announced for some time in 2003) gave rise to contradictory interpretations. It was understood by some refugees as an obligation to return, which they feared, whereas others saw it as an official guarantee of finding the conditions in their country of origin that existed before their flight.

23 A study of this site in the context of an analysis of the asylum policy of the Zambian government has been made by Véronique Lassailly-Jacob, 'Quelles réponses à l'afflux des réfugiés? L'exemple zambien', *Bulletin de l'Association des Géographes Français*, 2, 2002, pp. 211–22.

24 Lewis Mwanagombe, 'What becomes of Meheba after Angolan refugees go home?, *Zambia Today*, 23 March 1996.

25 Ibid.

7 Camp-Towns: Somalia in Kenya

1 Nuruddin Farah, 'A Country in Exile', *World Literature Today*, 2, 4 (Sept. 1998), p. 713.

2 I shall return further on to the form and meaning of this humanitarian fiction as a representation of the world and the individual (ch. 11).

3 Michael Pollak, *L'Expérience concentrationnaire. Essai sur le maintien de l'identité sociale*, Paris: Métailié, 1990, p. 10.

4 On the dynamic of African communities in colonial towns, see Georges Balandier, *Sociologie des Brazzavilles noires*, Paris: FNSP, 1955 (2nd edn, 1985). On the towns of apartheid, see in particular David Smith (ed.), *The Apartheid City and Beyond: Urbanisation and Social Change in South Africa*, London: Routledge, 1992, and Philippe Gervais-Lambony, *Territoires citadins: 4 villes africaines*, Paris: Belin, 2003. On contemporary urban ghettos and the emergence of a 'hyperghetto', see Loïc Wacquant, *Urban Outcasts: A Comparative Sociology of Advanced Marginality*, Cambridge: Polity, 2007. Several examples of urban segregation, and of overcoming it, are presented and discussed in Michel Agier, *L'Invention de la ville: banlieues, townships, invasions et favelas*, Paris: Éditions des Archives contemporaines, 1999.

5 The information presented in this chapter dates from 2000. Some of the material has been analysed in Agier, *On the Margins of the World*, and more systematically in my article, 'Between war and the city: towards an urban anthropology of refugee camps', *Ethnography*, 3, 3, 2002. Since this time, departures (for example the resettlement in the United States of 10,000 'Bantu Soomaali' in 2005) have been matched by new and

massive arrivals, in the wake of the resumption of violence in Somalia in 2006–7.

6 Making a total of 124,000 inhabitants in 2000 for the three Dadaab camps. The latest quantitative estimates by the UNHCR show 160,000 occupants in 2007.

7 Koranic instruction is conducted by a Libyan NGO, Al-Haramein.

8 Michel de Certeau, *L'Invention du quotidien, I. Manières de faire*, Paris: Gallimard, 1980 (2nd edn, 1990).

9 In a different way, as we shall see below, a part of the aid provided in the camps is designed for those women and men who were in the most fragile situation before the exodus.

10 Nathalie Gomes, 'Solidarité et réseaux dans l'exil. Les réfugiés somaliens clandestins au Kenya et en Éthiopie', in Luc Cambrezy and Véronique Lassailly-Jacob (eds.), *Populations réfugiées: de l'exil au retour*, Paris: Éditions de l'IRD, 2001, pp. 301–19.

11 Ibid.

12 Since the refugees have no right to work under Kenyan legislation.

13 This is the income level that a study by Save the Children on the health and food economy at Dadaab found in 1999 for what was seen as the richest group in the camp (Philippa Couts et al., *Kenya Refugee Study Food Economy: Updates of Ifo, Dagahaley and Hagadera Refugee Camps, Dadaab*, Final Report, Save the Children Fund, Nairobi, September 1999, 21-page ms.).

14 The same organization estimated that this so-called 'rich' category represented between 5% and 15% of the camp population, but this seems to be exaggerated, and I would suggest a figure below 5%.

15 Dominant under the Siad Barre regime until 1991, the Darood confederation was subsequently the victim of persecution and violence, and its members fled from Mogadishu and Somalia on a massive scale. The Darood – and particularly the Ogaadeen clans among them – represent the majority of Soomaalis in the Dadaab camps.

16 Around 30–35% according to the results of the Save the Children study cited above, which includes in this 'middle' category the workers employed by the NGOs who, I believe, can more pertinently be viewed separately, for reasons that bear more on questions of status and political weight within the life of the camps than on strictly economic factors.

17 Around 60% of the camp population, according to the same source.

18 See Liisa Malkki, *Purity and Exile: Violence, Memory and National Cosmology Among Hutu Refugees in Tanzania*, Chicago, University of Chicago Press, 1995, and 'Refugees and exile'.

19 Gaim Kibreab, 'Revisiting the debate on people, place, identity and displacement', *Journal of Refugee Studies*, 12, 4, 1999, p. 398.

20 Mohamed Mohamed-Abdi, 'Les bouleversements induits de la guerre civile en Somalie: castes marginales et minorités', *Autrepart*, 15, 2000, pp. 131–47.

21 This screening is an official individual examination that candidates must pass to be accepted for resettlement in a third country. It consists in checking the state of health of the refugees, but sometimes also their educational level, and their professional or linguistic skill. Sex and age may also intervene in the selection of candidates for resettlement.

22 As we have noted above in connection with the Liberian and Sierra Leonese refugees from the Mano River (ch. 5, p. 106).

23 Integrating the life of the Somalian refugees in Kenya into the wider ensemble of Somalia outside its national space is what enables the Somalian writer Nuruddin Farah to describe a 'country of exile' between Europe, Africa and America (see N. Farah, *Yesterday, Tomorrow: Voices from the Somali Diaspora*, London: Continuum, 2000).

24 Shortly after this study, the Belgian MSF (which took over from the French branch in Dadaab in the mid-1990s) was questioned as to the pertinence of its activities in these camps, now that the emergency was largely over. The Belgian medical organization eventually transferred its three clinics in the Dadaab camps to a Kenyan NGO.

8 In the Name of the Refugees: Political Representation and Action in the Camps

1 See ch. 6.

2 On the humanitarian and democratic stages, see Jacques Rancière, *Disagreement: Politics and Philosophy*, Minneapolis: University of Minnesota Press, 1999.

3 The fifteen types of vulnerability used by the UNHCR are as follows: 'single parent', 'single woman', 'unaccompanied child', 'separated child', 'child head of family', 'lost child', 'aged person in charge of minors', 'aged person alone', 'mental illness', 'physically handicapped', 'amputee', 'chronically ill', 'deaf and/or mute', 'blind', 'survivor of violence'.

4 This camp has been described above (ch. 5).

5 In another camp, that of Tobanda in Sierra Leone (which we shall discuss below), opened in April 2003, the UNHCR counted that September a figure of 20 per cent 'vulnerable'.

6 See ch. 7.

7 The BBC broadcasts two news programmes a day in Somali.

8 See ch. 6.

9 The Integrated Regional Information Networks is the information service of the UN's Office for the Coordination of Humanitarian Affairs.

10 The French version of this IRIN report specifies the camps of Kuankan and Kola. On Kuankan, see above, ch. 5.

11 See above, ch. 5, p. 110.

12 IRIN document, 'Refugees criss-cross a fluid and volatile border'.

13 Agamben, *Homo Sacer*, p. 133.

14 This is the case with refugee camps. As we have seen above in our inventory of the different forms of camp (ch. 2), the spaces we have called sorting centres (detention centres, transit zones) are often the site of a hidden violence.

15 Adding the refugees counted in the 'way stations' (transit centres) and a few urban refugees gives a total at this point in time of around 70,000 refugees registered by the UNHCR. There are actually far more Liberian refugees in Sierra Leone, undoubtedly three times as many if you count those living in Freetown, the medium-size towns and the border villages, who are not recognized by the UNHCR.

16 The camp is run by the Sierra Leonese branch of an international religious NGO, the Lutheran World Federation, to whom the UNHCR has delegated this task, in collaboration with NACSA (a Sierra Leonese social assistance body). As is often the case, the organization running the camp includes a number of Liberians among its officers, as well as its own nationals, the former being long-standing refugees who have acquired the status of immigrants authorized to work. Their situation is very different from that of the refugees in the camp who do occasional work for the NGOs active there, and receive – as we have seen – not a wage, which as refugees they are not allowed, but rather a scanty compensation known as an 'incentive'.

17 Female leaders, as we have seen above (the Boreah camp in Guinea's Forest Region), are rare but do exist.

18 The UNHCR calls a 'community' every group of twenty huts constructed around a collective tent in which the new refugees are held in order of arrival. When all the habitations are constructed, the collective tent is taken away. There are in this sense a hundred 'communities' of dwellings in the Tobanda camp. The 'community leaders' are generally refugees who assumed the function of tent chief on their arrival. The 'communitarian' rhetoric in vogue in the international milieus of the UN agencies and NGOs is thus something coming 'from above', and is taken over by the refugees in a new kind of political language.

9 Who Will Speak Out in the Camp?
A Study of Refugees' Testimony

1 See Alain Brossat, *Pour en finir avec la prison*, Paris: La Fabrique, 2001.

2 The whole ambiguity of the sense of suffering socialized in the 'speaking circles' (which certain NGOs have established in the refugee camps) and 'listening places' (established in the 'difficult quarters' of the urban periphery) is summed up in the profound doubt that is felt towards these experiences: do they actually contribute to producing authors emancipated from suffering, or on the contrary to imagining and fixing the social categories associated with a victim identity? The account of the

collective inquiry conducted by Didier Fassin into listening places on the social and urban margins in France (Didier Fassin et al., *Des maux indicibles: sociologie des lieux d'écoute*, Paris: La Découverte, 2004) gives an idea of the wealth of data and debates on this subject.

3 Hence the title of this chapter, 'Who Will Speak Out in the Camp?', a reference to the collective work edited by Marcel Detienne (*Qui veut prendre la parole?* Paris: Seuil, 2003), which focuses on the concrete spaces and situations where this speaking out takes place, and where politics is developed.

4 See above, ch. 5, pp. 104ff.

5 See the comparable case of the 'legitimacy' of the involvement in the war of the *kamajors*, the traditional Sierra Leonese hunters: Richards, *Fighting for the Rain Forest*.

6 See Jezequel, 'Libéria: un chaos orchestré'.

7 Marc Augé, *Les Formes de l'oubli*, Paris: Payot, 1998, p. 119.

8 Paul Ricoeur, *Memory, History, Forgetting*, Chicago: University of Chicago Press, 2004.

9 In the religious service I observed one Sunday morning at one of the five Pentecostal churches in this camp, I noted the following sequence: a testimony session during which five people took turns in relating a bit of their personal history, ending with thanks to God; a session to introduce new arrivals in the camp (and in the church), to which those attending responded 'welcome'; finally the *performance* of the pastor's sermon (30 November 2003). The sermon may sometimes be the occasion for critical commentary on the living conditions of refugees in the camp, the situation in their country of origin, the action of the 'UNs', etc.

10 This request is forwarded to the UNHCR when individuals can prove that they are in danger both in their country of origin and in the host country.

11 In 2002 the Maheba camp counted 58,000 refugees, mainly Angolan, but also 3,695 Rwandans (6.3%) and 1,441 Burundi (2.5%), these two nationalities being chiefly made up of Hutus (see ch. 6).

12 'The longest and most painful journey (Hutu refugees in search of asylum)'. The authors were A. Hagenimana, J. Nkengurukiyimana, J. Mulindabigwi and M. Goretti Gahimbare. The 77-page publication is not dated and no place of publication is cited, but it was produced in the Maheba camp in 2000.

13 Ibid., p. 3.

14 Ibid., p. 2.

15 Ibid., p. 1.

16 I have commented several times elsewhere on a number of dramatic pieces produced and presented in Europe with war or exile as their subject. See Agier, 'La vérité vraie: mises en scène de témoignages de guerre et d'exil', *Vacarme*, 2, 2003, pp. 79–82.

17 Both these alternative definitions of the story, referential and utilitarian, are put in question when suspicion as to the veracity of testimony fuels

tensions in Africa around the procedures of resettlement (see ch. 5), or justifies in Europe the increased rejection of asylum requests (see ch. 1). See also the study by Cécile Rousseau and Patricia Foxen on lying by people requesting asylum in Canada ('Le mythe du réfugié menteur: un mensonge indispensable', *Évolution Psychiatrique*, 71, 2006, pp. 505–20).

Part Three [Introduction]

1 In the sense of 'theories of practice', i.e. of describing and understanding the logics that underlie the practices and discourses observed in the course of these investigations.

10 'If This is a Town . . .'

1 Wim Van Damme, 'Do refugees belong in camps? Experiences from Goma and Guinea', *Lancet*, 346, 1995, pp. 360–2.
2 Erwann Queinnec and Jean Rigal, 'Aide alimentaire et carences vitaminiques dans les camps de réfugiés', in François Jean (ed.), *Populations en danger 1995: rapport annuel sur les crises majeures et l'action humanitaire*, Paris: MSF / La Découverte, 1995, p. 116.
3 Verdirame and Harrell-Bond, *Rights in Exile*, p. 271.
4 Michel Foucault, 'Des espaces autres', in *Dits et écrits*, vol. IV, Paris: Gallimard, 1984, pp. 752–62.
5 See Malkki, 'Refugees and exile'.
6 This is particularly the case with the camps in Guinea and Sierra Leone that we have described above.
7 See the example of the clinics in the three Dadaab camps in Kenya (see ch. 6).
8 In a political intervention on the occasion of the mobilization of European intellectuals in support of the 'boat people'.
9 See Zygmunt Bauman, *Wasted Lives: Modernity and its Outcasts*, Cambridge: Polity, 2004.
10 The out-places described here can be compared with two other figures of extra-territorial locality and relegation. Loïc Wacquant describes the 'excluding imprisonment' that characterizes the era of the 'hyperghetto', a territory of relegation where urban pariahs are confined, going beyond the figure of the traditional ghetto (Wacquant, *Urban Outcasts*, p. 242). Engin Isin and Kim Rygiel, for their part, list a series of frontier spaces, zones and camps as 'abject spaces': their common feature is to house in extraterritoriality occupants who are nothing, undefined individuals who are literally quite contemptible – 'neither subjects nor objects, but abjects'

(E. F. Isin and K. Rygiel, 'Of Other Global Cities: Frontiers, Zones, Camps', in Barbara Drieskens, Franck Mermier and Hieko Wimmen (eds.), *Cities of the South. Citizenship and Exclusion in the 21st Century*, Beirut: Saqi Books, 2007, pp. 169–76).

11 Foucault, 'Des espaces autres'.

12 Ibid., p. 756.

13 As shown by the events of the early months of 2008 in the CRAs of the Paris region.

14 Agamben, *Homo Sacer*.

15 For a more detailed critical analysis of Agamben's theses on the notion of bare life and the meaning of the camp, see the article by Maria Muhle, 'Le camp et la notion de vie', in Le Cour Grandmaison, Lhuilier and Valluy (eds.), *Le Retour des camps?* pp. 68–76. For the critique of a 'thanatopolitical' definition of present-day camps, see Brossat, 'L'espace-camp et l'exception furtive'.

16 See, in particular, Marc Bernadot, 'Les mutations de la figure du camp', in Le Cour Grandmaison, Lhuilier and Valluy (eds.), *Le Retour des camps?* pp. 42–55.

17 See Peschanski, *La France des camps*.

18 See Primo Levi, *Rapport sur Auschwitz*, presented with a critical apparatus by Philippe Mesnard, Paris: Kimé, 2005. This 'report on the hygienic and sanitary organization of the Monowitz concentration camp for Jews (Auschwitz, upper Silesia)' was written by Primo Levi in 1945–6, in collaboration with Leonardo Debenedetti.

19 Hannah Arendt, *The Origins of Totalitarianism*, New York: Harcourt Brace Jovanovich, 1968, Part Two, 'Imperialism', p. 279.

20 The camps of Argelès, Rivesaltes and Saint-Mitre embodied this history of camps long before Sangatte or the Zapis at Roissy. See Bernadot, 'Le pays aux mille et un camps' and *Camps d'étrangers*.

21 Olivier Clochard, Yvan Gastaut and Ralph Schor, 'Les camps d'étrangers depuis 1938, continuité et adaptations. Du "modèle" français à la construction de l'espace Schengen', *Revue Européenne des Migrations Internationales*, 20, 2, 2004.

22 See Rivière, 'L'asile aux antipodes'.

23 As mentioned above, Verdirame and Harrell-Bond (*Rights in Exile*, p. 334) emphasize that it is the camp situation as a deprivation of freedom of movement and work that makes possible all the other infringements of human rights.

24 See ch. 4, pp. 81ff.

25 P. Mesnard, 'Un texte sans importance', in Levi, *Rapport sur Auschwitz*, p. 40.

26 Louis Wirth (1897–1952), 'Urbanism as a Way of Life' (1938), reprinted in Jan Lin and Christopher Mele (eds.), *The Urban Sociology Reader*, Abingdon: Routledge, 2005, pp. 32–42.

27 Bernard Lepetit, 'La ville: cadre, objet, sujet. Vingt ans de recherches françaises en histoire urbaine', *Enquête*, 4, 1996, p. 32.

28 Isaac Joseph, 'Le droit à la ville, la ville à l'oeuvre: deux paradigms de la recherche', *Annales de la Recherche Urbaine*, 64, 1994, pp. 5–10.
29 Marcel Hénaff, *La Ville qui vient*, Paris: L'Herne, 2008, p. 83.
30 Ibid.
31 See ch. 6.
32 See ch. 7.
33 Hénaff, *La Ville qui vient*, pp. 78–9.
34 See, in particular, Mohamed Kamel Doraï, *Les Réfugiés palestiniens du Liban: une géographie de l'exil*, Paris: CNRS Éditions, 2006, as well as Bulle, 'Domestiquer son environnement', and Seren (ed.), *L'Urbanisation des camps des réfugiés dans la bande de Gaza et en Cisjordanie*.
35 For Marc Augé, what characterizes 'anthropological place' is the fact that a given space is the reference and support of a memory, an identity and a set of relationships (Augé, *Out-places*).
36 M. Detienne, *Comment être autochtone: du pur Athénien au Français raciné*, Paris: Seuil, 2003, p. 14.

11 'If This is a World . . .'

1 A foreigner in an irregular situation in the holding centre of Zeytinburnu, Istanbul, August 2006 (in Sophie Baylac, *Note sur la rétention des migrants et demandeurs d'asile en Turquie*, GISTI, October 2006).
2 Rancière, Disagreement: Politics and Philosophy, pp. 123ff.
3 See in particular, Marcel Mauss, 'Une catégorie de l'esprit humain: la notion de personne, celle de "moi"' (1938), in *Sociologie et anthropologie*, Paris: PUF, 1950, pp. 331–62; Louis Dumont, *Essays on Individualism: Modern Ideology in Anthropological Perpsective*, Chicago: University of Chicago Press, 1986; the collective work *La Notion de personne en Afrique noire*, Paris; Éditions du CNRS, 1973; Marc Augé, *A Sense for the Other*, Stanford: Stanford University Press, 1998; Alain Marie (ed.), *L'Afrique des individus*, Paris: Karthala, 1997.
4 I have mentioned elsewhere the strange experience of spending a few hours doing the 'tour' of the city of Freetown that local taxi drivers offer to foreigners. You pass the district of the UN armed forces, the town centre devastated by the war, and the camps for amputees (see M. Agier, 'La guerre', *La Sagesse de l'ethnologue*, Paris: L'oeil neuf éditions, 2004).
5 Marc Augé, *Pouvoirs de vie, pouvoirs de mort*, Paris: Flammarion, 1977.
6 Geneviève Freysse, *Les Deux Gouvernements: la famille et la cité*, Paris: Gallimard, 2000, p. 170.
7 Hannah Arendt, *Qu'est-ce que la politique?* Paris: Seuil, 1995, p. 146.
8 Michel Foucault, *The Thought From Outside*, New York: Zone Books, 1987. This text first appeared in 1966, in no. 229 of the magazine *Critique*. It thus anticipates the reflection developed a few years later in

'The discourse on language' (in English translation an appendix to *The Archaeology of Knowledge*).

9 Foucault, *The Thought from Outside*, p. 28.

10 See Mariella Pandolfi, 'Une souveraineté mouvante et supracoloniale', *Multitudes*, no. 3, 2000, pp. 97–105; and 'Contract of Mutual (in)Difference: Governance and the Humanitarian *Apparatus* in Contemporary Albania and Kosovo', *Indiana Journal of Global Legal Studies*, vol. 10, 2003, pp. 369–81.

11 Rancière, *Disagreement*, p. 126.

12 On the lines of the media 'revelations' of the existence of adolescent prostitution in the camps (see above, ch. 4, p. 81ff) which certain agents from the humanitarian and UN organizations took advantage of, and which gave rise to headlines in the newspapers – before they soon abandoned the subject – such as 'humanitarian rape', 'sordid humanitarianism', etc.

13 Like the images of 'illegals' trying to climb the fences at Ceuta and Melilla on the frontier between Morocco and Spain in 2005.

14 See Philippe Mesnard, *La Victime écran: la représentation humanitaire en question*, Paris: Textuel, 2002; Luc Boltanski, *Distant Suffering*, Cambridge: Cambridge University Press, 1999. Christiane Vollaire also analyses, supported by examples, the contemporary standards of 'humanitarian aesthetics' and the de-socializing functions of the images produced and publicized in order to cause scandal and emotion (Christiane Vollaire, *Humanitaire, le coeur de la guerre*, Paris: L'insulaire, 2007, pp. 66–83).

12 'If This is a Government...'

1 Paul Virilio, *The Original Accident*, Cambridge: Polity, 2007, p. 16.

2 See M. Agier, 'La main gauche de l'Empire: ordre et désordres de l'humanitaire', *Multitudes*, 11, 2003. This metaphor is borrowed from Pierre Bourdieu, who referred to social workers in the metropolitan countries as the 'left hand of the state', their unease arising from the desperate character of their work, which consists in constantly repairing the social and cultural damage inflicted by the 'right hand' – i.e. the managerial state applying to public services the economic principles of profitability and return on investment (see 'The abdication of the state', in P. Bourdieu et al., *The Weight of the World*, Cambridge: Polity, 1999, pp. 181ff.) There is the same relative position, the same unease, and often the same anger on the part of the volunteers for humanitarian action who set off to heal wounds at the other side of the world.

3 The theme of the single empire is not only proposed by neo-Marxist theorists of a structured and functional order on the planetary scale, who seek to develop a critical analysis and find places and forms of resistance

(see Michael Hardt and Antonio Negri, *Empire*, Cambridge, MA: Harvard University Press, 2001, and *Multitude: War and Democracy in the Age of Empire*, London: Hamish Hamilton, 2005). It also appears in literary fiction and futuristic films, where a single government (which may be American or already global, as the case may be) regularly governs the whole of planet Earth and confronts an enemy that can only come from outside, thus anticipating an extra-planetary alterity as the next form of extraterritoriality in general (for example *Independence Day*, *War of the Worlds*, *The Fifth Element*, etc.).

4 This constraining relationship, often unadmitted or unrecognized for ideological reasons, corresponds, in the view of Giorgio Agamben, to a 'secret solidarity' that humanitarian organizations maintain – even despite themselves – with 'the very powers they ought to fight' (*Homo Sacer*, p. 133).

5 Whereas the experiment is still in its origins in Europe and North Africa, as far as responsibility for the humanitarian apparatus of camps for illegals, asylum seekers and expellees is concerned.

6 See Jean-François Bayart, *Le Gouvernement du monde: une critique politique de la globalisation*, Paris: Fayard, 2004.

7 Virilio, *The Original Accident*, p. 16.

8 Established in the United States in 1946, CARE became an international network in the 1970s; Care France was founded in 1983.

9 The British organization OXFAM was established in 1942.

10 The original Save the Children organization was founded in London in 1919. The international Save the Children alliance dates from 1997.

11 Originally Action Contre la Faim, now the ACF (Action Against Hunger) Alliance.

12 Élisabeth Ferris, 'Le dispositif mondial d'aide humanitaire: une opportunité pour les ONG?' *Revue des Migrations Forcés* (Centre for Refugee Studies, Oxford), 29, January 2008, pp. 6–8.

13 Because, as Élisabeth Ferris notes (ibid., p. 7), 'the large international NGOs have more points in common with the UN agencies than with the national NGOs of the South'.

14 Dubernet, 'Du terrain au droit, du droit sur le terrain?'

15 Jean-François Bayart (*Le Gouvernement du monde*, pp. 96–109) refers to the 'indirect administration' that non-governmental systems generally carry out in world politics, without limiting this to the humanitarian domain. Commenting on the economic and political operation of the few very large international NGOs, Marc Abélès notes how 'the influence of the NGOs, the audience that they reach in the citizen body, derives from the fact that through them we hear the echo of an entire rejected humanity, those who appear as left behind by modernity' (Marc Abélès, *Politique de la survie*, Paris: Flammarion, 2006, p. 176).

16 Paul Virilio, *City of Panic*, Oxford: Berg, 2005, p. 108.

17 Naomi Klein, *The Shock Doctrine: The Rise of Disaster Capitalism*, New York: Metropolitan Books / Henry Holt, 2007.

244

18 Naomi Klein, 'The rise of disaster capitalism', *Nation*, 15 April 2005. This analysis is extended and documented in Klein, *The Shock Doctrine*, pp. 406–22.

19 See Mike Davis, 'The vultures of New Orleans. catastrophe capitalism', *Le Monde Diplomatique*, October 2005.

20 This may be as expatriate voluntary workers, as employees in the NGO offices, or as employees with host governments, the latter a position that is tending to expand and raise new problems of labour law. On the personal and professional trajectories of expatriate volunteers and head-office employees, a very original and detailed analysis is provided in Johanna Siméant and Pascal Dauvin, *Le Travail humanitaire: les acteurs des ONG, du siège au terrain*, Paris: Presses de Sciences Po, 2002.

21 Anne Vallaeys, *Médecins sans frontières, la biographie*, Paris: Fayard, 2004.

22 *L'aventure MSF*, France 5, Maha Productions, December 2006.

23 Among the numerous critical viewpoints of individuals and organizations publicly engaged in humanitarian action, we should mention the books by Rony Brauman (former president of MSF, now a researcher for the MSF foundation and a teacher associated with Sciences Po): *Le Dilemme humanitaire* (interview with Philippe Petit), Paris: Textuel, 1996; and, more recently, *Penser dans l'urgence* (interviews with Catherine Portevin), Paris: Seuil, 2006. MSF has published a number of volumes in the series 'Populations en danger', the most recent of which is Fabrice Weissman (ed.), *In the Shadow of Just Wars* (Ithaca: Cornell University Press, 2004). See also the work of Jean-Christophe Rufin, especially *Le Piège: quand l'aide humanitaire remplace la guerre* (Paris: Jean-Claude Lattès, 1994); and again, the periodical *Humanitaire* published by MDM (Médecins du Monde) since 2000, and the recent debate among staff and researchers connected with British and French NGOs in Karl Manchet and Boris Martin (eds.), *Critique de la raison humanitaire* (Paris: Le Cavalier Bleu, 2006). These are just a few of the many publications that regularly enliven the 'humanitarian movement'. The work of journalists close to the movement also contributes to the vigour of these debates (see, for example, Olivier Weber, *French doctors: la grande épopée de la médecine humanitaire*, Paris: Laffont, 1995; Stephen Smith, *Somalie: la guerre perdue de l'humanitaire*, Paris: Calmann-Lévy, 1993; and David Rieff, *A Bed for the Night: Humanitarianism in Crisis*, New York: Simon and Schuster, 2002).

24 Abélès, *Politique de la survie*, p. 193.

25 'L'action humanitaire: normes et pratiques. Politique, prescriptions légales et obligations morales', *Cultures et Conflits*, 60, 2005.

26 See, in particular, in this issue, Wolf-Dieter Eberwein, 'Le Paradoxe humanitaire? Normes et pratiques', *Culture et Conflits*, 60, winter 2005, pp. 15–37, and David Ambrosetti, 'L'humanitaire comme norme du discours au Conseil de sécurité: une pratique légitimatrice socialement sanctionée', *Culture et Conflits*, 60, winter 2005, pp. 39–62.

27 See Sami Makki, 'Les enjeux de l'intégration civilo-militaire: dynamiques transatlantiques de militarisation de l'humanitaire, incertitudes européennes', in B. Delcourt (ed.), *La Coopération civilo-militaire en Europe*, Brussels: Publications de l'ULB, 2008.

Conclusion

1 Jackie Assayag, 'La Terre est-elle ronde?' *L'Homme*, 185–6, 2008, p. 162.
2 For Hannah Arendt, conversation is 'the first concern of the citizen', as opposed to 'pre-political' constraint and command (*The Human Condition*, Chicago: University of Chicago Press, 1970).
3 This camp is described in ch. 8, pp. 156ff.
4 *Translator's note:* literally, 'ban-places', i.e. places of banishment, but punning with *banlieue*, i.e. 'suburb', with its contemporary connotations of disorder and riot.

Bibliography

Books and Articles

Abélès, Marc, *Politique de la survie*, Paris: Flammarion, 2006.

Agamben, Giorgio, *Homo Sacer: Sovereign Power and Bare Life*, Stanford: Stanford University Press, 1998.

Agier, Michel, *L'Invention de la ville: banlieues, townships, invasions et favelas*, Paris: Éditions des Archives contemporaines, 1999.

— 'Perte de lieux, dénuement et urbanisation: les *desplazados* de Colombie', *Autrepart*, 14, 2000, pp. 91–105.

— 'Between war and the city: towards an urban anthropology of refugee camps', *Ethnography*, 3, 3, 2002.

— 'La main gauche de l'Empire: ordre et désordres de l'humanitaire', *Multitudes*, 11, 2003.

— 'La vérité vraie: mises en scène de témoignages de guerre et d'exil', *Vacarme*, 2, 2003, pp. 79–82.

— 'La ville nue: des marges de l'urbain aux terrains de l'humanitaire', *Annales de la Recherche Urbaine*, 93, 2003, pp. 57–66.

— 'La guerre', in *La Sagesse de l'ethnologue*, Paris: L'oeil neuf éditions, 2004.

— 'Le ban-lieu du monde: marges, solitudes et communautés de l'instant', in Christine Macel and Valérie Guillaume (eds.), *Airs de Paris*, Paris: Éditions du Centre Pompidou, 2007.

— *On the Margins of the* World, Cambridge: Polity, 2008.

— 'Politiques urbaines sans auteur: une anthropologie des situations' (interview with C. Petcou and A. Querrien), *Multitudes*, 31, 2008, pp. 51–60.

— 'Violences et déplacements forcés en Colombie: apprendre à vivre avec la guerre', in Gilles Bataillon, Hamit Bozarslan and Denis Merklen (eds.), *Situations limites et expériences de l'incertain*, Paris: Karthala, 2008.

— (ed.) 'Une micropolitique de la ville: l'agir urbain', *Multitudes*, 31, 2008, pp. 11–121.

Agier, Michel, and Françoise Bouchet-Saulnier, 'Espaces humanitaires, espaces d'exception', in Fabrice Weissman (ed.), *À l'ombre des guerre justes: l'ordre cannibale et l'action humanitaire*, Paris: Flammarion/MSF, pp. 303–18.

Agier, Michel, and Jérôme Valluy, 'Le UNHCR dans la logique des camps', in Olivier Le Cour Grandmaison, Gilles Lhuilier and Jérôme Valluy (eds.), *Le Retour des camps? Sangatte, Lampedusa, Guantánamo...*, Paris: Autrement, 2006, pp. 153–63.

Agudelo, Carlos Efren, *Politique et populations noires en Colombie*, Paris: L'Harmattan, 2004.

Ambrosetti, David, 'L'humanitaire comme norme du discours au Conseil de sécurité: une pratique légitimatrice socialement sanctionée', *Cultures et Conflits*, 60, winter 2005, pp. 39–62.

Appadurai, Arjun, *Modernity at Large: Cultural Dimensions of Globalization*, Minneapolis: University of Minnesota Press, 1996.

Arendt, Hannah, *The Origins of Totalitarianism*, New York: Harcourt Brace Jovanovich, 1968.

— *The Human Condition*, Chicago: University of Chicago Press, 1970.

— *Qu'est-ce que la politique?* Paris: Seuil, 1995.

Assayag, Jackie, 'La Terre est-elle ronde?' *L'Homme*, 185–6, 2008, p. 162.

Augé, Marc, *Pouvoirs de vie, pouvoirs de mort*, Paris: Flammarion, 1977.

— *Non-places: Introduction to an Anthropology of Supermodernity*, London: Verso, 1995.

— *Les Formes de l'oubli*, Paris: Payot, 1998.

— *A Sense for the Other*, Stanford: Stanford University Press, 1998.

— *An Anthropology for Contemporaneous Worlds*, Stanford: Stanford University Press, 1999.

— *Le Temps en ruines*, Paris: Galilée, 2003.

Balandier, Georges, *Sociologie des Brazzavilles noires*, Paris: FNSP, 1955 (2nd edn, 1985).

Bauman, Zygmunt, *Liquid Modernity*, Cambridge: Polity, 2002.

— *Wasted Lives. Modernity and its Outcasts*, Cambridge: Polity, 2004.

Bayart, Jean-François, *Le Gouvernement du monde: une critique politique de la globalisation*, Paris: Fayard, 2004.

Bazin, Jean, 'Interpréter ou décrire: notes critiques sur la connaissance anthropologique', in J. Revel and N. Wachtel (eds.), *Une école pour les sciences sociales*, Paris: Cerf/EHESS, 1966.

Bensa, Alban, 'De la micro-histoire vers une anthropologie critique', in Jacques Revel (ed.), *Jeux d'échelles: la micro-analyse à l'expérience*, Paris: Gallimard-Seuil, 1996, pp. 37–70.

Bernadot, Marx, 'Le pays aux mille et un camps: approche sociohistorique des espaces d'internement en France au XXe siècle', *Les Cahiers du Cériem* (Université de Rennes-II), 2003.

— 'Les mutations de la figure du camp', in O. Le Cour Grandmaison, G. Lhuilier and J. Valluy (eds.), *Le Retour des camps? Sangatte, Lampedusa, Guantánamo...*, Paris: Autrement, 2006, pp. 42–55.

— *Camps d'étrangers*, Paris: Éditions du Croquant, 2008.

Boltanski, Luc, *Distant Suffering*, Cambridge: Cambridge University Press, 1999.

Bouillon, Florence, Marion Fresia and Virginie Tallio, *Terrains sensibles: expériences actuelles de l'anthropologie*, Dossiers africains, Paris: EHESS, 2005.

Bourdieu, Pierre, 'The abdication of the state', in Pierre Bourdieu et al., *The Weight of the World*, Cambridge: Polity, 1999, pp. 181ff.

Bouteiller-Paquet, Daphné, 'Quelle protection subsidiaire dans l'Union européenne?' *Hommes et Migrations*, 1238, 2002, pp. 75–87.

Brauman, Rony, *Le Dilemme humanitaire*, Paris: Textuel, 1996.

— *L'Action humanitaire*, Paris: Flammarion, 2000.

— *Penser dans l'urgence*, Paris: Seuil, 2006.

Brossat, Alain, *Pour en finir avec la prison*, Paris: La Fabrique, 2001.

— 'L'espace-camp et l'exception furtive', *Lignes*, 26, 2008.

Bulle, Sylvaine, 'Domestiquer son environnement: une approche pragmatiste d'un territoire confiné: le camp de réfugiés de Shu'faat à Jérusalem', *Asylon(s)*, online magazine of the TERRA network, 2, 2007, http:/terra.zero.net/article672.html.

Caloz-Tschopp, Marie-Claire, *Les Sans-etat dans la philosophie d'Hannah Arendt*, Lausanne: Payot, 2000.

Cambrezy, Luc, *Réfugiés et exilés: crise des sociétés, crise des territoires*, Paris: Éditions des Archives contemporaines, 2001.

Cambrezy, Luc, and Véronique Lassailly-Jacob (eds.), *Populations réfugiées: de l'exil au retour*, Paris: IRD éditions, 2001.

de Certeau, Michel, *L'Invention du quotidien, I. Manières de faire*, Paris: Gallimard, 1980 (2nd edn, 1990).

Cigerli, Sabri, *Les Réfugiés kurdes d'Irak en Turquie*, Paris: L'Harmattan, 1998.

Clifford, James, and George Marcus (eds.), *Writing Culture: The Poetics and Politics of Ethnography*, Berkeley: University of California Press, 1986.

Clochard, Olivier, Yvan Gastaut and Ralph Schor, 'Les camps d'étrangers depuis 1938, continuité et adaptations: du "modèle" français à la construction de l'espace Schengen', *Revue Européenne des Migrations Internationales*, 20, 2, 2004.

Corbet, Alice, 'Les campements de réfugiés sahraouis en Algérie: de l'idéel au réel', *Bulletin de l'Association des Géographes Français* ('Territoires d'exil: les camps de réfugiés', ed. Véronique Lassailly-Jacob), 2006, 1, pp. 9–21.

Davis, Mike, *City of Quartz*, London: Verso, 1990.

— 'The vultures of New Orleans. catastrophe capitalism', *Le Monde Diplomatique*, October 2005.

— *Planet of Slums*, London: Verso, 2006.

Dedenis, Julien, 'La territorialité de l'espace des camps des réfugiés sahraouis en Algérie', *Bulletin de l'Association des Géographes Français* ('Territoires d'exil: les camps de réfugiés', ed, Véronique Lassailly-Jacob), 2006, 1, pp. 22–34.

Detienne, Marcel, *Comment être autochtone: du pur Athénien au Français raciné*, Paris: Seuil, 2003.

Detienne, Marcel (ed.), *Qui veut prendre la parole?* Paris: Seuil, 2003.

Doraï, Mohamed Kamel, *Les Réfugiés palestiniens du Liban: une géographie de l'exil*, Paris: CNRS Éditions, 2006.

Dozon, Jean-Pierre, *Frères et sujets: la France et l'Afrique en perspective*, Paris: Flammarion, 2003.

Dubernet, Cécile, 'Du terrain au droit, du droit sur le terrain? Origines et trajectoires du label "déplacé interne"', *Asylon(s)*, online magazine of the TERRA network, 2, November 2007, http://terra.rezo.net/article670.html.

Dumont, Louis, *Essays on Individualism: Modern Ideology in Anthropological Perpsective*, Chicago: University of Chicago Press, 1986.

Eberwein, Wolf-Dieter, 'Le Paradoxe humanitaire? Normes et pratiques', *Cultures et Conflits*, 60, winter 2005, pp. 15–37.

Elias, Norbert, and John Scotson, *The Established and the Outsiders: A Sociological Enquiry into Community Problems*, London: Frank Cass, 1965.

Ellis, Stephen, *The Mask of Anarchy: The Destruction of Liberia and the Religious Dimension of an African Civil War*, London: Hurst, 1999.

Fabian, Johann, *Time and the Other: How Anthropology Makes its Objects*, New York: Columbia University Press, 1983.

Farah, Nuruddin, 'A country in exile', *World Literature Today*, 2, 4 (Sept. 1998).

—— *Yesterday, Tomorrow: Voices from the Somali Diaspora*, London: Continuum, 2000.

Fassin, Didier, 'La cause des victimes', *Les Temps Modernes*, 627, 2004, pp. 73–91.

Fassin, Didier et al., *Des maux indicibles: sociologie des lieux d'écoute*, Paris: La Découverte, 2004.

Ferris, Élisabeth, 'Le dispositif mondial d'aide humanitaire: une opportunité pour les ONG?' *Revue des Migrations Forcés* (Centre for Refugee Studies, Oxford), 29, January 2008, pp. 6–8.

Filhol, Emmanuel, *Un camp de concentration français: les Tsiganes alsaciens-lorrains à Crest, 1915–1919*, Grenoble: Presses universitaires de Grenoble, 2004.

Foucault, Michel, 'Des espaces autres', in *Dits et écrits*, vol. IV, Paris: Gallimard, 1984.

—— *The Thought from Outside*, New York: Zone Books, 1987.

Fresia, Marion, 'Aide humanitaire et production de services publics en Afrique de l'Ouest: le cas de la gestion des populations mauritaniennes réfugiées au Sénégal', *Le Bulletin de l'APAD*, 23–4, 2002.

—— 'Des "réfugiés-migrants": les parcours de l'exil des réfugiés mauritaniens au Sénégal', *Asylon(s)*, online magazine of the TERRA network, 2, 2006, http://terra.rezo.net/article675.html.

Freysse, Geneviève, *Les Deux Gouvernements: la famille et la cité*, Paris: Gallimard, 2000.

Geertz, Clifford, *Works and Lives: The Anthropologist as Author*, Stanford: Stanford University Press, 1988.

Geffray, Christian, *La Cause des armes au Mozambique: Anthropologie d'une guerre civile*, Paris: Karthala, 1990.

Gervais-Lambony, Philippe, *Territoires citadins: 4 villes africaines*, Paris: Belin, 2003.

Godding, Jean-Pierre (ed.), *Réfugiés rwandais au Zaïre*, Paris: L'Harmattan, 1997.

Gomes, Nathalie, 'Solidarité et réseaux dans l'exil: les réfugiés somaliens clandestins au Kenya et en Éthiopie', in Luc Cambrezy and Véronique Lassailly-Jacob (eds.), *Populations réfugiées: de l'exil au retour*, Paris: Éditions de l'IRD, 2001, pp. 301–19.

Guichaoua, André, *Exilés, réfugiés, deplacés en Afrique centrale et orientale*, Paris: Karthala, 2004.

Hardt, Michael, and Antonio Negri, *Empire*, Cambridge, MA: Harvard University Press, 2001.

—— *Multitude: War and Democracy in the Age of Empire*, London: Hamish Hamilton, 2005.

Hartog, François, *Régimes d'historicité: présentisme et expériences du temps*, Paris: Seuil, 2004.

Hazan, Éric, *Notes sur l'occupation: Naplouse, Kalkilyia, Hébron*, Paris: La Fabrique, 2006.

Hénaff, Marcel, *La Ville qui vient*, Paris: L'Herne, 2008.

Henry, Douglas, 'Réfugiés sierra-léonais et aide humanitaire en Guinée', *Politique Africaine*, 85, 2002, pp. 56–63.

Hoffmann, Odile, *Communautés noires dans le Pacifique colombien: innovations et dynamiques ethniques*, Paris: IRD/Karthala, 2004.

Isin, Engin F., and Kim Rygiel, 'Of other global cities: frontiers, zones, camps', in Barbara Drieskens, Franck Mermier and Heiko Wimmen (eds.), *Cities of the South: Citizenship and Exclusion in the 21st Century*, Beirut: Saqi Books, 2007, pp. 169–76.

Jezequel, Jean-Hervé, 'Libéria: un chaos orchestré', in Fabrice Weissman (ed.), *À l'ombre des guerres justes*, Paris: Flammarion/MSF, 2003, pp. 171–90.

Joseph, Isaac, 'Le droit à la ville, la ville à l'oeuvre: deux paradigms de la recherche', *Annales de la Recherche Urbaine*, 64, 1994, pp. 5–10.

Khoury, Elias, *La Porte du soleil*, Arles: Actes Sud, 2002.

Kibreab, Gaim, 'Revisiting the debate on people, place, identity and displacement', *Journal of Refugee Studies*, 12, 4, 1999.

Klein, Naomi, 'The rise of disaster capitalism', *Nation*, 15 April 2005.

— *The Shock Doctrine: The Rise of Disaster Capitalism*, New York: Metropolitan Books / Henry Holt, 2007.

Laacher, Smaïn, *Le Peuple des clandestins*, Paris: Calmann-Lévy, 2007.

Larzillière, Pénélope, *Être jeune en Palestine*, Paris: Balland, 2004.

Lassailly-Jacob, Véronique, 'Des réfugiés mozambicains sur les terres des Zambiens: le cas du site agricole d'Ukwimi, 1987–1994', in Luc Cambrezy and Véronique Lassailly-Jacob (eds.), *Populations réfugiées: de l'exil au retour*, Paris: IRD éditions, 2001, pp. 269–99.

— 'Quelles réponses à l'afflux des réfugiés? L'exemple zambien', *Bulletin de l'Association des Géographes Français*, 2, 2002, pp. 211–22.

Le Cour Grandmaison, Olivier, Gilles Lhuilier and Jérôme Valluy (eds.), *Le Retour des camps? Sangatte, Lampedusa, Guantánamo . . .*, Paris: Autrement, 2006.

Lepetit, Bernard, 'La ville: cadre, objet, sujet. Vingt ans de recherches françaises en histoire urbaine', *Enquête*, 4, 1996, pp. 11–34.

Leservoisier, Olivier, and Laurent Vidal, *L'Anthropologie face à ses objets: nouveaux contextes ethnographiques*, Paris: Éditions des Archives contemporains, 2008.

Levi, Primo (with Leonardo Debenedetti), *Rapport sur Auschwitz*, with a critical apparatus by Philippe Mesnard, Paris: Kimé, 2005.

Makaremi, Chowra, 'Vies "en instance": le temps et l'espace du maintien en zone d'attente. Le cas de la "Zapi 3" de Roissy-Charles-de-Gaulle', in *Asylon(s)*, online magazine of the TERRA network, 2, November 2007, http://terra.rezo.net/article664.html.

Makki, Sami, 'Les enjeux de l'intégration civilo-militaire: dynamiques transatlantiques de militarisation de l'humanitaire, incertitudes européennes', in B. Delcourt (ed.), *La Coopération civilo-militaire en Europe*, Brussels: Publications de l'ULB, 2008.

Malkki, Liisa, *Purity and Exile: Violence, Memory and National Cosmology among Hutu Refugees in Tanzania*, Chicago: University of Chicago Press, 1995.

– 'Refugees and exile: from "Refuge Studies" to the national order of things', *Annual Review of Anthropology*, 24, 1995, pp. 495–523.

Manchet, Karl, and Boris Martin (eds.), *Critique de la raison humanitaire*, Paris: Le Cavalier Bleu, 2006.

Marie, Alain (ed.), *L'Afrique des individus*, Paris: Karthala, 1997.

Mauss, Marcel, 'Une catégorie de l'esprit humain: la notion de personne, celle de "moi"' (1938), in *Sociologie et anthropologie*, Paris: PUF, 1950, pp. 331–62.

Mesnard, Philippe, *La Victime écran: la représentation humanitaire en question*, Paris: Textuel, 2002.

— 'Un texte sans importance', in Primo Levi, *Rapport sur Auschwitz*, Paris: Kimé, 2005, pp. 9–47.

Messiant, Christine, 'Fin de la guerre, enfin, en Angola. Vers quelle paix?' *Politique Africaine*, 86, 2002, pp. 183–95.

'Migrations en Europe: les frontières de la liberté', *Multitudes*, 19, 2005.

Mohamed-Abdi, Mohamed, 'Les bouleversements induits de la guerre civile en Somalie: castes marginales et minorités', *Autrepart*, 15, 2000, pp. 131–47.

Muhle, Maria, 'Le camp et la notion de vie', in Olivier Le Cour Grandmaison, Gilles Lhuilier and Jérôme Valluy (eds.), *Le Retour des camps? Sangatte, Lampedusa, Guantánamo . . .*, Paris: Autrement, 2006.

Noiriel, Gérard, *Réfugiés et sans-papiers: la République face au droit d'asile, XIXe–XXe siècle*, Paris: Hachette, 1999.

La Notion de personne en Afrique noire, Paris; Éditions du CNRS, 1973.

Pandolfi, Mariella, 'Une souveraineté mouvante et supracoloniale', *Multitudes*, 3, 2000, pp. 97–105.

— 'Contract of mutual (in)difference: governance and the humanitarian *apparatus* in contemporary Albania and Kosovo', *Indiana Journal of Global Legal Studies*, 10, 2003, pp. 369–81.

Peschanski, Denis, *La France des camps: l'internement, 1938–1946*, Paris: Gallimard, 2002.

Piette, Albert, *Ethnographie de l'action: l'observation des details*, Paris: Métailié, 1996.

Pollak, Michael, *L'Expérience concentrationnaire: essai sur le maintien de l'identité sociale*, Paris: Métailié, 1990.

Queinnec, Erwann, and Jean Rigal, 'Aide alimentaire et carences vitaminiques dans les camps de réfugiés', in François Jean (ed.), *Populations en danger 1995: rapport annuel sur les crises majeures et l'action humanitaire*, Paris: MSF / La Découverte, 1995.

Rancière, Jacques, *Disagreement: Politics and Philosophy*, Minneapolis: University of Minnesota Press, 1999.

Revet, Sandrine, *Anthropologie d'une catastrophe: les coulées de boue de 1999 au Venezuela*, Paris: Presses de la Sorbonne nouvelle, 2007.

Richards, Paul, *Fighting for the Rain Forest: War, Youth and Resources in Sierra Leone*, Oxford: Currey, 1996.

Ricoeur, Paul, *Memory, History, Forgetting*, Chicago: University of Chicago Press, 2004.

Rieff, David, *A Bed for the Night: Humanitarianism in Crisis*, New York: Simon & Schuster, 2002.

Rivière, Philippe, 'L'asile aux antipodes', *Le Monde Diplomatique, Manières de Voir*, 62, 2002.

Rodier, Claire, 'Zone d'attente de Roissy: à la frontière de l'État de droit', *Hommes et Migrations*, 1238, July–August 2002.

Rodier, Claire, and Emmanuel Blanchard, 'Des camps pour étrangers', *Plein Droit*, 58, December 2003 (Special issue: 'L'Europe des camps').

Rolland, Stellio, 'De l'individuel au collectif: des strategies de survie des déplacés colombiens aux regroupements communautaires', *Asylon(s)*, online magazine of the TERRA network, 2, November 2007, http://terra.rezo.net/rubrique124.html.

Rousseau, Cécile, and Patricia Foxen, 'Le mythe du réfugié menteur: un mensonge indispensable', *Évolution Psychiatrique*, 71, 2006, pp. 505–20.

Rozelier, Muriel, *Naplouse Palestine: chroniques du ghetto*, Paris: Presses de la Renaissance, 2007.

Rufin, Jean-Christophe, *L'Aventure humanitaire*, Paris: Gallimard, 1994.

— *Le Piège: quand l'aide humanitaire remplace la guerre*, Paris: Jean-Claude Lattès, 1994.

Sanbar, Elias, *Figures du Palestinien: identité des origines, identité de devenir*, Paris: Gallimard, 2004.

Siméant, Johanna, and Pascal Dauvin, *Le Travail humanitaire: les acteurs des ONG, du siège au terrain*, Paris: Presses de Sciences Po, 2002.

Smith, David (ed.), *The Apartheid City and Beyond: Urbanisation and Social Change in South Africa*, London: Routledge, 1992.

Smith, Stephen, *Somalie: la guerre perdue de l'humanitaire*, Paris: Calmann-Lévy, 1993.

Smouts, Marie-Claude (ed.), *La situation postcoloniale: les 'postcolonial studies' dans le débat français*, with a preface by Georges Balandier, Paris: Presses de Sciences Po, 2007.

Sossi, Federica, 'Une tragédie en trois actes', *Vacarme*, 39, spring 2007, pp. 56–9.

— 'Entre l'espace et le temps des nouvelles frontières', *Lignes*, 26, 2008, pp. 132–44.

Temime, Émile (with Nathalie Deguigné), *Le Camp du Grand Arénas: Marseille, 1944–1966*, Paris: Autrement, 2001.

Temime, Émile, and Geneviève Dreyfus-Armand, *Les Camps sur la plage: un exil espagnol*, Paris: Autrement, 1995.

Vallaeys, Anne, *Médecins sans frontières: la biographie*, Paris: Fayard, 2004.

Valluy, Jérôme, 'La fiction juridique de l'asile', *Plein Droit* (GISTI review), 63, December 2004.

— 'La nouvelle Europe politique des camps: genèse d'une source élitaire de phobie et de repression des étrangers', *Cultures et Conflits*, 57, 2005, pp. 13–69.

— (ed.), 'L'Europe des camps: la mise à l'écart des étrangers', *Cultures et Conflits*, 57, 2005.

Van Damme, Wim, 'Do refugees belong in camps? Experiences from Goma and Guinea', *Lancet*, 346, 1995, pp. 360–2.

Varikas, Eleni, *Les Rebuts du monde: figures du paria*, Paris: Stock, 2007,

Verdirame, Guglielmo, and Barbara Harrell-Bond, *Rights in Exile: Janus-faced Humanitarianism*, New York and Oxford: Berghahn, 2005.

Virilio, Paul, *City of Panic*, Oxford: Berg, 2005.

— *The Original Accident*, Polity, 2007.

Vollaire, Christiane, *Humanitaire, le coeur de la guerre*, Paris: L'Insulaire, 2007.

Wacquant, Loïc, *Urban Outcasts: A Comparative Sociology of Advanced Marginality*, Cambridge: Polity, 2007.

Weber, Olivier, *French doctors: la grande épopée de la médecine humanitaire*, Paris: Laffont, 1995.

Weber, Serge, *Nouvelle Europe, nouvelles migrations: frontières, intégration, mondialisation*, Paris: Éditions du Félin, 2007.

Weissman, Fabrice, 'Sierra Leone: la paix à tout prix', in F. Weissman (ed.), *In the Shadow of Just Wars*, Ithaca: Cornell University Press, 2004.

Wirth, Louis, 'Urbanism as a way of life' (1938), in Jan Lin and Christopher Mele (eds.), *The Urban Sociology Reader*, Abingdon: Routledge 2005, pp. 32–42.

Reports

Amnesty International, *Displaced in Darfur: A Generation of Anger*, 22 January 2008.

Baylac, Sophie, *Note sur la rétention des migrants et demandeurs d'asile en Turquie*, GISTI, October 2006.

Coordination française pour le droit d'asile, 'Quelles solutions pour une protection internationale des exilés et réfugiés d'Irak?' Paris, December 2007.

Couts, Philippa, et al, *Kenya Refugee Study: Food Economy. Updates of Ifo, Dagahaley and Hagadera Refugee Camps, Dadaab*, Final Report, Save the Children Fund, Nairobi, September 1999, 21-page ms.

European Parliament, *The Conditions for Third-Country Nationals (Detention Camps, Open Centres as well as Transit Centres and Transit Zones), with a particular focus on provisions and facilities for persons with special needs in the 25 EU member states*.

Hagenimana, A., J. Nkengurukiyimana, J. Mulindabigwi and M. Goretti Gahimbare, *L'Itinéraire le plus long et le plus pénible (les réfugiés hutu à la recherche de l'asile)*, n.d. [2000], n.p. [Maheba], mimeographed.

International Organization for Migration, *Iraq Displacement 2007 Year in Review*, www.iom-iraq.net/idp.html.

Laporte Weywada, Thomas, *Liberia – Halfway through the Return Process*, Monrovia: ACF, June 2006.

Office for the Coordination of Humanitarian Affairs, *The Humanitarian Impact of the West Bank Barrier on Palestinian Communities*, Jerusalem, Update 7, June 2007.

Office for the Coordination of Humanitarian Affairs / UNHCR, *IDP Return Survey of Official Camps*, Preliminary Report, HIC-Liberia, May 2004.

Osservatorio sulle vittime dell'immigrazione, *Effeti collaterali: rapporto sulle condizioni dei migranti di transito in Algeria*, Fortress Europe / ARACEM, Rome, October 2007, http://fortresseurope.blogspot.com/2006/01/revue-de-presse.html.

Parlement européen, *Conditions des ressortissants de pays tiers retenus dans des centres (camps de détention, centres ouverts, ainsi que des zones de transit) au sein des 25 États membres de l'Union européenne*, December 2007, 'Rapports pays: Pologne'.

Powles, Julia, 'Tales of fish ... a field report: Angolan refugees in Zambia, September 1992 to July 1993', ms., n.p., 1993.

Rahmi, M., E. Rabant, L. Cambrezy and Mohamed-Abdi M., *Environment, Cartography, Demography and Geographical Information System in the Refugee Camps, Dadaab, Kakuma – Kenya*, vol. III, *Demography, Data Processing and Cartography*, n.p.: UNHCR/IRD, 1999.

Seren, Hélène (ed.), *L'Urbanisation des camps des réfugiés dans la bande de Gaza et en Cisjordanie*, research report, GEMDEV, Programme de recherche urbaine pour le développement (PRUD), Palestinian Diaspora and Refugee Centre (SHAML), project 93, n.p. [Paris?]: n.d. [2004?].

UNHCR, *Annual Report*, 1997 and 2000.

UNHCR, *Protecting Refugees: The Role of the UNHCR*, Geneva: UNHCR, 2007.

255

INDEX